THE BETRAYED PROFESSION

JOHNS HOPKINS

The Johns Hopkins University Press

2715 N. Charles Street
Baltimore MD 21218-4319

THE BETRAYED PROFESSION
Lawyering at the End of the Twentieth Century

By Sol M. Linowitz
with Martin Mayer

0-8018-5329-X $15.95 paperback

Publication date: March 8, 1996

This book is sent to you for review. Two copies of your review will be appreciated.

The Betrayed Profession

Lawyering at the End
of the Twentieth Century

SOL M. LINOWITZ
WITH MARTIN MAYER

The Johns Hopkins University Press
Baltimore and London

Copyright © 1994 by Sol M. Linowitz and Martin Mayer
All rights reserved
Printed in the United States of America on acid-free paper

Originally published in a hardcover edition by Charles Scribner's Sons, New York, 1994
Reprinted by arrangement with Scribner, a Division of Simon & Schuster Inc.
Johns Hopkins Paperbacks edition, 1996
05 04 03 02 01 00 99 98 97 96   5 4 3 2 1

The Johns Hopkins University Press
2715 North Charles Street
Baltimore, Maryland 21218-4319
The Johns Hopkins Press Ltd., London

Library of Congress Cataloging-in-Publication Data will be found
at the end of this book.

A catalog record for this book is available from the British Library.

ISBN 0-8018-5329-X (pbk.)

To Anne, June, Jan, and Ronni, who thought
I should do it

"Like any profession which considers its function to be that of serving the public, the legal profession must strive for, and will be measured by, three standards: its independence, its availability, and its learning."

—PAUL A. FREUND

Contents

PREFACE

This is a book I hoped I wouldn't have to write. I decided to do so only after I concluded that there were some things I very much wanted to say about my profession, where it is and where it is heading.

The book would not have come into being without the valuable research and help of my collaborator, Martin Mayer. Martin and I have been friends for over twenty-five years, during which time he produced over a dozen books, including *The Lawyers* and *Emory Buckner*. He knows how much I appreciate all he did to help make this book a reality.

The idea for the book arose after I made a speech about lawyers at the hundredth anniversary of Cornell Law School in 1988. (It was also, incidentally, the fiftieth anniversary of my graduation from the law school.) In my talk I expressed my disappointment and concern at what has been happening to the practice of the law in the years since I left law school. The speech evoked a surprisingly widespread response—including approving letters from seven of the Supreme Court justices and proposals from several book publishers.

My main purpose in doing the book is to set forth with accuracy and honesty what I have seen going on in the practice of law for over five decades and to offer some suggestions as to how we lawyers might rekindle pride in our profession and restore the practice of law to the respected position it once occupied.

A number of lawyers and nonlawyers alike will, I expect, take issue with some of the things I have to say, and this is as it should be. I certainly don't claim to have all the answers, but I do believe I am raising a number of the right questions.

I am grateful to my wife, Toni, and our daughters, Anne, June, Jan, and Ronni, for pressuring me to keep at the book, and for periodically reassuring me that what I had to say was worth saying. Teresa Schwartz, associate dean of the George Washington University Law School, was immensely helpful with her ideas and suggestions, and especially thoughtful in putting together a group of George Washington University law students with whom Martin Mayer and I talked. My thanks also go to a number of others—both lawyers and nonlawyers—with whom we spoke and who gave us their frank opinions and comments. I owe a special vote of thanks to my administrative assistant, Marge Fitzgerald, who made sure everything came out right, and to Douglas Rutzen, who went over the entire manuscript and told me just what he thought. It was a pleasure working with Edward T. Chase, my editor at Scribners, and I thank him for his encouragement and wise guidance.

CHAPTER 1

LIVING THE LAW

1

"I came to learn and understand the noble history of the profession of the law. I came to realize that without a bar trained in the conditions of courage and loyalty our constitutional theories of individual liberty would cease to be a living reality. I learned of the experience of those many countries possessing constitutions and bills of rights similar to our own whose citizens had nevertheless lost their liberties because they did not possess a bar with sufficient courage and independence to establish those rights by a brave assertion of the writs of habeas corpus and certiorari. So I came to feel that the American lawyer should regard himself as a potential officer of his government and a defender of its laws and Constitution. I felt that if the time should ever come when this tradition had faded out and the members of the bar had become merely the servants of business, the future of our liberties would be gloomy indeed."

The words are those of Henry Stimson, a great figure New York bar, who served both Theodore Roose

Franklin Roosevelt as secretary of war (then the name for what we now call the secretary of defense) and Herbert Hoover as secretary of state. They appear in the preface to his memoirs, which he prepared in 1948 with the help of the young McGeorge Bundy, who would later become John F. Kennedy's national security adviser and the president of the Ford Foundation. Among the oddities of these memoirs is that Stimson (like Henry Adams, in some ways a comparable figure) refers to himself throughout as "Stimson" rather than as "I." But when he wanted to pay tribute to the law, he used the first person.

Henry Stimson would have been shocked and saddened by the state of the bar today, and especially by the common, public, even proud utterance in and out of bar associations that "law is a business like other businesses." Whether or not the business of America was business, as Calvin Coolidge said, the spirit of America has been the rule of law. For generations, Americans prided themselves that ours was a nation of laws, not of men, and that no one, not even the president of the United States, was above the law. Law established the bounds of the behavior society was willing to permit, and the process by which behavior seen as beyond those bounds could be punished. Our Constitution, in many ways a commercial document, established a legal order at the center of economic activity—it is, after all, the rules of the "free market" that keep the market free. Fair contracts that expressed the true intention of the parties were not a game, where the lawyer for one side or another won advantages for his client by cleverness, but the fundament of civilized economic activity.

The law we spoke of was not an "adversary system" but a framework for cooperative activity. Karl Llewellyn of the Columbia Law School, a founder of the "legal realism" school that now sees everything from the perspective of litigators, wrote in 1942 that "the essence of [legal] craftsmanship lies in skills, and wisdoms; in practical, effective, persuasive, inventive skills for getting things done, any kind of thing in any field; in wisdom and judgment in selecting the things to get done; in skills for moving men into desired action, any kind of man, in any field; and then in skills for *regularizing* the results. . . . [W]e concentrate on the areas of conflict, tension, friction, trouble, doubt— and in those areas we have the skills for working out results. We are the troubleshooters. We find the way out and set up the method of the way, and get men persuaded to accept it. . . ."[1] Economists recognized this *regularity* of outcome in commercial law as a "merit good"—something that produces benefits to an entire society without imposing costs. For the market system, as the Russians are learning, cannot work without the housing of a stable legal order.

Lawyers have also, always, been fiduciaries, actors on behalf of others, who put the interests of those others ahead of their own. This was not a matter of altruism: their license to practice law implied the acceptance and enforcement of fiduciary obligations. The satisfactions of practicing law were in the knowledge that others depended upon your judgment, your loyalty, and your abilities, and that at the end of the day you knew that you had, in fact, helped your client. In my generation, we thought of the law as a *helping* profession, not a continuation of war by other means.

Moreover, it was understood that a good lawyer helped his clients not to evade the law but to obey it. "The tested character of a sound lawyer of experience and independence," said Chief Justice Charles Evans Hughes, "is a priceless *public* asset." Former federal judge Simon Rifkind, who left the bench in the 1940s because he couldn't raise his children on a judge's salary and was still practicing law in his nineties in 1993, once wrote:

> The advocate has more than a private fiduciary relationship with a client; he also has a public trust. . . . In his counseling and planning functions, the attorney not only expedites his client's wishes and lightens the work load of the courts; he en-

forces the law as well. . . . [T]here are simply not enough governmental officials charged with the responsibility of enforcing
our laws to relegate the assessment of legality solely or even primarily to adjudicatory forums. The smooth functioning of our
society requires the private attorney to pass his client's proposal
through the filters of every relevant area of the law, so that the
client can proceed confidently on a legal course of action, and
so that the chaos of a multiplicity of improperly planned, ultimately illegal, courses of action can be avoided.[2]

Elihu Root, like Henry Stimson a great lawyer of the early
years of this century—secretary of war before Stimson, secretary of state when Stimson was secretary of war, later a U.S.
senator—put the matter more simply: "About half the practice
of a decent lawyer," he once said, "consists in telling would-be
clients that they are damned fools and should stop."

Today there are too few lawyers who see it as part of their
function to tell clients (especially new clients) that they are
damned fools and should stop: Any such statement would interfere with the marketing program. The public pays, because the
rule of law is diminished. Coal companies falsify the data from
the gauges that measure air quality in the mines, tobacco companies sponsor research that confuses people about the dangers
of smoking, automobile companies conceal data about product
defects, makers of breast implants misstate the results of their
tests of the toxicity of silicone. Such antisocial behavior is not
new, but we had counted on law and regulation to prevent it.
Asked the other day whether business behavior is worse today
than it was at the turn of the century, a distinguished lawyer
and historian said, "No. But in those days it was legal." We
made such deceptions illegal for a reason, and we counted on
the nation's lawyers to tell their clients the law. Too many times,
lawyers have been willing to look the other way, or even plan
out the defenses in advance, while their clients violated the
law.

Lawyer bashing is an old and almost honorable occupation, though Shakespeare's most quoted attack comes, in fact, from the mouth of a self-interested and disreputable revolutionary. When I was still young I found attacks on lawyers irritating but not disturbing, for I was certain of my respect as well as my love for my profession, and I was confident that whatever misbehavior might be discovered in its lower depths, its leadership was ethically as well as intellectually admirable. In recent years, through experience as well as observation, I have lost some of that confidence and some of my respect—but not my love—for my profession.

American society today is being corroded by a pervasive cynicism. *Most* of our political campaigns are poisoned by charges or implications of corruption. People don't trust companies, unions, the police, legislators, newspapers—they just don't trust. As recently as 1963, Everett Hughes wrote that the central feature of professionalism was a doctrine of *credat emptor*—"let the buyer trust"—rather than the commercial maxim of *caveat emptor*—"let the buyer beware."[3] Society counts on the law, and on lawyers as its servants, to spread such feelings of trust through the community. Instead, too often, we help weaken them.

2

Of course, law as I knew it and lived it in the middle decades of this century had its own gross imperfections, some of which affected me personally. At Cornell Law School, from which I graduated in 1938, I was first in my class and editor-in-chief of the *Cornell Law Quarterly*. In the fall of my senior year, I sat down with Professor Arthur John Keeffe, who was in charge of placement, to discuss what I should do when I graduated. He made it clear to me that I was most unlikely to find a job with any of the well-known law firms in New York, except the handful of explicitly "Jewish" ones. I knew perfectly well that if I hadn't been Jewish, I would have been offered multiple jobs, and I resented it. I'd say to Professor Keeffe, "What about *this* firm?" and he'd say, "You'd be hitting your head against the wall."

My discovery that the legal profession would not let me compete on the basis of ability was an all too familiar experience in the 1930s, and for many years thereafter, for aspiring lawyers who were not White Anglo-Saxon Protestants. When my fellow Trentonian Leon Higginbotham, Jr., later chief judge of the United States Court of Appeals for the Third Circuit, graduated from Yale Law School in 1939, the alumni representative from Philadelphia felt he could recommend him only to a firm of "two colored lawyers." Until 1943, like most professional (and sports) associations, the American Bar Association explicitly banned African-Americans from membership; the first blacks were not admitted until 1954. In 1956, eighteen years after I left Cornell, Mario Cuomo on graduation from St. John's Law School could not even get an interview with any of the eighty-four New York firms to which he applied. As late as 1963, there were only 1,700 women in American law schools, as against almost 60,000 in 1992. Women were not admitted to Harvard Law School until 1950, or to Washington and Lee School of Law until 1972. There were only two women in my class at Cornell Law School, and to tell the truth we felt somewhat uncomfortable when they were around. It never occurred to us to wonder whether *they* felt uncomfortable.

Nobody in those days thought of bigoted exclusion from the higher levels of legal practice as an "ethical" problem. For those who were excluded, it would have been pretentious; for others, with few exceptions, it was the way of the world—unfair, perhaps, but unchangeable. After all, you couldn't ask lawyers to be partners with people with whom they did not feel "comfortable." Professor Philip Schuchman of the University of Connecticut wrote unpleasantly if accurately in 1968:

We teach ethics, as thoughtful men from Aristotle to Bentham have known, in much the same way we train children and dogs. We beat them when they are bad and sometimes reward them when they are good—not necessarily good and bad for the children or the dogs, but good and bad for those in a position to administer the beatings and parcel out the rewards. . . . Should the young lawyer not have chosen his grandparents too wisely, he must look elsewhere [than the big law firms] for employment in his chosen profession. If at that point the aspirant may begin to wonder about the ethics of his chosen profession, it only proves how ingenuous he is and hence unfit for employment in a [big law firm]. . . . The question is legitimately posed, why certain of our ethical precepts are in the canons and others are not. Is this willy-nilly the course of nature, or is it just the kind of unilateral law-making so often seen in the world of big business just carried over to the world of big law?[4]

The leaders of the legal profession of my youth would have scoffed at the notion that people have a *right* to counsel, even in criminal cases, where someone's liberty was directly at stake. Abe Fortas's triumph in *Gideon* v. *Wainwright* was still a generation away. We did have a "contingent fee" system by which the victims of accidents could sue someone whose negligence had caused the accident and pay their lawyer out of the proceeds, but the leaders of the bar didn't do that and didn't think much of it: They were of the opinion that contingent fees led to "ambulance chasing." The idea that manufacturers were liable to users for dangerous defects in their products was still very recent when I went to law school in the 1930s. Some cities had "legal aid" societies that went back to the Progressive era, and some legal aid societies might help a tenant being evicted by a landlord—but as a *profession* lawyers did not feel obligated to defend tenants against landlords (who, of course, had lawyers because they could pay a lawyer's fees). We spoke of equal justice under law, but a lot of that was lip service. A. J. Liebling once wrote that freedom of the press belongs to those who own one; the legal profession I revered behaved as though justice under law was for those who could afford to hire a lawyer.

Thinking back, then, to my profession as it was more than a half century ago, I have to temper my enthusiasm with recognition of the narrowness of both my own focus and the focus of others at the bar, including the best of them. Together with the abuses and failures has come progress in the elimination of indefensible bigotry by lawyers and in the representation of those long excluded from the protection of the law. Such bigotry was common enough among businessmen, bankers, and lunch counter proprietors as well as among lawyers, and our society had to make the behavior that sprang from this bigotry broadly illegal before it could be stopped at the law firms.

In reforming the bar, then, those of us who fear the ethical decline of the profession must also make sure that our unhappiness does not become a way to further the agenda of those who have no compunction about depriving poor potential antagonists of their day in court. Professor Monroe Freedman of Hofstra University in New York, a law professor who advises on ethical practice, remembers being offered quite a lot of money to condemn "ambulance chasers who were bringing reputable mine owners to their knees by going around to mining towns and testing people for brown lung disease." In 1988, in a keynote address at the Cornell Law School Centennial (also the fiftieth anniversary of my own graduation), I spoke with dismay about those lawyers who had come all the way from America to descend like vultures upon the miserable survivors of the Union Carbide disaster in Bhopal, India, to sign them up as plaintiffs. Freedman, commenting on my address (which was reprinted in the *New York State Bar Journal*), pointed out correctly that it would have been even more disturbing if these poor fellows had been left without any legal assistance at all.

Above all, we must not blame the moral decline of the leadership of the bar on the admission of "lesser breeds." It would be bigotry as shameful as the behavior we have criminalized to contend that once you let Jews and Catholics and women and blacks into the profession you can't keep the standards. What has diminished the law in recent decades is not the wider variety of humanity among the practitioners but the loss of humanity in the practice itself.

3

Historically in the United States, members of the legal profession were the leaders of their communities and of the country. John Adams, Thomas Jefferson, James Madison, John Jay, John Marshall—how many of our Founding Fathers were lawyers! Abraham Lincoln, too, and Franklin Roosevelt. Our icons were lawyers. In no other constitutional system were the courts so important as in ours, and lawyers were officers of the court. To be a lawyer was, for me and for those I admired, a great *responsibility*. The relationship between lawyer and client was sacred—sanctified indeed by our law, which made the confidentiality of communications between lawyer and client almost as privileged as the communication between parishioner and clergyman. One owed loyalty to one's client, but first one owed deference to the court and obedience to the law.

It was from his role as an officer of the court that the lawyer derived his authority. Only a lawyer could exert legal powers, bring suit on behalf of his clients, subpoena witnesses to appear at his rather than their convenience, and compel the production of documents their possessor would much rather keep secret. These powers were not inherent in his license to practice law; they were awarded to him on specific application for their use in each case by the courts before which he practiced. It was understood that he was not to use these gifts of the court for his own advantage or to help further the designs of clients whose cause could not make at least a *prima facie*—"first look"—claim that the law was on their side. The purpose of the elaborate "pleadings" by which lawyers introduced their clients' cases to the courts was to establish a reason why these "impositional powers" of the judge should be placed at the disposal of a litigant. Judges expected that, as officers of the court, lawyers would *always* make some investigation of their clients' claims before asking for such powers—that, in the fine phrase of Chief Justice Warren Burger, "a lawyer's signature on a pleading or motion was something like a signature on a check; there was supposed to be something to back it up."[5] It was not until the 1980s that the judges of the federal courts found it necessary to write a rule holding lawyers liable if they presented "frivolous" claims.

Unfortunately, the idea that a lawyer as an officer of the court must exercise an independent professional judgment has fallen into disfavor. Driven by a distrust of what they consider "elitism," by a feeling that what older lawyers consider professionalism is really only an expression of social class superiority, legal academics in large numbers have taken to equating professionalism in law with subservience to the client. Richard L. Abel, professor of law at the University of California at Los Angeles, writes:

> Lawyers are hired guns: they know they are, their clients demand that they be, and the public sees them that way. As more lawyers are employed by or represent increasingly powerful clients, this identification grows even stronger. Lawyers must stop denying the identification and embrace it. Instead of seeking to justify their actions by reference to process values that allegedly produce truth and justice, lawyers must concede—indeed, affirm—that they actively promote the objectives of their clients and justify their own behavior in terms of the substantive justice of their clients' goals.[6]

Professor Monroe Freedman of Hofstra University Law School, once chairman of the ethics committee of my own District of

Columbia Bar Association, insists that the "intended implica-
tion [of the phrase "officer of the court"] is that the lawyer
serves principally as an agent of the state." But this is entirely
backward. The question to be asked is how the lawyer derives
his authority to act on behalf of his client to the disadvantage of
others, and the answer to that question is that by the acceptance of his license to practice law he has also accepted a responsibility to act as more than an advocate.

Indeed, even today we have significant areas of law where
lawyers must pledge *not* to do what their clients would wish
them to do. Judges will often agree to order the opponents of a
party to a lawsuit to let that party's lawyers interrogate them
and scour their files in unsupervised "discovery" proceedings
prior to trial. Such access to the other party's secrets may, however, be hedged with a "confidentiality agreement" by which
the lawyer promises not to communicate the contents of those
files to anyone, including his clients. House counsel for corporations will be limited in what they can do when litigation requires this sort of discovery, because courts will be reluctant to
give mere employees of the company, whether or not they have
law degrees, access to confidential files of its rival.

Some part of the structure of the "legal services industry," as
the Department of Commerce calls it (it is Standard Industrial
Classification 81), still requires that lawyers be independent.
The "autonomy" of the client, his continuing power to make for
himself the decisions that affect his cause—much acclaimed by
modern legal philosophers and in the codes of ethics adopted
since the 1960s—expresses an unreality. The client who comes
to the lawyer, like the patient who comes to the doctor, has
done so because he cannot handle his problem himself. Ac-
knowledging this, he abdicates some part of his autonomy. The
state, in licensing lawyers and doctors (and architects), certifies
the competence of the professional to deal with the problems of
those who seek help. In return for providing this certification,
and the access to authority that accompanies it, the state correctly imposes professional obligations.

A client cannot himself subpoena witnesses or documents, simply because he is not a lawyer. The lawyer is forbidden by his oath from farming out his power to laymen. If the lawyer is acting on the instruction of a layman rather than through the exercise of his judgment applied to the layman's problem, there is no logical reason why the witness should respond to the subpoena or provide the documents. For those who feel that the value of law is the imposition of reason on human activity, the argument that the lawyer serves society by exclusive service to his client contains an inherent and hopeless contradiction. The Hobbesian world in which every man's hand is against every other man's hand is not conducive to the rule of law.

The relationship of lawyer and client is not that of soldier and general. A much better analogy is, as noted, to the relationship of parishioner and clergyman, where it is understood that the clergyman is not subservient to the parishioner—even when that parishioner is the largest contributor to the church. Like the ministry, law is a *calling*. As the clergyman advises on the moral nexus of his parishioners' problems, the lawyer tells clients what the law permits them to do.[7] Louis D. Brandeis was the premier corporation lawyer of Boston, representing the "traction" companies (streetcars) and the public utilities. This did not make him any less a crusader for popular causes: His clients bought his professional services, not him. "Instead of holding a position of independence, between the wealth and the people, prepared to curb the excesses of either," he told a Harvard meeting in 1905, "able lawyers have, to a great extent, allowed themselves to become adjuncts of great corporations and have neglected their obligation to use their powers for the protection of the people. We hear much of the 'corporation lawyer,' and far too little of the 'people's lawyer.'"[8] He defined his own career very simply: "I would rather have clients," he said, "than be somebody's lawyer."

Even those whose firms fought persistently against all social legislation, getting much of it declared unconstitutional, re-

tained their independence. It was of the nature of the profession in the nineteenth and early twentieth centuries that
lawyers working on commercial matters came in to manage the
scavenger phase rather than the creation phase. The great users
of investment capital were the railroads and the public utilities,
which had to be built with money from the public before they
could generate earnings. Promoters and bankers alike were
subject to great temptation to exaggerate their markets, over-
build—and, indeed, raise more money than needed for the job,
keeping the surplus for themselves. When the cash flow was insufficient to leave any income for the stockholders, the bankers
blamed competition between the railroad companies and
sought "consolidation," usually by issuing more bonds to buy
out stockholders. Testifying before the Hadley Commission appointed by President Taft, Paul D. Cravath (of the firm now
known as Cravath, Swaine & Moore) noted his own belief that
"[t]he modern tendency to bring about railroad consolidation
through the issuance of bonds in payment for the stocks of the
railroads acquired is economically dangerous, because it results
in having a disproportionate amount of obligations bearing a
fixed rate of interest. . . . In acting as counsel for gentlemen in
these transactions, it has been my duty not to give advice about
political economy, but as to the law. . . . I may hold views totally
at variance with those of my clients on such matters."[9]

Cravath was supposedly a dedicated servant of powerful corporations, but he was nobody's lackey. He was a lawyer; his
clients bought his work, not his opinions, and not his citizenship. Those who claim that there never really were any "good
old days" tell us that law always was a business and the old-
timers just don't realize it. But I wonder how many of my colleagues in Washington today would be willing to tell a
presidential commission or congressional committee that they
disagreed with their clients and hoped Congress would change
the law in ways they would disapprove.

Today the prevailing view in the profession is that what matters in the lawyer's world is "winning." In my time, a Joseph Welch (of Boston's Hale and Dorr) could pierce the McCarthy image to its heart with his call of "Have you no shame?" when the junior senator from Wisconsin tried to blacken the reputation of one of Welch's young assistants. Today a number of lawyers would argue that the lawyer as advocate must do whatever *can* be done to win his client's cause.

In 1988, a lawyer for R. J. Reynolds Co., describing the tactics his firm used to get plaintiffs to drop tobacco cases, wrote the company: "The aggressive posture we have taken regarding depositions . . . continues to make these cases extremely burdensome and expensive for plaintiffs' lawyers. To paraphrase General Patton, the way we won these cases was not by spending all of Reynolds's money, but by making that other son of a bitch spend all of his."[10] New York Public Advocate Mark Green says that such tactics are common in divorce matters: "It's a war of attrition where the loser is the one whose assets have been exhausted. Usually that's the woman."[11]

When I was young at the bar, lawyers who did such things (and there were some) might have been feared—but they were not admired. It was a cliché of the profession in those days that a so-so settlement was better than a good lawsuit. "Persuade your neighbors," Abraham Lincoln wrote in advice to younger lawyers, "to compromise whenever you can. Point out to them how the nominal winner is often a real loser—in fees, expenses and waste of time. As a peacemaker a lawyer has a superior opportunity of being a good man."[12] Paul Freund wrote: "The lawyer-client relation in counseling has about it something of the attitude of a sympathetic critic to a work of art—immersion and withdrawal—immersion lest he be pedantic and unfeeling, withdrawal lest he become bemused and sentimental."[13] Toward the end of his life, speaking on the topic of the continuing education of the bar, Judge Learned Hand called for "imagination" on the bench, at the bar, and in the legislature. "You must be able successfully to realize how other people in the society with which you are concerned are likely to respond to the adjustments that you propose. . . . We are not merely advocates, and we must not always be advocates. Adult education means that we have got rid of inveterate advocacy."[14]

Even when a lawyer is an advocate, it is by no means clear that he must be an advocate only for his client. The American Academy of Matrimonial Lawyers has promulgated a code of ethics urging that in divorce cases a lawyer, whether representing the father or the mother, must consider himself an advocate for their children.[15] The Arizona court of appeals has ruled that the lawyer for the guardian of an incompetent ward has duties to the ward that may transcend his duties to his client.[16] The Securities and Exchange Commission since the early 1970s has treated lawyers who help their clients lie on registration statements as unprivileged co-conspirators. In the backwash of the S&L disaster, lawyers have paid fines to the government and compensation to victims of fraud by their S&L clients because they had entered what they knew or should have known to be false arguments before banking regulators. Eminent authorities on legal ethics have defended some of these lawyers, arguing that they had done only "what a lawyer does for a client." One remembers the classic definition of a diplomat as someone "sent to lie abroad for his country"—but one should remember also that the man who uttered that definition was recalled from his post and cashiered.

In *Nix* v. *Whiteside* in 1986, the Supreme Court held that a lawyer's refusal to help a client give perjured testimony did not, as his subsequent lawyer argued, deprive him of his Sixth Amendment right to assistance of counsel or of his right to testify in his own defense. Professor Bennett Gershman of Pace University complained that "to the extent that *Nix* authorizes defense counsel to engage in conduct which effectively drives his client off the witness stand, it constitutes an insensitive and unwarranted intrusion into a defendant's right to testify in his own behalf. Crucial to notions of civilized justice are concerns for a defendant's individual freedom and dignity. Such concerns ought to be respected, even at the risk of false testimony." This is by no means a universal belief: Texas judge Thomas M. Reavley writes: "I am as sympathetic with the claim that a lawyer is obligated to protect and advance the right of her client to commit perjury as I am with the claim that we should protect and advance the right of a man to beat his wife and children."[17] But there has grown up substantial academic acceptance of such behavior.

The profession of law as I recognize it has no place for the lawyer who in the interests of "winning" will seek knowingly to hoodwink the court. We did not when I was young destroy the village in order to save it. Nor does the profession of law as I recognize it have a place for the lawyer who sells his conscience as well as his services to the client that pays him. Sir Walter Scott wrote a bit of doggerel verse about the Scottish laird who refused to shake the hand of his king:

> *My castles are my king's alone*
> *From tower to foundation stone.*
> *The hand of Douglas is his own.*

The sense that the law is basically about fair play does of course survive, especially in the rural parts of the country, where, as lawyer Paul Stritmatter of Hoquiam, Washington, put it, "a lawyer represents folks, not entities." John S. Moore of nearby Yakima Valley noted: "Around here, everybody pretty well honors the 't'ain't fair rule. If another lawyer tries to take unfair advantage, you go up to the judge and say, ''T'ain't fair, Judge,' which is usually enough. When you call another lawyer and agree on something, you don't worry that you have to get it in writing."[18] This is the way it was everywhere not very many years ago, even in the big cities, where the lawyers didn't know each other or the judge. Nobody spoke in those days of "scorched earth" or "take no prisoners," and no one could have imagined that law professors would solemnly defend such tactics with the argument that if they are *not* employed the lawyer has not sufficiently represented his client's interest.

Judge Charles Wyzanski put the question of the trial lawyer's role most subtly. He wrote in the 1950s:

> Of course, when playing a game—especially if you are playing in a representative capacity—you must keep your eye on the ball, and *within the rules* try to win that game. Nothing else counts. And this is because the objects and procedure are defined. The limitations are the conditions of the art. Style is performance within the prescription. Or to use a lawyer's phrase, it is 'due process.'. . . But life is not a game. Nor is it (for me) the opposite: a struggle of deadly serious implications. That is, it is not a wager for Heaven or Hell. No such gamble is offered to man. He plays for less substantial stakes—for an ethically satisfactory life while on earth.
>
> Man has a chance to make a *moral* pattern—not merely something he likes, or something that has the beauty of the dance, or the virility of an ascent of Everest. If he restricts himself to what he likes and the way his taste runs, of course we may get a Learned Hand or a Paul Valéry, but we may get Al Capone or Hitler. And to tell the young to make a pattern without at the same time telling them it is to be a moral pattern is to run the risk of which direction they arbitrarily will select. To advise them to make a *moral* choice is not to tell them *what* choice they must make. It is only to stress that in your way through life you must try to build some coherent structure drawn from the experience of the race, from your background, from your personal insight.[19]

All this seems far from the discussions of legal ethics one overhears at the luncheon tables. Law firms confront questions about whether the Xerox room and the messenger service should be profit centers, whether to create a "class action" against a record company based on the revelation that a duo of rock singers had faked a recording, whether travel time to and from a client's office should be charged at regular hourly rates. Should the law firm give up representation of a smaller client in order to take on a larger one with whom there might be a conflict? Should law firms own and operate consulting services and other businesses to which they can refer clients? Is it legitimate for a lawyer to bill different clients at full rates for the same quarter hour because he made phone calls for both of them during a single fifteen-minute period? All these are questions one hopes Judge Wyzanski's young lawyer would have answered properly, but the fact that they arise is itself a demonstration that something has gone very wrong. There are much more important questions that go unasked.

I believe we did better in the past, and we can do better today. Law is an honorable calling that can employ all a man's or woman's talents—and better instincts, too. "Fair and square," Americans used to say when they talked about winners and winning. At the great law firms, and among many of the smaller firms and solo practitioners, it was, I think, understood and internalized that when you won at law, it should be fair and square. Surely those who sought the honor of leadership in their profession prized their reputation above all.

Law, of course, is not alone in the deterioration of its morals and manners. Much of American life has lost our old reverence for reputation. I understand, I hope, and I will explain my understanding in subsequent chapters, why the profession I love has changed so drastically and disappointingly in the past half century. Looked at through the rearview mirror, much of what happened seems to have had an awful inevitability about it. But understanding does not in this case bring forgiveness, for what looks at first glance inevitable was often, really, no more than the easy way out. The doctrine that professionalism means respect for the client's "autonomy" and commands doing whatever the client wants is, after all, most convenient. Nobody ever lost a client by doing exactly what the fellow wanted, but much lucrative legal work has been sacrificed by lawyers who regretfully told prospective clients that this was something they were not willing to do.

The president of the Canadian Bar Association in a speech to the American College of Trial Lawyers in 1990 said wistfully: "Not very long ago a lawyer was a lot more than a human punch clock churning out billable time units. He or she was an adviser in the truest sense of that word—a trusted counsellor to clients who more often than not were also family friends. I suppose those days are gone forever and there is precious little to be gained from maudlin reflections on the way we were."[20] I think there is more than maudlin reflection to be done, and there is something to be gained by stepping back and looking at where we are through a lens of time. This book is written in the faith that we lawyers can, if we care, restore those values we used to preach and even tried to live by, in the belief that lawyers should lead the way to a more ethical America. I am an idealist, and I always have been. Quite apart from the personal satisfactions idealism brings, my idealism has also been the foundation of my career as a lawyer. Lawyers prosper when troubled people seek them out, and most troubled people like the thought that there are ethical solutions to their problems.

But when I cry out for a stop to so much of what is going on in the practice of law today—and when I suggest ways and means to restore our dignity—I am being at least as practical as I am idealistic. For as a practical matter, neither clients nor the political public will long endure what so many Americans now regard as abuses of their trust by lawyers. Justice Sandra Day O'Connor insists: "Both the special privileges incident to membership in the profession and the advantages those privileges give in the necessary task of earning a living are means to a goal that transcends the accumulation of wealth. That goal is public service, which in the legal profession can take a variety of familiar forms. This view of the legal profession need not be rooted in romanticism or self-serving sanctimony, though of course it can be. Rather, special ethical standards for lawyers are properly understood as an appropriate means of restraining lawyers in the exercise of the unique power that they inevitably wield in a political system like ours."[21]

Socrates pointed out more than 2,400 years ago that orators as distinct from teachers persuade rather than enlighten. When the orator Gorgias is announced as a visitor to Socrates, the great philosopher's first question is "Ask him who he is." Similarly, legal ethicist Geoffrey Hazard finds a need in modern America to give the legal profession "an identity and a place in the social system. My root question is 'Who is "we" when it is said "We lawyers"?'"[22]

The time has come for lawyers to answer that question, determine who we are, where we are, how we got here, and what we can do about it—in our own interest, in our clients' interest, and in the interest of the nation.

CHAPTER 2

A GREAT PROFESSION
LOSES ITS WAY

1

I n the 1992 presidential campaign, both George Bush and
Vice President Dan Quayle sought to make the behavior of
my profession one of the major issues of the national election. The vice president in particular quoted enormous numbers, hundreds of billions of dollars, when proclaiming the
losses the country was suffering because doctors had to practice defensive medicine for fear of lawsuits and corporations
did not dare to bring out new products. Elimination of malpractice suits against doctors was a centerpiece of the Bush
White House cost-containment program that would make universal health insurance affordable in America. Restrictions on
environmental and consumer safety lawsuits would help American enterprise compete against foreign manufacturers not bur-
dened with such costs.

On the whole the country has refused to take the antilawyer
crusades seriously, I assume partly because there are more peo-

ple who fear they might become the victims in an accident or of a poorly manufactured product than there are stockholders in insurance companies, and partly because people sense that the country has more serious problems. "Courts in America," John Heilemann of *The Economist* argued in that magazine's generally negative 1992 review of lawyering worldwide, "have powerful protectors of individual liberties and agents of social change—think of civil rights, or consumer protection. For all their complaints, Americans hold dear the ease with which they can use their courts. And well they should. People in many countries would dearly love to be so litigious."[1]

But I cannot deny that there was something to what the critics were saying, and the argument crossed party lines. In his first congressional address, President Clinton went out of his way to comment negatively on the lawyers who had found ways to take for themselves a high fraction of the money supposedly set aside to clean up toxic waste repositories—and his comment drew what may have been the loudest applause of a very well received speech.

Too many in my profession have taken a calling that sought the good society and twisted it into an occupation that seems intent primarily on seeking a good income. The change has been very widely if sometimes wistfully accepted. When Alexander Forger, managing partner of the great New York firm Milbank Tweed, told his partners "We are not a trade or business; we are a profession," he described his statement as "a hysterical note from the past."[2]

The Supreme Court has said that the Constitution protects lawyers' rights to advertise their services, and all around the country lawyers advertise the miracles they can accomplish for those who ring their doorbells. A New York firm headed by a former judge advertises on the radio: "Have you or someone you know been injured in any type of accident? Just call toll-free, 1-800-EX-JUDGE. . . . Let the ex-judge help you get everything you're entitled to. . . ."[3] On a less grating level, different in degree but not necessarily in kind, bar associations present conferences on "marketing" legal services; the National Law Firm Marketing Association now has more than 750 members. Marketing consultants, *The Wall Street Journal* reports, "exhort lawyers to heed the gospel of legal salesmanship in the competitive '90s: The client rules."[4]

Law firms own and operate subsidiary "consulting services" that enable them to profit by supposed "synergies" between the practice of law and other, often unprofessional, services. Law is a service "industry"—the president of the District of Columbia Bar Association (which has more than 44,000 members) claimed in his 1991 inaugural address with pride that law was "the biggest, healthiest industry in town."[5] And what seems to characterize the perceived leadership of the profession is too often not a reputation for public service, probity, judgment, or scholarship but a reputation for representing the biggest clients and charging the highest fees.

The press has been quick to recognize achievement measured in such terms. In 1986, the firm of Finley, Kumble, Wagner, Heine, Underberg, Manley, Myerson and Casey, new but huge (approaching a nationwide network of a thousand lawyers), received an admiring profile in *Fortune*: "Traditionalists deplore Finley Kumble's nontraditional ways. It raids the competition, rewards on merit rather than seniority and operates like a big business. . . . In a profession notorious for a cavalier attitude toward cash flow, Finley Kumble is a taut financial ship. . . . Finley Kumble has no more skeletons in its closet than any other major firm. Is white shoe status just around the corner?"[6] This was a firm that included among its partners both a former governor of New York State and a former mayor of New York City (Hugh Carey and Robert Wagner) and two men who had been among the most influential members of the United States Senate (Russell Long and Paul Laxalt). Eighteen months after the publication of the *Fortune* article, Finley Kumble was bankrupt, several of its former partners were facing criminal charges, and all of them were being sued by bankers who had loaned the firm a total of more than $100 million. In 1992, the partners in Finley Kumble, now employed elsewhere, paid out $40 million to former clients suing for malpractice. But the sad fact is that the lessons have not been learned. The aspiring Finley Kumbles of the 1980s are still there, and many of them are still aspiring; and the magazines that acclaimed them once would in all likelihood do so again.

The American Bar Association's Commission on Professionalism reported in 1986 that only 6 percent of corporations rated "all or most" lawyers as deserving to be called "professionals."[7] Only 7 percent thought professionalism was increasing among lawyers, and 68 percent thought it was decreasing. No fewer than 55 percent of the nation's state and federal judges responded to a similar questionnaire with the view that lawyer professionalism was in decline. A 1993 poll by the *National Law Journal* found that almost a third of Americans thought lawyers were "less honest than most people."[8] Can we really live with those numbers?

2

Respect for lawyers begins with the public's sense that they are independent professionals. Clearly, professionals who can make their own decisions about what they will or will not do are more worthy of respect than people who are always ready to do what they are told. But the sad fact is that the ideal of lawyers' independence is too often honored in the breach. Professor Abel and his colleagues are right to deny a meaningful professionalism to those who "remain autonomous in selecting their means but only by allowing others to determine their goals."[9] There always have been and always will be hired guns, just as there always have been and always will be ambulance chasers.

And it is of course expected, quite properly, that a lawyer will use his arts and his mastery of process in the interest of his clients. Emory Buckner, Felix Frankfurter's best friend at the bar and founder with Elihu Root, Jr., and Grenville Clark of the firm now known as Dewey Ballantine, gave the young men of his office a motto: "When we are for the plaintiff, nothing can stop us; when we are for the defendant, nothing can start us."[10] Frankfurter himself, en route to his professorship at the Harvard Law School almost a hundred years ago, took the dependence on others as reason to shun private practice because it meant "putting one's time in to put money in other people's pockets."[11]

But it is impossible to square the insistence of Abel and others that lawyers justify their behavior by proclaiming the "substantive justice of their client's cause" with the assertion that lawyers "always embraced the interests of any client willing to pay them," that the profession follows the British "'cab rank' rule, which requires English barristers to represent any client who seeks their services (and can pay their fees)." If you have the client simply because you were next on the cab rank, you can be truly convinced of the justice of his cause (and thus the injustice of his antagonist's cause) only by autohypnosis, which is not the mark of professionalism. And the best lawyers, the ones we should wish to regard as our models, have in the end accepted clients very largely through judgments as to whether or not they were willing to be associated with this person's cause. Buckner was by no means alone in his "personal rule . . . never to argue a cause unless I believe the Court should decide in my favor or, at least, that my argument is entitled to a dissenting opinion."[12] Anyway, the cab rank rule is probably a fiction imposed by one culture on the habits of another. Justin Stanley, a leading Chicago lawyer who is a former president of the American Bar Association, has pointed out that British barristers do not accept clients directly, but through the agency of solicitors. The best of them will refuse to take cases they feel should not be brought, and they will refuse to deal with solicitors whose judgment they distrust.

Lawyers who are incontestably employees have become a major portion of the profession. Ours is an era of bureaucracy; governments at all levels and large private corporations have found that legal training prepares people well to administer rules. Many lawyers now work on a salaried basis for employers who are not members of their profession. When they work as lawyers, representing their corporate employers as a law firm would, such lawyers are not practitioners with clients, they are "somebody's lawyer." But even these can—and should—retain a respect for their "mystery" in the medieval sense: the fellowship they have joined through study and apprenticeship.[13]

Every profession, George Bernard Shaw wrote, looking at it from the outside, is a conspiracy against the layman.[14] But from within, what Shaw calls a "conspiracy"[15] is benign and reflects the practitioner's devotion to the skills and canons of his profession.* Professionals are people who make decisions and take responsibility for them. A professional does not "take orders" and does not prostitute his judgment. Clients find work well done or ill done according to the results, but lawyers know better: Great work can be done in a losing cause, or in setting up a deal that in the end does not come through, or in finding an argument that some later court (but not yours, not now) decides is the true expression of the law. Professionals do not accept as definitive opinions on their performance or their conduct from outside the circle of their peers—this is, indeed, why the ethics of the leadership are so crucial to the performance of the rank and file. If a lawyer does something truly admirable, the praise he cherishes is that of his colleagues. If he does something disgraceful, the shame is his loss of reputation among his peers.

The highest expression of the fellowship of the bar has al-

*My use of the masculine pronoun throughout this book reflects customs of the time when I began writing about legal subjects. I intend no discrimination or desrespect: Ask my four daughters!

ways been the partnership of lawyers. *Partner* was, and for most of us still is, a word with deep meanings. You chose people as partners because they added, or in everyone's view would add, strength or luster to the firm. Not long after World War II, the general counsel of American Airlines offered that company as a client to the firm of Sullivan & Cromwell (he had been an associate at the firm fifteen years earlier) if he were taken into the partnership. Edward Green, the firm's elder statesman on the finance side, said: "Making partners just to get clients is the beginning of the end," and American Airlines was sent elsewhere.[16]

Partnerships were, of course, entirely voluntary and not required by the economics of the practice of law: As late as 1948, more than three fifths of all lawyers were solo practitioners.[17] Like marriages, partnerships were traditionally for life, and they were not casually broken. Nor were partners compelled to retire at any age. New York Family Court Judge Kathryn A. McDonald has attributed some of the decline in the moral fiber of her city's bar to the forced retirement of senior partners "who had the wisdom and leisure to serve as mentors."[18]

Juniors in law firms in the years right after World War II stood in awe of the partners—not of the money the partners made but of their knowledge—knowledge of the law, knowledge of the world. Youngsters worked usually as assistants to one partner, on his matters, but they met the others at the firm, at lunches or dinners or just through casual conversations in the office. Professor Mary Moers Wenig of the University of Bridgeport Law School remembers the 1950s at the Wall Street firm of Cahill Gordon, when neophytes like herself tried to find work that would put them in the library at four o'clock. One or more of the partners would come in for the tea the library served every day at that time and would shoot the breeze for the edification of the juniors, making them feel part of a larger enterprise.

As late as 1975, there were fewer than four dozen firms with more than a hundred lawyers, totaling 6,558 lawyers in all; by 1993 there were more than 250 such firms totaling more than 66,700 lawyers.[19] Today many of these firms have large numbers of partners scattered all over the United States, Europe, Latin America, the Middle East, and Asia, and several times as many associates as partners; contacts are formal, structured, rare. Managing committees run the firms, delegating much of their authority to a managing partner who may be so busy with internal administrative detail that he no longer practices law. A world in which partners don't know each other is not a world that nourishes professional standards. Lawyers can't know much about what their partners are doing three thousand miles away—but they can read the numbers that show how profitable that office is. And it is these firms, still growing, housing most of the nation's best-paid lawyers, that set the tone for the modern practice of law.

Years ago, law was a profession with many satisfactions, and lawyers lived well, but law was not considered a route to great wealth. A large fraction of the income of a firm was "on retainer" from clients who paid a flat annual fee to have access to a lawyer whenever they needed one. If a client required a great deal of work during the year, his lawyer would sit down with him and explain why the retainer didn't cover what had been done for him. But the notion of sending time sheets and hourly rates to a client of some years' standing would have chilled the blood of the old-timer—and, no doubt, of his client. The rich paid more, the less rich probably paid less.

There was, of course, another side to the story. Except for the infrequent cases taken pro bono, without fee, because the lawyer believed in the cause, the poor essentially got no legal services at all—unless they had a good case for major money damages, which a lawyer might be prepared to take for a fee that came out of the proceeds. And even then, access to the best-regarded lawyers was rare because "contingent fees" were frowned upon: The philosophers of the profession argued that lawyers' advocacy should be hedged about with ethical restraints and that contingent fees gave a lawyer illicit pecuniary reasons to violate those restraints. Disapproval of having an interest in a client's cause was by no means a matter of class prejudice; it was a rule the leaders of the bar applied to themselves in their corporate practice. Paul Cravath forbade anyone who worked at Cravath, Swaine & Moore from owning stock in any client corporation.

Partners shared and shared alike, or pretty much alike. The compensation schedule in the old-fashioned law firm was essentially that of the Japanese civil service: Your share was a function of your seniority. Dominant figures violated the rules. One of the most charming stories about Cravath (a protean figure, he was unpaid general counsel of the National Association for the Advancement of Colored People and chairman of Fisk University as well as the Metropolitan Opera) tells of the day when some of the younger partners waited for him to discuss compensation questions, and Cravath, after hearing their complaints, waved them off with the comment that as long as they didn't touch his 50 percent they could do whatever they liked. The key fact was that nearly all members of a firm moved in lockstep up the ladder of seniority. This helped keep partnerships together, because partners were not competing against each other, and gave the young something to anticipate.

Before 1900, "clerks" were paid nothing: Learning the law was a process of apprenticeship, and the apprentices were to be grateful for the opportunity. After World War I, clerks in all the larger offices were upgraded to the status of "associates" and were salaried, but the salaries were modest. When Cravath began to pay more in 1924, the other law firms called for a meeting, and an agreement was reached to prevent any firm from offering more to new law school graduates than any other firm. The associate's salary was part of the firm's fixed costs at a time when payment for legal work was usually on retainer. Provided the work was done properly, the client had no reason to care whether it was done by a partner or by an associate. Usually, nobody told him whether a given piece of work was done by a partner or an associate. No doubt the associates were pressed hard. But that was part of the game of competing for partnerships. The competition was felt to be fair. Virtually all new partners came from the ranks of the associates, and an entering associate's chance of gaining a partnership in a growing firm was as good as one in three or one in four. The rule was "up or out"; with rare exceptions, associates who didn't "make partner" were expected to leave the firm—but often the firm took responsibility for placing the associates who did not become partners into good jobs with clients or with other firms that were not quite as large and almost as good.

Associates, then, were almost family; but so were clients. Taking on a client was not just acquiring a piece of business; it was the beginning of a relationship. And the relationship, however personal in its origins, was regarded as one between the firm and the client. Other partners and even juniors might attend meetings of the client with the lawyer who was the primary contact with the firm, to make sure that the other people in the firm had their own personal relationships with him. The client was not charged for their time at the meeting. (I was general counsel and then chairman of the board at Xerox while senior partner in a Rochester law firm; and the president and CEO of Xerox, Joseph C. Wilson, was my closest friend. When I left to become ambassador to the Organization of American States for President Lyndon Johnson, my firm kept Xerox as one of its largest clients.)

By the same token, one did not wish to have a relationship with everybody who sought one. Buckner, who had enjoyed telling his young associates about their force as plaintiff's counsel and their inertia as defense counsel, also wrote for their benefit that "clients are not entitled to lawyers who disbelieve their stories." Today the cant outside and even inside the profession is that everybody is "entitled" to dedicated advocacy by the lawyer of his choice. My own view is Buckner's: A lawyer should not undertake the representation of someone whom he does not trust and whose story he does not believe. Professionalism requires a lawyer to tell any client that he will not introduce evidence he believes to be false or seek to discredit by trickery testimony he believes to be true, and if the client wants other services, the lawyer should urge him to seek representation from a lawyer who considers him truthful. Roy Grutman, who was a partner in the giant Finley Kumble firm, and who professes in his memoirs a totally cynical attitude toward the law, nevertheless writes that "accepting a client is ultimately a moral decision."[20]

Good lawyers don't have to take bad clients. Edward Bennett Williams, the brilliant trial lawyer, once sought to explain his representation of people like Frank Costello by saying, "Everyone is entitled to a lawyer." "Yes," was the response, "but they are not entitled to *you*."

I believe Ron Brown was ill-advised when he told a Senate committee during his confirmation hearings as secretary of commerce that he was "proud" of his representation of Baby Doc Duvalier, the tyrant and despoiler of Haiti. In defense of his representation, he said, "You're judged not by your clients but by your advocacy."[21] It is true that, in the Washington of the 1980s, Ron Brown's willingness to work for a man like Duvalier was not extraordinary behavior, and no one should judge a man outside the context of his times. But it was not something to be proud of.

Money is, of course, at the heart of the problem. Law as a profession can carry many burdens, but it cannot carry a code of values that ranks money very high among the virtues. The full implications of the changes in compensation by the firms were not understood for a generation. Less than twenty years ago, the journalist Paul Hoffman could still write: "Unlike business executives or college professors, the Brahmins of the Bar don't shop around for better-paying positions. A partner at Sullivan & Cromwell won't drop a hint to the powers at White & Case that he's available for a little more money. And, as if by an unwritten agreement, there is almost no 'raiding' by one firm of another's talent."[22]

Now there is a great deal of what is politely called "lateral entry" at almost all the big firms. Judge Simon Rifkind of Paul Weiss, now in his nineties but still to be found at the office every day, bitterly regrets the changes. "This was a better world and a better profession," he said, "when clients didn't know what other law firms charged and lawyers didn't know what other lawyers made." Steven Brill, inventor and owner and editor of *American Lawyer*, says: "It's all my fault. Before we began publicizing the money the partners in the big law firms made, a man might be satisfied with the two hundred thousand dollars a year he was receiving from Milbank Tweed. But when he read in *American Lawyer* that a classmate of his who had gone to Cravath, Swaine & Moore was making four hundred thousand dollars, he demanded more. That wasn't like Finley Kumble—he could move to Cravath and still be in his country club. So he moved." The greatest vice of the Supreme Court decision that permitted advertising may have been that by inference it legitimated lawyers' talking to reporters.

The worst damage is done invisibly, within the firm, where collegial relations become secondary to financial return and the young are inducted into a business rather than a mystery. The division of a law firm's "profits" among the partners has become far less equal than it once was. Increasingly, revenues are allocated to those whose work is perceived as actually generating them—which does not by any means imply that they go to those who do the work: The "rainmakers" who have the client contacts are generally more heavily rewarded than those whose labors buttress the firm's reputation for quality. Clients are increasingly seen as the "property" of the partners who have the highest level of direct personal contact with them. If these partners leave the firm, it is assumed that "their" clients may well follow them. It is thus also expected that if one partner's clients decline as sources of revenues for the firm while another's rise, the shares within the firm will soon be adjusted. When Finley Kumble went marauding in the 1980s, buying up rainmakers from other firms and sometimes entire firms, it became acceptable for partners to inform their firms that if their share was not increased they would take their clients elsewhere.

The Committee on the Profession of the City Association in New York made a list of horribles:

> [F]or example, there is the case of the partner who agrees with his or her partners to a new long term lease and to substantial expenditures for new offices, then promptly departs with a large book of business.
>
> A case involving partner dismissal would be that of the hardworking partner, a rainmaker, who contributes greatly to building up a firm, has an unexpected heart attack or cancer and is dropped by his partners. . . .
>
> [T]here is the lateral transfer by a young partner who has built his or her practice as the protégé of an older lawyer, then departs unceremoniously with the clients to take an offer from another firm. A similar case is that of a partner in one department who departs the firm with clients introduced to him or her by his or her partners from other departments, when the latter had been continuing to serve those clients in their own special areas. There is the aging partner who has been the mainstay of the firm and then is systematically stripped of perquisites as he ages, even though continuing to practice full time. There are the partners in mid-career who are functioning effectively but are dropped to improve the bottom line for other partners, effectively ending their careers.

After much discussion—for there were those who argued that "the market should be permitted to work"—the committee generally agreed that "disloyal behavior by lawyers which injures a firm's ability to serve its clients is unprofessional."[23]

On the other hand, a number of law firms had become institutions that did not worry about the loyalty of their employees. Associates were paid a salary set at the beginning of the year, and the employing firm benefited by their labors according to the number of hours they worked that could be "billed" to clients. In many firms, associates became not so much the hope for the future as the cash cow for today. Of the ten large law firms with the greatest "profits per partner" in the United States in 1992, according to the annual *American Lawyer* summary of the hundred largest firms, only one (Wachtell Lipton) had more partners than associates, and five had more than three associates per partner. The chance of "making partner" diminished—and when the revenues of the large firms turned down in the 1990–91, a number of them decided to eliminate associates rather than cut the profits per partner.

Lawyers are, of course, fiduciaries—trustees—for other people's money. By far the most common cause of disbarment has been "commingling"—treating the client's money as one's own and "borrowing" it. Yet the question has to be raised whether there is really a great difference in ethical terms between such universally condemned misappropriations and the actions of a lawyer who deliberately overbills a client. A client is not a customer, and a client's relationship with his lawyer should never be one of *caveat emptor*. It seems to me that "marketing" the services of a law firm puts one perilously close to peddling the profession.

For me, the worst vice of the "marketing" approach, corrosive of relations both within the firm and with clients, is the acceptance of business that ought to be refused. It does not matter to Kellogg's Corn Flakes whether the purchaser is John Gotti or Cardinal O'Connor—but it should matter to a law firm whether or not what its client wants should be done for him. The savings-and-loan scandal is laced with stories about the participation of reputable law firms that knew their clients were doing improper things but tried to squeeze their actions into the framework of permissive government regulations so they could be, with luck, legally defensible. Now that the regulators have decided not only that the dishonesty was punishable but that the lawyers bear some responsibility for abetting it, a cry has arisen from some members of the profession that the rules have been changed in the middle of the game and the new rules are "unfair."

But in the end professionals have to stand responsible for their own actions, and the cry "My client made me do it" must fall on deaf ears. Harris Weinstein, who as general counsel for the Office of Thrift Supervision brought most of the cases against the law firms that represented the S&Ls, found himself "hard pressed . . . to understand how we can claim that a lawyer is free to deceive a third party when the client could not. If that were the rule, if a lawyer were permitted to do that, what would be left of the liability risked by the client's deception? Any client could overcome that liability simply by hiring a lawyer to do the dirty work for him."[24]

Indeed, to the extent that the lawyer's obligation of confidentiality will keep him from revealing what his client has done, professional ethics may require him to resign as this client's counsel—an embarrassment most easily avoided by not taking such clients to begin with. Lawyers certainly should not represent clients who come to them to break the law—and I would argue that they should avoid even those clients whose ambition is to profit from a defect in the law. An English businessman who has written novels asked recently about the obligations of a lawyer who has found a drafting error, a loophole in the law, or a wrongheaded court decision that would enable his client to make money doing things Congress or the state legislature had intended to prohibit. Wasn't a lawyer ethically required to tell his client of this discovery? The question is too clever by half, as the British like to say, but the answer can be plain and simple: A lawyer does have an obligation to tell his client that there is a loophole that can be exploited to his profit. And according to the client's decision about what to do with this information, the lawyer should decide whether or not he wants him as a client.

Dealing with the problems of a lawyer representing a company before a regulatory agency, Judge Stanley Sporkin of the District of Columbia asked: "What should counsel's role be where counsel is retained to keep his or her regulated client in business for as long as possible notwithstanding the lack of merit of the client's legal position? . . . The problem becomes exacerbated where counsel's 'playing the rules' can keep a known dangerous substance or product in the marketplace for virtually unlimited periods of time. . . . [T]he time seems ripe to review some of the questionable tactics employed by lawyers to assist their clients in the all-out takeover wars. To just name some of the measures employed suggests that perhaps less than ethical conduct was sometimes involved. 'Scorched earth,' 'poison pills,' 'greenmail,' and the 'pac man' defense are just some of the terms that raise serious questions whether the legal system was always ethically served. . . . While there is little that can be done about the past, we as members of the organized Bar can start the debate as to what the appropriate rules should be for the future."[25]

"Rules" may not be the answer: Attitudes will count for more. Quoting Max Weber, Professor Geoffrey Hazard of the Yale Law School notes "a transformation of the profession from a 'traditional' institution—one in which authority derives from 'the sanctity of age-old rules' to a 'bureaucratic' institution—one regulated by a 'system of abstract rules which have . . . been intentionally established.'. . . As a member of a traditional institution, a lawyer would first think 'Doing X is unprofessional,' and perhaps on second thought wonder whether X was barred by the Canons. As a member of an institution whose character is defined by law, the lawyer's first thought is more likely to be 'Does Rule Y prohibit/require doing X?'"[26]

Before we can write good rules, the profession must recognize as its leaders those whose careers illustrate the traditional rather than the bureaucratic standards.

3

In recent years we have seen a shift of emphasis from a client's hiring a firm to his hiring an individual member of a firm with the kind of expertise he seeks. This reflects the fact that law is so much more complicated, there is so much more of it, and a client tends to come to a lawyer not for general guidance in legal matters but for help with a special problem. The firms expand, hoping to attract business from their clients beyond this one partner's specialty. Partners are recruited from other firms to fill gaps, bringing new associates and new clients with them.

Ellen Joan Pollock reports that Milbank Tweed in 1987 commissioned the consulting firm of Zand Morris & Associates "to do a marketing report." They came back with word that "potential clients were not looking for 'quality and integrity' when choosing their counselors. . . . Superior work product could no longer be used as an effective selling point. . . . In fact, executives were looking for entrepreneurial lawyers who took initiative and made a discernible impact on transactions. . . ."[27] At that time, the conclusion Milbank Tweed drew was that it needed merger-and-acquisition specialists, because that was the hot area of law for corporations. Other firms drew the conclusion that they needed real estate specialists, because the real estate business was growing at a mad pace in the late 1980s. In the end, these decisions created problems for a number of firms when the merger-and-acquisition business shrank drastically after the indictment of Michael Milken and the collapse of Drexel Burnham—and the real estate market imploded.

Behind these practical concerns lay a subtle shift that has

been affecting all the American professions and many of our businesses—the shift from relationship to transaction. Deals have a beginning and an end; after their end, they are history. In the process of deal making, the prime question is getting the deal done; the focus is not so much on the continuing relationship of the parties (let alone their professional advisers) as it is on the transaction itself. The "deal" syndrome—the atomized transaction for which the law firm's fee will be greatly enlarged as part of the package if the deal is accomplished—tends to give lawyers an unprecedented stake in getting the deal done even if in their professional judgment there may be a doubt as to whether the deal *should* be done. In a world of transactions that have a beginning and an end, the parties are forever starting with a clean slate. Events do not cast shadows forward, and memories vanish. And the world of transactions sires a world of products bought and sold in anonymous marketplaces, where producer and consumer must be wary of each other—a world where the word *trusting* is too often followed by the word *fool*.

Relationships take time, and there are many bits and pieces that must fit together for them to make sense. In the 1980s we were in a hurry, and we disliked complexity. In banking, in business, in advertising, in medicine, in law, we atomized our relationships. Lawyers worked on specific cases for a fee that was built up from hourly charges for legal and nonlegal personnel, plus expenses. Newton Minow, once chairman of the Federal Communications Commission and later a senior partner in the Chicago firm of Sidley & Austin, expresses a particular distaste for "the feeling that the meter is running." The paradigm, as has happened so often in the history of law as a profession, came from medicine. In 1970, a doctor explained the loss of public affection and esteem for his profession by positing first an earlier time when someone who didn't feel good came to a doctor who cured him—and then the observable present, when someone who doesn't feel good goes to a doctor, and the first thing the doctor does is to give him a disease. Then the doctor treats the disease. And ever-increasing numbers of people no longer admire doctors.[28]

The loss of personal contact in the law derives also from changes in the real world outside the relationship of client and lawyer. In corporate practice the clients are now enormous multifaceted conglomerates, and the law firms that represent them—in New York, Houston, Seattle, Tokyo, London, and Brussels—meet not with the CEOs or even the COOs but with the general counsel or even a deputy to the general counsel, whose job is to decide what legal services his employer needs and to buy them. "It used to be," Henry King, managing partner of Davis Polk & Wardwell, told an *American Lawyer* symposium, "that my seniors in the firm dealt a great deal with overall issues confronting companies. They met with boards; some of my partners, though not members of the board themselves, attended every board meeting of every major company that we were involved with. It was a turn-on: They were involved in big issues.

"Today, that's being done by house counsel. The outside lawyer is involved almost exclusively in transactional matters. . . . And that has put greater pressure on the practice. It's 'Get the deal done.'"[29]

Of course, nostalgia is too easy. "Businesslike management" of law firms has too often come to mean maximizing the firm's profits. But the inefficiently operated law office benefited neither client nor lawyer. Too many hours could be devoted to the preparation of inadequate documents that were not even ready on time, requiring a request for postponement which one's gentlemanly antagonist always granted. In short, the significance of a word like "businesslike" reduces to the individuals on both sides of the relationship. The fact that these individuals are often on a lower organizational level than CEO and senior partner does not necessarily diminish the importance of trust and respect. But it does mean that the well-rounded relationship between a client and his "counselor at law" has become much less common. Thus the counseling function has become less central to a business practice. Thirty years ago, several of the larger firms did not have a partner—certainly not a senior partner—who concentrated on litigation. Adversary proceedings were a late, if not last, resort.

One way or another, those days will return. Lawyers still live and practice in a legal order that assumes they are professional and can therefore be trusted with other people's money and secrets. (Note the difference between the restrictions the law placed on a bank trust department and the confidence reposed in a lawyer as trustee.) Until recently, it would have been unthinkable that a lawyer would have interests that might conflict with those of his client.

Now conflicts sometimes grow so severe that courts must remind lawyers that the privilege of confidentiality in communications between client and lawyer exists to benefit the client, not the lawyer—and that a client claiming that his lawyer approved the behavior that got him in trouble has the right to introduce evidence supporting his claim whether the lawyer likes it or not.

These days even eminent lawyers and law firms find themselves in troublesome situations.

Former federal judge Abraham Sofaer of Hughes Hubbard, who was State Department legal adviser when the United States government demanded economic sanctions against Libya in 1986, signed on in July 1993 to represent the Qaddafi government in litigation arising out of Libya's involvement in the destruction of Pan Am flight 103. To accept Libya as a client, Sofaer had to get a special license from the Treasury Department's Office of Foreign Assets Control exempting him from the embargo he himself had crafted. Though he eventually resigned the client, his quoted initial reaction when questioned about his Libyan relationship was "I don't know what people are so excited about."

As both counsel for the Bank of Credit and Commerce International and chairman of First American Bancshares (covertly controlled by BCCI in contravention of American law), my friend, the distinguished and all but universally respected Clark Clifford, assured a Senate committee that he had never knowingly made inaccurate representations to the government as to the relationship between his client and his bank. He was indicted by state and federal grand juries in New York and Washington, but the charges against him were withdrawn by the U.S. Attorney in Washington, and because of his ill health, he was not brought to trial in New York. His partner, Robert Altman, did stand trial in New York and was acquitted of the charges. Many were bewildered as to how a lawyer like Clark Clifford, who commanded the highest respect of his profession, could have become involved in such a confused and confusing situation.

Cravath, Swaine & Moore represented General Development Corporation, which sold poorly built, greatly overpriced houses on low-value land to people living in lower-middle-class neighborhoods in the eastern states, and financed the sales in ways that anticipated that they would eventually foreclose on the property and sell it again. According to public records, Cravath's fees for helping to structure and defend this activity ran as high as $5 million a year. The defense of the officers of the corporation (the chairman was a Cravath alumnus) was that every step of the transaction had been vetted by Cravath, and thus the scheme as a whole could not be illegal. A jury did not agree and convicted them. If a pollster selected a thousand knowledgeable lawyers in the United States and asked them to name the best law firm in the country, Cravath would surely be among those with the highest number of votes. Why was such an estimable firm engaged in helping a corporation that was conducting such a business?

Early in 1992, the firm of Kaye, Scholer, Fierman, Hays & Handler, one of the most prominent and respected in New York, paid the Federal Deposit Insurance Corporation $41 million toward the taxpayers' $2 billion of losses in insured deposits in Lincoln Savings and Loan. The firm had already agreed to pay $20 million to individuals in retirement colonies in California to whom the parent company of Lincoln, controlled by Charles Keating, had sold worthless subordinated debentures for which Kaye Scholer had written the prospectus and approved the selling program. The former managing partner of Kaye Scholer agreed to accept disqualification from ever again representing an insured bank or S&L. (It should be noted, however, that a New York Attorney Disciplinary board found no basis for claiming he had violated ethical rules.) The charge against Kaye Scholer was that its partners had conspired with Lincoln to frustrate bank examiners. As Federal Judge Stanley Sporkin pointed out in an opinion in a separate court action, an internal memorandum of the firm placed in the record indicated that the firm was aware of the innacuracy of Lincoln's statements.

In April 1993, the *ABA Journal* published an article titled "The Tangled Web: When Ethical Misconduct Becomes Legal Liability," listing a number of the large (more than $19 million) settlements law firms have paid in recent years to settle claims of alleged malpractice. Great firms—Blank, Rome, Comisky & McCauley in Philadelphia; New York's Rogers & Wells; Chicago's Lord, Bissell & Brook; Baltimore's Venable, Baetjer & Howard; Denver's Sherman & Howard—all made settlements relating to savings and loans debacles or arising out of their representation of clients charged with misusing customers' or investors' or government insurance funds. The representation of such clients by such highly regarded law firms has been embarrassing not only to the firms but to the legal profession as a whole. "In many cases," says Allen Snyder of Hogan & Hartson, who served on the District of Columbia Board of Professional Responsibility and now defends law firms charged with misconduct, "ethics and malpractice merge or are closely related."[30]

Years ago there was a popular puzzle featured in American

newspapers that asked readers, "What is wrong with this picture?" Tests not unlike that puzzle have been used by psychologists to give them guidance in assessing how individuals react to situations of stress. The profession of law in the early 1990s presents such a puzzle, and the answers that are found will decide its future. In 1992, for the first time since World War II, the total income of the large law firms declined. An "industry" that had been recessionproof—that had expanded its income by 10 or 12 percent a year even through the deep decline of the economy in 1981–82—suddenly felt the bite of adversity. Some firms disintegrated, giving the bankruptcy courts cases of a kind they had never seen before. Many sloughed off associates, the young lawyers lured from the best schools with the promise of the highest salaries, now simply sent out to make their own way in the world. More than a few simply fired partners, sometimes publicly.

This shocking decline may in truth be an opportunity, for it compels the leaders of the great firms to look at their "business" again, in a different way. The fact is that law simply cannot operate as a business, because except for the very simplest, commoditylike legal tasks (the uncontested divorce, the routine will) there cannot be a market price for legal services. Markets require standardized categories, weights and measures, and comparabilities that a profession cannot offer. The first question a professional must answer is what services his client needs, and the market cannot determine that. Consumers have no way to know whether a lawyer can promise (let alone deliver) value for money, no way to judge whether what they are buying is a quality product or a lemon, no way to really know whether other lawyers would do precisely the same work for them and what they would charge for it. Professional services are sold by input rather than by output simply because output is unmeasurable by the consumer.

The decline in lawyers' revenues in 1992 should be seen as a warning that a heavy price will be exacted in the future if the profession persists in converting itself to a business. When lawyers worked on retainer, income was relatively steady but work load fluctuated. Relationships imply sustenance, a calculation of costs and benefits over a period of time. Dependence on transactions rather than relations implies less stability, years of boom and years of bust as the world generates more or fewer transactions that require intensive legal service. Efforts to maintain profits on the downslope of the business cycle will generate bitterness among employees who are made to bear a disproportionate share of the burdens, and resentment and resistance among clients who find their legal bills per transaction remaining high or even rising as their own profitability is squeezed. Their reaction, inevitably, will be to do more and more of their legal work in-house, where they can fix their costs, taking it away from the law firms that represent them. In the relationship of lawyer and client, there is much to be said from the lawyer's point of view for legal fees that are part of the client's fixed costs rather than part of his variable costs.

Professor Stephen Gillers, who teaches ethics at the New York University Law School, has made a specialty of ethical counseling to law firms. He argues that in an economic sense the correctives for today's vices are already on the scene. In the aftermath of the S&L disaster and a number of dishonestly presented initial public offerings of stocks, lawyers are being sued for restitution to the victims of their now-bankrupt clients. For the profession as a whole, malpractice insurance rates are climbing into the sky. Like automobile drivers, law firms will eventually have "experience ratings" that will control how much malpractice insurance costs them, and questions of fair dealing will no longer be only for idealists. Perhaps the best control of abuse in the world of "class action" lawsuits—where law firms ask a court to declare them the representatives of all those who may have been injured by some action of a corporate defendant, though at present they may have as clients only a few of their friends—is the one found by federal judge Vaughn

Walker in the Northern District of California. He asked all the recognized firms that had applied to be the lawyers for a class to put in a bid of what they would charge the clients if they won, and awarded the potentially lucrative job of lead counsel to the firm with the lowest bid.

The clients, Professor Gillers points out, are becoming resentful. A study by Professor Maurice Rosenberg of Columbia University indicates that the cost of legal services, which were once a minimal expense for American corporations, have risen to 5 percent of an average corporate budget. Companies are being asked to pay more than they believe they should—or more than they think the services of the law firms are worth. When every other supplier to their companies is being asked to cut back, they have no compunctions about making the same requests to the lawyers who have become in their eyes nothing more than vendors of legal services. As part of the "marketing" orientation that now suffuses the big firms, some of which have acquired "marketing departments," it is now relatively common for firms to compete for a given piece of "legal work," each making its own pitch to clients in presentations known as "beauty contests." At first, these presentations were confined to the showcasing of the "rainmaker," the former high government official or well-publicized expert who would devote his efforts to this client's cause if this firm was hired. Later, more elaborate efforts were mounted, including easel displays of how well the firm had done in similar matters. Eventually, as the day follows the night, clients—like Judge Walker in the class action context—began to ask the participants in the beauty contests to name their price.

This seems perfectly reasonable "business practice" to non-lawyers; manufacturers compete by shaving their margins, and people expect to pay more for great wine or cars or hotel rooms than they would pay for lesser goods and services. The best lawyers should, of course, command premium payments for their services by comparison with less brilliant practitioners.

But clients are not told, to say the least, that their lesser fees will buy them the services of lesser lawyers. In a number of instances in 1992, the losers of beauty contests were convinced, perhaps correctly, that their rivals had bought a piece of a client's business by offering a loss leader, a price that did not come near paying the costs of the work. If the partners in that firm had indeed agreed to reduce their incomes to get this business, one cannot quarrel. But other clients may well feel that they are entitled to similar consideration with respect to the bills submitted to them.

Acceptance of the proposition that law is a business will inevitably lead to the kind of government regulation that other businesses suffer—only more so, because of lawyers' "impositional powers." If lawyers cannot by themselves reestablish a climate of professionalism, government will set the parameters of behavior. Unbridled advocacy of the interests of drug dealers and S&L chieftains has already created laws that confiscate lawyers' fees. The widely shared outrage over the fraction of the asbestos settlement fund that goes to lawyers rather than victims may make some bad law indeed before we are done. Bankruptcy judges will come under increasing pressure, and perhaps legal restraint, to police the stripping of the bones of the bankrupt that can follow the assignment of a well-regarded law firm to such a case.

The issues should trouble many more than lawyers. Governments that assume the whip hand over lawyers can more easily whip others. More than the self-image and personal satisfaction of lawyers can be lost if law firms that have declared themselves to be businesses become subject to government regulation as businesses.

CHAPTER 3

My Profession: Remembrance and Assertion

1

Coming to the bar as a young man, I was an idealist because I had to be. The eldest of my immigrant parents' four sons, I had been destined to seek the American dream. As an undergraduate at Hamilton College, where I was the only Jewish member of my class, I helped pay my bills by reading to the venerable Elihu Root, one of the nation's first corporate lawyers and a great servant of his country, who was the last senator elected by the New York State Legislature before the Constitution was amended to provide for the direct election of senators. Root's term as an appointed senator ended in 1915, and he thereupon departed; he had been elected to the state legislature many years before and, after his decades of achievement, considered it beneath his dignity to run for office again. But this did not mean an end to his public service; he became chairman of the convention that wrote the new New York State constitution.

In his old age, Root retired to Hamilton, where he had been a student, and became an icon of the college. He interrupted my reading to him one day to ask what I planned to do after I finished school. I said I was debating between becoming a lawyer and becoming a rabbi. "Become a lawyer," he urged. "I have found that a lawyer needs twice as much religion as a minister or a rabbi."

Root had never been one to take his clients' goals as his own. Archibald Cox, the lawyer whose probing into Watergate as a special prosecutor *within* the Justice Department came close enough to the truth for Richard Nixon to insist that he be fired, quotes Root as having said to a client, "The law lets you do it, but don't. . . . It's a rotten thing to do."

2

My first job as a lawyer was from that tradition. My trip to New York during my last year at Cornell had produced one offer, from Root, Clark, Buckner & Ballantine, the Root being Elihu Root's son. But I decided I would rather practice in Rochester, where there seemed to be a camaraderie among lawyers I missed in the New York offices I visited. I accepted an invitation from the firm of Sutherland and Sutherland, which was strikingly like the image of a law firm I had acquired from *The Saturday Evening Post* when I was in high school. The magazine regularly featured a short story telling the adventures of a pair of brothers, Tutt and Mr. Tutt, who were small-town lawyers, one shrewd and one scholarly, through whose practice the author, Arthur Train, created the persons and life of the town and its surrounding countryside. This was Norman Rockwell America, and Rochester was not a small town, but in my early years as a junior in the little firm of Sutherland and Sutherland I kept finding myself in situations straight out of Train's fiction.

This was a four-man law firm, all members of the family except for myself. Its senior partner was Judge Arthur E. Sutherland, who had been a New York State Supreme Court judge. (In New York, the "Supreme Court" is a trial court.) He had not long before broken out of the larger Rochester partnership called Sutherland and Dwyer to form a new firm with his two sons—Andrew, a real Tutt, a great raconteur and fly fisherman who rolled his own cigarettes and loved the theatrics of the courtroom; and Arthur, Jr., Mr. Tutt, much more serious, a man who read Latin for pleasure and would become a law professor first at Cornell and then at Harvard, where he wrote a history of the law school. Arthur, Jr., had been a law clerk to Justice Oliver Wendell Holmes, Jr. He had argued before the U.S. Supreme Court the landmark case of *Nebbia* v. *New York*, which established the Holmesian doctrine that if a state could make a case that a regulation had a reasonable public purpose, the Supreme Court would not interfere. In this case, the state had established a minimum price for milk. Nebbia, who had a grocery, gave away a free loaf of bread with each bottle of milk he sold. The state sued Nebbia and won, and Arthur handled the appeal. He was, as law clerks often are in later life, on the opposite side of the matter from his old mentor, and he lost— but he had been excited by his brush with history, and I was excited to be in his office.

At Sutherland and Sutherland, tea was served in the office library every afternoon at four, and I would sit around listening to the conversation of father and sons. I was invited to the Sutherlands' homes (Arthur, Jr., even found me a violin to play so I could accompany him when he played the guitar and sang), and I felt myself part of a fellowship. The same courtesies were extended to George Williams, another Cornell Law graduate who came to the Sutherland firm a year later.

In 1920, in one of Judge Sutherland's most famous courtroom victories, he had represented the men's clothing manufacturer Michaels Stern in a labor matter. The Amalgamated Clothing Workers Union had been trying to organize the company's Rochester factory and, failing to win management's recognition, had called the workers out on strike. Sutherland got an injunction to prohibit picketing by the union, which brought suit to vacate the injunction, and Sutherland filed a countersuit for damages done to Michaels Stern by the picketing. Felix Frankfurter, then a Harvard law professor, was the adviser to the union's leader, Sidney Hillman, and he recruited his friend Emory Buckner of Root Clark to share the representation of the union. Among Sutherland's advantages in the trial was the fact that the judge hearing the case was sitting in the chair Sutherland had only recently vacated. Frankfurter, who had teaching duties, came only to argue motions (which were denied) for the admission of testimony by economists on the economic effects of unionization and to conduct the direct examination of Hillman. A long-established Rochester legend says that during that direct examination Sutherland kept prowling the well of the court behind Frankfurter, who finally turned to see what he was doing—at which point the former judge boomed out, in a voice that could be heard throughout the courthouse, "Your Honor, I call to your attention the fact that counsel is dishonoring the flag by standing with his back to it."

Despite such courtroom shenanigans, Sutherland and Frankfurter got on well, and Buckner and Sutherland became good friends who had drinks together at the conclusion of each day's work in a five-week trial. "It shows you," Frankfurter said years later, "how little laymen understand; my wife was shocked that Buckner and Sutherland were great friends."[1] It was and is part of professionalism that the lawyer does *not* identify with his client to the extent of sharing his client's antagonisms. And it is both the glory and the limitation of the trial lawyer that he becomes an actor on a stage, making the most of a script only part of which he had the chance to write.

Often I would go to trials with Andrew Sutherland and watch him at work. He was a canny, foxy, folksy trial lawyer who could twist juries around his finger. He always presented himself as a country boy, and when his opponent was a New York City lawyer he would make much of the differences between the "big city" and our "small town." One of his greatest talents in a courtroom was his ability to pretend surprise when he got the answers he had carefully encouraged his witness to give him. He would give the jury a startled look to make sure they understood the significance of the answer. An insurance company lawyer once told me that when Andrew represented plaintiffs in a negligence case, the company's settlement offer went up immediately.

I revered the Sutherlands and did not think any the less of them because, like all trial lawyers, they saw the trial itself as, in part, a game. They played the game well and within the rules. In those days, a much higher percentage of the ordinary practice was related to trials, but for that very reason we distinguished between what was proper for a lawyer to do in the context of a lawsuit and what was proper for him to do outside the adversarial context. Outside the courtroom, we knew, the practice of law is not a game.

Upon retirement from the bench, Judge Sutherland had accepted a part-time appointment as an official referee of the court, which meant that he heard certain assigned matters, mostly matrimonial. One of my jobs was to accompany him to the hearings and prepare rough drafts of opinions from the evidence that had been presented. He had a researcher's interest in the sexual aspect of marriage breakups, and I learned a good deal about the sexual proclivities of Rochesterians.

My first appellate case was a matrimonial matter passed to me by Arthur Sutherland, Jr. A lady had hired a detective to keep an eye on her husband, and the detective reported back that her husband had taken a woman to their house, turned on the lights on the ground floor, then turned them off as the lights went on in the upstairs bedroom. Some minutes later, the lights in the upstairs bedroom went off, those on the ground floor went on again, and the couple departed. Such was the testimony of the private investigator. At the trial, the case had turned on whether the lights were on long enough in the upstairs bedroom for the husband and his girlfriend to have used the bed, and the aggrieved wife had won, which meant she got a divorce and a favorable settlement of the family's assets. In the first appeal, the court reversed the original decision on the ground that the evidence was suggestive but not probative. The wife appealed, and I was asked to handle the husband's side of the case before the Court of Appeals, New York's highest tribunal.

I went to Albany, at twenty-five years of age, to appear before the Court. As the case was called, the chief judge, Irving Lehman, asked who represented the defendant. I said, "I'm here, sir." The judge asked, "Who is with you, young man? Who is going to argue the case?" I said, "I am, sir," and he said, "Well, then, advance to the court." He and the other judges joshed me in a kindly way, asking my opinion as to how long I thought the lights had to be off in the downstairs and on in the bedroom to prove the plaintiff's case. I must have given the right answer, because we won.

Judge Sutherland had attracted significant clients to the firm, including Union Trust Co., a bank later absorbed into Marine Midland, and several insurance companies. We did the usual routine work of law firms: real estate closings, wills and estates, contracts, divorces. Everything, even the work for the banks and corporations, had a human context. Lawyers in the 1930s still saw, knew, and represented the people of the community, not its money. Erwin Griswold, later dean of the Harvard Law School and solicitor general of the United States, grew up in his father's law office in Cleveland, a firm with twelve lawyers. "Many of my father's clients," he remembers, "were the widows of his clients."

One of my most interesting cases in those early years was a suit by the heirs to a very sizable estate to keep the "remainder" of the estate—after the payment of specific bequests— from going to a Pennsylvania charity. The argument, which I made because the family was our client and not because I liked it, was that under Pennsylvania law at the time an unincorporated charity could not be the beneficiary of a will. This position was, of course, precisely contrary to the wishes of the man whose will was being challenged. I pointed this out to our clients, urging them to find a basis for settlement, but they were adamant. After extended hearings on the issue in surrogate's court, a decision came down largely in our favor. When the charity gave every evidence of appealing to a higher court, I finally persuaded our clients to make a settlement, and we all felt better.

As I became more familiar with the city, I began to attract my own clients. One of them was a farmer who had a sizable farm and came in regularly with a litany of failed crops, broken machinery, overdue mortgages, too much rain, too little rain, et cetera. I tried to be helpful, even gave him ideas he might use to make his farm a more businesslike proposition, but to no avail. After one listening session, I said to him, "Do you think the problem could be that you just are not a good farmer?" He stared at me, got up, and left without either a word spoken or a bill paid.

One of my most important early clients, a lifesaver in the years after World War II, was Superba Cravats, a tie manufacturer that at one point had an exclusive contract with Du Pont to make neckties from Dacron. I was general counsel of the company, and I made my first contact with patent lawyers when I tried to get Superba a patent on washable neckties made of Dacron. As an expression of appreciation for my efforts, Superba gave me a sizable collection of unmarketable Dacron ties.

When you came to the Sutherland office, you entered a room with two desks and six hard wooden chairs. There were two secretaries available for dictation from all the lawyers in the office, though as the junior I had to wait until the Sutherlands had finished their own dictation. There were no dictating machines in those days, and if there had been I am sure they would have been banned from the office. Like all lawyers, I drafted my memoranda or briefs on long, "legal-size" lined pads. Then I would dictate from the outline on the pad to Tommy or Helen. The office library was a large room filled with bookshelves containing statutes and judicial opinions. When we needed further legal material, we went to the county courthouse next door, which had an excellent and sizable library. Meetings with clients normally occurred in the office, though occasionally I would visit a client's office and sometimes go out to lunch with him. (Later, when I became general counsel of Xerox, I had another office there, though I still spent most of my time in my law office.) In those days, lunches were normally social rather than business occasions.

I started at $25 a week in 1938, and was raised to $30 a year later, when I married. When I became a partner, I had a drawing account each week and a share of the firm's profits at the end of the year. Money was not my primary interest—Root Clark had, in fact, offered me twice as much before I accepted the job with the Sutherlands. I enjoyed the practice of law in Rochester, particularly the relationships of the lawyers with each other. We worked in an atmosphere of trust and respect, and many matters were settled with handshakes and phone calls, without a written record of agreement. This was not simply because we were a small office dealing with other small offices: It was Rochester. In 1958, when I merged what had become "my" firm into what then became Harris, Beach, Keating, Wilcox, Dale & Linowitz, I was partner in a firm of more than fifty lawyers, and we knew each other not only as colleagues but as friends.

Such experiences were by no means unique. Even in the great metropolis, partnerships were permanent and congenial. John Nelson, a real estate lawyer who was forced out of New York's Milbank Tweed at the age of sixty-five, remembered that in his peak years at the firm the older partners had been retained in a senior status, chipped in from their experience and guided the younger people. He described what they did as "They opened their mail [and] tottered around," and in most cases, of course, their partnership share was greatly reduced, but they remained part of their firm. Younger partners were protected, too. As Steven Dickerman, who runs a legal placement service in New York, told *The Wall Street Journal*: "When there were tough times, the older partners would take less. There was no thought of firing partners."

For most of us, the bar itself was a fellowship. It was from this period that we get Harrison Tweed's famous encomium: "I have a high opinion of lawyers. With all their faults, they stack up well against those in every other occupation or profession. They are better to work with or play with or fight with or drink with, than most other varieties of mankind."[2] We lunched together, swapped stories, had picnics together, staged amateur theatrics at bar association meetings, celebrated holidays, applauded each others' triumphs, and supported each other in adversity. We trusted each other. We were a community at the bar.

How different the world of the law firms is today! The early 1990s saw bloodlettings, partners dismissed at such firms as Chicago's Winston & Strawn, New York's Skadden Arps, and Los Angeles's Latham & Watkins, among others. Partnership agreements that specified a two-thirds majority vote before a partner could be expelled could easily be circumvented by a compensation committee that cut the partner's share until he could no longer afford to stay, so few fought back. James M. Asher, supervising partner at Rogers & Wells, told the *Journal* that the partners had brought it on themselves by becoming nomads, moving from one partnership to another because their new partners promised them more money. The restructurings of 1992 were necessary, he argued, so that the firms could survive, but once this job was done the firms should regain their "distinctive nature as partnerships."[3] Blair Perry, dismissed from the Boston firm of Hale and Dorr at the age of sixty-one, two years after it had given him special recognition for introducing a practice in high-tech intellectual property, told his partners when they asked what he was going to do: "I'm going to stand out in front of the building with a tin cup and a sign that says 'Former Partner at Hale and Dorr' and see how much I can collect."[4] In my day, we knew that personal relationships once violated were never the same again. Even John Foster Dulles, who told the associates at Sullivan & Cromwell who went off to World War II that they might or might not have a job when they returned, paid the partners who served in the armed forces all through the war.

Obviously, the socialization of the bar was in fact that of an all-male, all-white, mostly Protestant club. Even in my time, there were cadres of sole practitioners from the ethnic neighborhoods of the city who did not have commercial clients and participated only marginally in these festivities. The maintenance of camaraderie when the comrades encompass a wider variety of mankind is more difficult, which does not defend the ease with which my profession retreated from that goal.

3

My first move to the larger arena of the law, in one big jump, was the result of World War II. Pearl Harbor Day was my twenty-eighth birthday, and I celebrated the next day by calling the air force and the navy, seeking a commission. My eyesight and my trick knee made me resistible to both services, and I began making inquiries at war-related Washington bureaus that I knew were hiring lawyers. Finally, the Office of Price Administration asked me to be chief of its Rent Control Court Review branch. Here, in truth, I *made* law. The United States had never known nationwide rent control before, and we had to answer endless questions: What is a fair rent? Could we freeze different rents for similar properties in the same area? What is due process in setting rents?

Once the constitutionality of rent control had been accepted, we had a public policy to carry out—but that policy was to hold down an important price in the nation's economy, not to punish anyone. I met a number of times with landlords from various parts of the country to get their views on shaping the new regulations. At the peak of the work, I had responsibility for scores of lawyers, many of them significantly older than I was, working under me. I was paid more than I had been making at Sutherland and Sutherland, but what mattered was not the status or the salary. The exhilaration was the feeling that I was really doing something to serve my country.

We had to set up an appeals process for landlords, through administrative procedures in our agency and then in the courts. A special federal appeals court, called the United States Emergency Court of Appeals, had been formed from the nation's Federal Circuit Courts of Appeals to hear these cases. They were to be argued locally for the convenience of the protesters, so we traveled the country with the judges on the trains—for air travel by government employees was restricted in those days to those who were working more directly in the war effort. A personal fellowship developed, even though we punctiliously kept our relationships impersonal. The chief judge was Fred Vinson, later Chief Justice of the United States, and when we would meet in later years, at a legal convention or, after I moved to Washington, on a social occasion, there would be a "Hello, Sol" in the manner of people who have shared a memorable experience. (And, incidentally, I won all my cases.)

After two years, I did succeed in getting into a naval officer's uniform, in the general counsel's office at the Navy Department. My most interesting assignments involved renegotiating contracts with suppliers. One of these cases was, in retrospect, especially memorable: an attempt to prevent the railroads from charging premium prices for the loaded freight cars they were taking to Hanford, Washington. Their defense was that the freight cars they sent to Hanford had to deadhead back without cargo. As part of my preparation, I asked my superiors what was in those freight cars and was told that the contents could not be divulged for national security reasons. Rather to my surprise, I won this case—but the railroads might have had a point here, for the material going to Hanford was (as I later learned) uranium to be enriched for the atom bomb.

I was demobilized soon after the end of the war at the request of President Truman himself, because the New York City landlords had won a case before the Emergency Court of Appeals declaring the rent control program unconstitutional. OPA wanted its old appeals bureau head back to handle what could be one of the most important cases in its history. This became my most public triumph in a courtroom, for the case commanded considerable attention and opposing counsel was a roster of the great law firms of New York. Charles Evans Hughes, Jr., son of the former chief justice, was lead counsel. When the case was called, the landlords' lawyers milled around their table, men of wealth and status, and I entered alone for the government. It was David and Goliath—the lone, young, slight government lawyer facing the massed artillery of Wall Street. And I won—the decision was reversed. As the result of the publicity, the Democratic party in Rochester offered me its nomination for Congress; but I wanted to be a lawyer.

When I returned to Rochester after the war, Judge Sutherland had retired; his son Arthur, now a colonel, had decided to teach rather than practice law; and his son Andrew, having seen the horizon, had decided there were other things he would rather do. With the very few clients Andrew had retained, George Williams and I had to reinvent the firm, and we did, under its new name of Sutherland, Linowitz & Williams. If I had anything special as a lawyer to offer the Rochester business community, it was that I now knew more than most Rochester lawyers about how the government worked. For example, a charter aircraft company in Rochester claimed it had not been paid by the government for flying services performed under contract, and I took the matter to Washington for them. We quickly negotiated a satisfactory settlement, and it did Sutherland, Linowitz & Williams some good. But in truth there wasn't much work that first year back.

Having time on my hands and a continued civic interest, I became active in the City Club, eventually its president, and also head of the Rochester branch of the American Association for the United Nations and of the Rochester Chamber of Commerce. In those days, the outstanding lawyers virtually without exception were donors of their time to civic causes, board members and officers of the hospitals, symphonies, universities, libraries. It was quietly suggested to me that a young lawyer who acquired a reputation for civic virtue might find his name known to older colleagues when they were looking for someone to whom they could refer work. But the direct exploitation of such connections to solicit work would have been beyond the pale.

From 1949 to the mid-1950s, when television was new in Rochester, I ran and moderated a Saturday evening discussion program called "The Court of Public Opinion," where politicians and experts debated issues of the time. We were on just before Sid Caesar's comedy show, which meant that in addition to the serious-minded of the community we got a large audience of people who had turned on the set early. Before I agreed to do the show, I went to the Rochester Bar Association to make sure there was no objection to my appearing on a regularly scheduled television show. They requested that I not be identified in the show as a lawyer, and I never was.

The friends I made in the civic organizations would to a large extent become the foundation of both my personal and my professional life in Rochester for the next twenty years. And, clearly, the two were connected. My best friend, Joe Wilson, was someone I met through the City Club. His father had founded a little photographic paper company called Haloid, and Joe would build it into Xerox. This was one of those rare situations where the lawyer was present at the creation: Joe took me with him to Columbus, Ohio, on a dreadful winter's day in 1947—it was the first time I represented him—when he visited the Battelle Memorial Institute to see what little its scientists had accomplished with Chester Carlson's still very primitive xerography process and to arrange a license for Haloid to develop it into a commercial product. (It speaks volumes for the Battelle scientists' expectations for xerography that the one use they reserved for the institute was children's toys.) We paid $10,000 for a one-year license with an option to renew at $12,500 in 1948, $20,000 in 1949, up to $35,000 in 1951. Battelle promised to spend that money on research in the fundamental process, and Joe promised that Haloid would work on treated papers and toners to improve the results of the process. I drew up what was a complicated contract that would become more complicated as time went on.

I was involved from the start in the strategic planning for a product that my friend and client Joe Wilson believed in with a true passion, though really it didn't exist for the first ten years we worked on it. Joe's wife, Peggy, was religious and he wasn't; on Sunday morning, while she and the children went to church, he and I would walk around the reservoir, mostly talking business. (I didn't, of course, charge for this time.) In 1949, he objected to the legal bills from Sutherland, Linowitz & Williams. They were too low, he said, and added 20 percent to them.

No doubt my view of what law practice can be and should be was importantly influenced by the extraordinary nature of my relationship with Joe, Haloid, and Xerox. I was in the fullest sense Joe's "counselor." Many of the decisions he had to make related to legal matters. The business was built on Carlson patents that were running out; we had to do things to strengthen our patent position not only to make a practical machine but to keep our rights intact. There was an immense amount of work to do, more than Haloid could finance from its own resources. We decided to license some rights to companies with greater research capacity—RCA, Western Electric, GE, IBM—under arrangements that would give us access to their improvements on our process while limiting the use they could make of those improvements. We defended ourselves further by insisting that we also had to make available to our other licensees on the same terms whatever any one licensee might find. Any of these companies could have gobbled us up for breakfast (we were a public company with shares traded over the counter), and I designed our contracts with each giant in such a way that any other giant that wished to take us over would have antitrust embarrassments.

Carlson, crippled by arthritis, emotionally worn by the years of futile struggle to get someone to take an interest in his invention, came to work with us in Rochester and participated in our decision making. In 1953, Joe established a "royal commission" of Battelle and Haloid people to look into our patent situation and recommend what we should do to improve it, and he asked me to chair it. As a result of the commission's work, Haloid hired two more patent attorneys in-house (making a total of three) and authorized me to engage outside patent counsel. I researched the capabilities of patent law firms to choose those who could best handle our complicated problems (this was entirely at my initiative; if a firm had come to me to solicit our business, I would have lodged a complaint with the bar association), and finally hired the firm of Kenyon & Kenyon.

Joe asked me to become an officer of Haloid, vice president for licensing and patent development, and in the end, because he was my best friend and he'd had a heart attack, and because he promised me that I could do most of the work from my law offices and continue to serve my other clients, too—I accepted.

In 1955, Joe and I and our wives went to Europe together (it was the first trip abroad for all of us), and we negotiated a

broad joint company agreement with the J. Arthur Rank interests, which had grown out of their theatrical and movie business in England. The Xerox copier remained tantalizingly on
the horizon year after year (fourteen years elapsed before we
were in a position to market the Model 914 that transformed
American offices—"Invention," I once said, explaining the phenomenon, "became the mother of necessity"). We searched for
other profitable uses for the process, and each year there were
new contracts to write, new tactics to develop within the central strategy.

My friendship with Joe and my knowledge of the business
made me, I am sure, a better lawyer and made him a better
client. Whether the problem was patents, stockholder relations,
antitrust regulations, labor relations, international arrangements, acquisitions, or sales contracts, I could not intelligently
frame the legal problem without knowing a great deal about the
business. In 1958, when I merged our little law firm into the
larger firm of Harris Beach (where I spent almost half my
working week even after I became chairman of the board of Xerox), I had at my beck and call technically capable lawyers who
could work all the more efficiently because I could outline the
work they were to do. Companies such as IBM and General
Electric would sometimes hint that perhaps Xerox should employ higher-powered New York counsel, but Joe trusted me.

When we needed experience not available in my firm, I retained other firms. I consulted about the Xerox antitrust problems
with Whitney North Seymour at Simpson Thacher in New York,
and took legal problems abroad to Coudert Brothers in Paris, in
large part because I had come to know Alexis Coudert and Charles Torem. Struve Hensel, who was one of Coudert's senior partners, had been my boss in the Navy Department.
But everything started with and returned to my personal relationship with Joe Wilson, which grew even closer when I became
chairman of the board of Xerox.

Over the years, most of my professional relationships on the corporate level have also involved significant personal relationships with the decision makers of the companies. In Rochester, I was a director of Security Trust Company and Rochester Savings Bank and Superba Cravats while our firm did legal work for them—and while I was chairman of Xerox. I left Rochester for Washington, first to be ambassador to the Organization of American States for President Lyndon Johnson and then to be senior partner of Coudert Brothers in Washington. While at Coudert, I served on the boards of Time, Inc.; Pan American World Airways; Marine Midland Bank; and Mutual Life Insurance Co. of New York, and represented them in various legal matters.

When I retired from these boards (always a ceremonial occasion when people are required to say nice things about you), my fellow directors usually referred to what one of them called my "gadfly" services—my insistence on pressing management to explain and defend its plans, decisions, and results. Such quizzing, I felt, was something I was obliged to do and was able to do because I was a lawyer and had expertise in the determination of relevance.

I was not the first Rochester lawyer to become chairman of the board of a client company. Jean Hargrave, a name partner in the largest law firm in the city, had previously abandoned the practice of law to become chairman of Eastman Kodak. Even earlier, Winthrop Aldrich had left Milbank Tweed to become chairman of Chase Bank, and a few years later Irving Shapiro would become chairman of Du Pont. One day I asked Hargrave why so many lawyers were becoming chairmen or CEOs of companies, and he said, "Not to deal with legal problems but to know when there *is* a legal problem."

Over the years, sitting on various boards, I have time and again heard matters presented in narrative fashion without an awareness that there might be important legal factors involved. Once there was a merger that management had pursued for some period of time before laying the matter before the board. As I listened, I realized that there was a real conflict of interest, and an antitrust problem, and therefore the strong possibility of costly litigation. An apparently sophisticated management had not seen it. On another occasion, the corporation was about to buy a piece of property owned by another company in which one of our board members played a leading role, and management had not thought to question it. On yet another board, the CEO routinely asked for approval of a contract that would have failed to cover respective patent rights (which later proved to be extremely valuable).

There are and always have been legitimate arguments against having the corporation's lawyer on the board; boards do not give advice, they make decisions. If the lawyer sits on the client's board and the board gets into a dispute with the CEO to whom he normally relates, he may be unable to represent either side. (To avoid this limbo, Sullivan & Cromwell historically always told a corporate client on the day that the firm undertook its representation that if a dispute arose the firm would necessarily represent the company rather than any individual in the company's management.) What a lawyer learns about his client's business while serving on a board cannot be held back from antagonists in a lawsuit by the claim of lawyer-client privilege. Law firms are partnerships; if a lawyer is on a board held liable for the misbehavior of the corporation, his partners may be compelled to share his liability. There is the old wheeze that a lawyer who represents himself has a fool for a client. Proxy statements sent to shareholders to solicit their votes for a slate of directors must reveal the directors' compensation, which in the case of the lawyer includes all the fees paid to his firm, a number neither the lawyer nor the CEO always likes to see on the public record. Lawyers who work for corporations as in-house general counsel often feel that the provision of legal advice to the board is their function and that there is some degree of conflict of interest when a lawyer, much of whose income derives from his relationship with this client, sits on its board. Certainly, there are lawyers who go on boards for the purpose of holding or getting business for their firm.

Despite all this, I believe it is entirely appropriate for an outside counsel to sit on clients' boards, because his advice has its greatest impact before the board makes its decision—and his influence on the CEO is greatest if that worthy knows that his directors will independently, automatically, ask counsel's views on whether a proposal is legal or wise. Such service does not, in fact, make a lawyer an insider; he retains his independence. Board membership is, however, not essential. Howard Trienens of Chicago's Sidley & Austin was for a number of years (the years of the big antitrust suits) general counsel of AT&T while maintaining his status as an outsider and partner of his law firm. He felt that he did not want to have a vote as a director, but he did want to be at the board functions, the parties, and the picnics, as well as at the meetings, to relate effectively with the directors so they could ask each other questions in an informal context.

Corporate lawyers who are happy in their work will almost invariably speak of their personal relationships with their clients. It isn't that much fun just making money for corporations, and it's no fun at all swotting through deposition after deposition hoping to find diamonds in a nondescript soil. "We smooth out difficulties," said John W. Davis, J. P. Morgan's and later AT&T's lawyer said, describing the work of the profession. "[W]e relieve stress; we correct mistakes; we take up other men's burdens and by our efforts we make possible the peaceful life of men in a peaceful state."[5] That's what a *corporate* practice looked like as late as the 1950s, and even today the best lawyers know they can practice happily only in a human context. "Clients come to you," said Newton Minow, "because they have a problem, and for this day that problem is the most important thing on their minds. They need somebody who is not only technically proficient, but somebody who cares about them."

The truth is that personal relations make legal services not only more pleasant but also more effective. Stephen M. Bundy of the University of California suggests that one of the reasons

Pennzoil prevailed over Texaco in its $10 billion litigation over the purchase of Getty Oil was that the Pennzoil lawyers were closer to the Pennzoil management:

> Pennzoil was represented at trial and on appeal by the same counsel—Joseph Jamail, Baker & Botts, and W. James Kronzer. Jamail was a close friend of Hugh Liedtke, the chairman and chief executive of Pennzoil. He had easy access to Pennzoil's senior management and they had confidence in him. Pennzoil's president, Baine Kerr, was a former partner in Baker & Botts, and the firm also had a close, long-term relationship with Pennzoil's internal legal department. . . . Texaco's situation was different. Prior to the case, Texaco's Texas trial counsel had no professional or personal contact with Texaco. Even before the jury verdict, trial counsel often dealt with senior management through the hierarchical structure of Texaco's in-house legal department. . . .[6]

Texaco's position, in short, was weakened by its lack of continuing relationships with the lawyers who were trying to protect it. And the modern way of organizing the practice of law will multiply the number of times this epitaph is written. Bundy sees "an increasingly important class of matters in which outside counsel is less likely to play a strong role in informing and checking senior management." In the absence of independent advice, companies are measurably more likely to get into trouble. In my own practice, I have never been able to function effectively unless I knew that my advice was getting to the actual client as I have given it. I believe that many problems in corporate law practice today are the result of the divorce of the "counselor" from the person who needs the counsel.

I write as a Washington lawyer, from the vantage point of a practice much more concentrated in counseling than lawyers elsewhere in the country are likely to find. When I joined Coudert Brothers a quarter of a century ago, I was leaving a post in the State Department dealing with Latin America, and I brought with me the experience of earlier work in Latin America in connection with the introduction of Xerox there. The clients who came to my office were at first in large part companies that wanted advice and contacts relating to Latin American countries. Occasionally, they sought influence; a group of oil companies once came calling to offer an enormous fee for my help in influencing some foreign political leaders to make concessions they knew they should not make. I thanked the companies for their attempted generosity and wished them well in finding another lawyer. From time to time, I was approached by a number of corporations to undertake what was essentially lobbying work on their behalf. I declined because I did not feel comfortable trying to profit from my friendships and relationships in the government.

Law to me never was and must never be a collection of techniques a technician is paid to apply for the benefit of a client. Obviously, no lawyer today can know everything his client needs to know in dealing with the hugely expanded library of government rules and regulations, touching on so many phases of business activity. Specialization is unavoidable, and with specialization comes depersonalization. My time as a practicing lawyer has been a time when the mechanics have increasingly supplanted the humanists. It is important to understand why and how this occurred. By studying the factors that have turned what was to a large extent a learned profession into what is virtually a clanking factory that works night and day to generate and sell private law and lawsuits, perhaps we can learn to fight back, to regain the nonpecuniary satisfactions that lawyers once sought and found in the law.

CHAPTER 4

THE CLIENTS CHANGE

1

In 1977, Alfred D. Chandler, Jr., of the Harvard Business School, published *The Visible Hand*, which soon became a classic history of American enterprise and the "managerial revolution" that created large corporations. Nowhere in its six hundred pages is there a mention of a contribution to this history by a lawyer or a law firm performing professional tasks. Lawyers, the visiting Alexis de Tocqueville had observed in the early nineteenth century, were the aristocracy of the new republic on the western side of the Atlantic—but aristocrats, of course, in America as in Europe, did not have much to do with trade. It was largely in their role as legislators—law *writers*—that lawyers such as Daniel Webster made their mark on the conduct of business in America.

In 1901, when J. P. Morgan put together U.S. Steel in a four-hour meeting in his grand library in New York, the participants were steelmaker Charles Schwab, banker Robert Bacon, and stock market operator John ("Bet-a-Million") Gates.[1] No lawyers. William Nelson Cromwell was called in later to draw up the terms of the securities that would be kept by the bankers and the securities that would be sold to the public as the result of the deal, and he was paid well for his work; but he wasn't present at the creation. (A few years later, in one of relatively few episodes in which the lawyer was a prime mover, Cromwell would put together the plan that led to the surgery on Colombia that produced Panama and the agreement to build a Panama Canal. For this his fee essentially was the $5 million he made on dealing in the stock of the canal company.)[2] When Theodore Vail, the master builder of AT&T, decided that he had better come to terms with William Howard Taft's attorney general, George Wickersham, rather than wait for the newly elected Woodrow Wilson to make new antitrust policy, he sent his operations vice president, N. C. Kingsbury, to negotiate a deal by which AT&T got out of the telegraph business and pledged to connect independent companies to its long-distance service. The government was represented by lawyers, but AT&T was not.

Law in the United States then mostly covered the sale and purchase of real property and the problems of real people. Wills and estates were the fundament of most large practices, and the construction of intricate "trusts" to manage what successful people left behind them was the most highly skilled of legal occupations. Even banks, which had to "perfect" their claim to the collateral behind a loan and sometimes go to court to collect it, were most likely to seek the services of outside law firms in connection with trusts and claims by the beneficiaries of trusts. This body of expertise, of course, bled into commercial life. Trustees transferred the ownership of stock certificates from sellers to buyers (as, indeed, on an automated basis through a specialized central processor, they still do), and for years much of this work was done in law offices. Then lawyers adapted the trust rules that enabled individuals to set up estates to keep their holdings under one cover after death, to make possible a more concentrated ownership of American industry—until antitrust laws outlawed their easiest devices and set functional rather than legal tests to measure the effects of the reorganizations. The first New York firm to have as many as ten lawyers (Sullivan & Cromwell) pioneered such work, but it didn't have much resonance for other practitioners.

Lawyers normally served as intermediaries between the state that chartered limited-liability corporations and the company that wanted such a charter (though their most important function in many states was to get the law governing corporations written or amended for the benefit of their clients; thus, Cromwell persuaded New Jersey to write its corporation law in such a way that shareholders had no right to see the corporation's books).[3] And lawyers brought suit for their clients to compel the execution of contracts that businessmen had made with each other. But the clerk in the state office could handle an incorporation if you didn't come with a lawyer, and the contracts usually enforced the customs of the trade rather than specific clauses drawn by counsel for specific purposes. The business lawyer's expertise was most heavily solicited to secure injunctions—judges' orders forbidding people to do what a company didn't want them to do, under the unlimited penalties judges can impose on those "in contempt of court"—against labor unions seeking collective instead of individual bargaining for a company's workers, against competitors infringing on trademarks or patents, against retailers selling in ways the company didn't like.

There was a constant demand for "reorganization," a task that could be accomplished through the federal courts with existing management remaining in control as receivers appointed by the judge. There was no federal bankruptcy law in those days, but it was easy to get the case into federal court under "diversity jurisdiction" simply by arranging for a lawsuit to be brought by an out-of-state holder of an unsecured bond on which interest had not been paid. The New York bankers, having sold the owners their bonds, never had any trouble finding an owner from another state who could bring suit in federal court. These were enormous cases for lawyers because different firms were needed to represent the interests of the company being reorganized, the stockholders, the various classes of bondholders, and the bankers who would in the end create and sell the new securities of the reorganized company.

Companies had little need for lawyers to defend them against lawsuits brought by aggrieved individuals because common law rules allowed relatively few opportunities for individuals to sue companies. Law in courts came to be regarded as a way the powerful kept the weak in their place, and, given the sympathy of the judges, mostly it did. Until Justice Cardozo wrote his opinion in *McPherson* v. *Buick* in 1916, someone damaged by a defective product could not sue the manufacturer because only those "in privity" with the customer could be held liable—and since the store hadn't done anything wrong there was no point suing the store. In most states, "contributory negligence"—the fact that there was something the victim could have done to prevent the accident—was a defense to claims growing out of personal injury into the 1950s. Ordinary people suffering bad luck of that sort looked not to lawyers but to politicians and to local leaders with clout. This lack of legal services available to ordinary people strengthened the political machines that dominated our cities.

Apart from the acquisition of patents and trademarks, companies rarely needed a lawyer in their dealings with the executive branch of government because government didn't do much to regulate the conduct of business. When the government did try to tell businesses what they could and couldn't do, lawyers were more likely to move to get the rules declared unconstitutional than they were to negotiate their content. Here, too, the weapon might be the injunction, by which a court ordered an agency of government not to bother a lawyer's client by enforcing a law or regulation. Parodying a European cliché that the person who wrote a nation's songs had more influence on its people than those who wrote its laws, Finley Peter Dunne's newspaper character Mr. Dooley said he didn't care who wrote the nation's laws as long as he could get an injunction.

So the law practice I entered in 1938 was focused on people rather than soulless corporations because that's what most lawyers in America did. Legal representation of business clients was in large part a personal matter. Most property was still held by individuals, and most businesses, even quite large businesses, were essentially the lengthened and protected shadows of the people who owned them—still, often (though not so often as fifty years earlier), the people who had started them. Sometimes it was hard to know whether the president's personal lawyer was the lawyer for the business or whether the lawyer for the business handled the president's personal matters.

The most rewarding clients were those where one got both the human satisfaction of the individual relationship and the fees from a business relationship. Leo Gottlieb, in his history of Cleary, notes that after he and his partners left their old firm of Root Clark in 1941, their first new client was Bing Crosby: "[T]he work we did for him during the five-year period added up to a respectable volume of interesting and satisfactorily re-munerative professional services and we found Crosby to be an intelligent and agreeable client."[4] Later this highly conservative firm became the lawyer for the Beatles in their case against their former manager: "This initial retainer led to a long series of complex litigations, both in the United States and in London, the ultimate outcome of which was a settlement of all claims and counterclaims on a basis that was highly favorable to the Beatles and greatly appreciated by them and their respective regular counsel. Very large sums were involved in the litigations and the settlement, and our bills for professional services, which were also large, were promptly and cheerfully paid."[5]

Gottlieb's book is surprisingly forthcoming about how his firm got its clients. He gives a formidable list of those that came through personal relationships with individuals who had observed one or another of the partners in work-related action. Fairchild Aircraft came to Cleary because Sherman Fairchild had served on the Pan Am board with Cleary partner Henry Friendly. Schlitz came because Cleary partner Bob Barnard "was a good friend of the inside General Counsel at Schlitz." Lily–Tulip Cup was acquired by Fowler Hamilton "on the recommendation of Ira Schur, who was then the managing partner of S. D. Leidesdorf & Co." Hamilton's work as director of New York Telephone Co. and Mutual Life Insurance Co. of New York resulted in "our being retained on a number of conventional legal matters." George Ball's acquaintance with Jean Monnet generated much work from the French government (including the negotiation of a loan for which the collateral was 1,174 gold bars stored in the vaults of the Federal Reserve Bank of New York), and the early representation of the first institutions later to form the European Common Market. Gottlieb himself was friendly with the Guggenheims, which meant that the firm represented not only Chilean Nitrate and the newspaper *Newsday* but also Federated Department Stores, CIT Financial, and Pepsi-Cola.

Perhaps the first intimate involvement of lawyers as lawyers in the plans of a large corporation came in Atlanta, where the Coca-Cola Company had a panoply of problems of the kind lawyers were most likely to resolve. As a matter of fact, most of what modern law firms do for modern corporations was done for Coca-Cola eighty, ninety, even a hundred years ago. The story is instructive both because of the involvement of the government and because of the detail in which it is known.[6] The product (which in its early years contained cocaine and caffeine in some quantities) had been sold originally as a patent medicine for people who did "brain work" and whose brains got tired. In 1895, Frank Robinson, who ran Coca-Cola advertising, persuaded the company's proprietor, Asa Candler, that a refreshing drink would have a much larger market than a remedy for exhaustion, but three years later, when the government put a tax on patent medicines to help pay the costs of the Spanish-American War, the commissioner of internal revenue remembered the previous advertising and hit Coca-Cola for the tax.

Candler's brother John was a lawyer (indeed, though he never stopped representing Coca-Cola, he took occasional days off from his private practice to sit as a justice of Georgia's supreme court). In 1904, he hired a twenty-two-year-old Columbia Law School graduate named Harold Hirsch, who took Coca-Cola under his wing for more than thirty years. When the Copyright Act of 1905 permitted people who had been using a trademark for ten years or more to register it for their exclusive use, Coca-Cola was one of the first names in the door. Hirsch, who became the company's general counsel in 1909 while continuing to be part of the Candler law firm, began a crusade to discipline all who had the temerity to sell a soft drink under a name anything like Coca-Cola. Over the next quarter of a century, he filed by his own estimate one trademark-infringement case a week. In 1923, the firm published and made available to law libraries all around the country a 650-page book of decisions in Coca-Cola infringement cases, and two further books on the subject updated the state of the law for the benefit of lawyers whose clients might wish to get into the cola business.

It was Hirsch who insisted that the company needed a specially shaped bottle and commissioned several glassworks to come up with a prototype. Hirsch then copyrighted the "hobble-skirt" bottle as well as the logo and the diamond inscription on the bottle. He tried and failed to copyright the caramel coloring. He hired teams of investigators (usually recent law school graduates) to go around the country, order Cokes, and pour some of the contents into a specially prepared sack for chemical analysis back in Atlanta. When the contents were not the Coca-Cola syrup, Hirsch's young lawyer would get an injunction compelling the soda fountain to use genuine Coca-Cola syrup whenever a Coke was served to a customer.

From 1911 to 1917, Coca-Cola needed Hirsch to fight off a

concerted attack on its vitals by the recently established Food and Drug Administration, which charged that the caffeine in the drink was a dangerous drug. This ended up in the Supreme Court, where Charles Evans Hughes, in his last opinion before running for president, overturned previous decisions for the company and remanded the matter back to the lower courts for retrial. Hirsch then negotiated the sort of compromise that would become standard in such disputes with the government—Coca-Cola signed a "consent decree" without admitting any wrongdoing and agreed to reduce the caffeine content of the beverage.

When a syndicate of investors headed by the Trust Company of Georgia bought out Candler in 1919, the new chairman, Robert Woodruff, asked Hirsch to become a member of the Coca-Cola board. Because he had his own bottling franchise and Woodruff was making controversial changes in the company's contracts with its bottlers, Hirsch arranged for a new law firm to represent the bottlers. This was King & Spalding, an Atlanta firm that would later, after Coca-Cola had acquired most of the "parent bottlers" itself, become Coke's lawyers.

The legal work done for Coca-Cola over the years was in large part at the initiative of the lawyers, who had one of their own at the center, understanding fully when and where legal questions had to be foremost. King & Spalding had (and probably still has, for there have been only two changes in CEOs in that company in the twentieth century) considerable input into the policies of the Coca-Cola Company. Everything that would create the modern corporate law department and the modern corporate law firm was present, in sizes ranging from embryonic to elephantine, in Atlanta in the first four decades of this century. Even the lawyer's ultimate disappointment—that it's the client who decides, whether the lawyer approves or not—was part of the story. When Coca-Cola's Robert Woodruff decided that Pepsi-Cola's Walter Mack was too tough a nut for a lawsuit to crack (both men had been in the trucking business before they took over soft drink companies), Woodruff invited Mack to his suite at the Waldorf-Astoria, and the two of them signed off on their own document giving Pepsi the right to use the word *cola*. And there wasn't anything the company's devastated general counsel—or King & Spalding—could do about it.[7]

2

"By far the greatest single part of the practice of the firm since 1928," Robert Swaine wrote of Cravath, "has had to do with the efforts of clients to comply with federal legislation and to accommodate their businesses to the vagaries of the many federal regulatory agencies and executive departments."[8] Although this seems a little disingenuous, considering how much time was spent by the firm fighting federal legislation and the rules of the regulatory agencies, the point is well taken: What has built large law firms has been government action. Government has an all but unlimited supply of lawyers. Time is a cost item to the private client in a dispute, but to the directors of a government agency involved in legal process, time in effect is revenue, because the agency's actions to control those subject to its jurisdiction are put forward to justify the budget the Congress votes it. The discovery that the government may have a reason for action under the law is a moment of satisfaction for the agency, a moment of dismay for the client.

Even at the turn of the century, the most time-consuming cases in the "large" seven- and eight-man metropolitan offices (plus unpaid clerk-apprentices) were customs cases and the occasional antitrust case. Henry Stimson wrote that before his time as U.S. attorney, which started in 1906, "the function of the United States Attorney had been one that a good lawyer could faithfully execute with half his time and almost no assistants."[9] What had made the difference, he wrote, was the

Elkins Act of 1903, which had authorized federal judges to impose penalties for railroad freight rebates: "Now, in 1906, the United States was asserting its latent strength; its lawyers were expected to do successful battle with the corporate giants of the time. No longer would it be the major business of the United States Attorney to pursue petty smugglers and violators of the postal laws." If the Henry Stimsons of this world—thirty-eight years old, formerly a partner of Elihu Root, founder of the firm that became Winthrop, Stimson, Putnam & Roberts— were going to be engaged on the side of the government, businessmen were going to need able lawyers indeed, not to help them evade the law but to help them understand it so they could keep out of trouble.

World War I brought government seizure and operation of the railroads, a panoply of emergency regulations, and many opportunities to represent foreign governments, which in various ways funded significant elements in their war effort through the American market. All these developments stimulated the growth of law firms, especially in New York and Washington. When the war ended and the government tried to cancel procurement contracts for arms and matériel and shipping no longer needed, there was much negotiation and litigation to establish the significance, if any, of the failure of the original contracting parties to write a termination clause.

After the war, there was much business relating to foreign debts and to the disposition of German property seized by the Alien Property Custodian, plus a great deal of issuance of securities, which required a lawyer's certification of their legality. After 1920, railroad consolidations required the approval of the Interstate Commerce Commission, which was also given new power to control the fees lawyers and bankers could charge for their work on such matters. (In one widely publicized case from the early 1900s, the lawyers and bankers had taken for themselves more than a third of the value of the securities to be issued; the modern leveraged buy-out artists, so acclaimed in the 1980s and reviled in the 1990s, were really amateurs beside their ancestors.) Some control over the issuance of other securities was taken by the states under "blue sky laws" accepted as constitutional by the Supreme Court in 1917. A handful of New York law firms grew quite large—forty, fifty, sixty lawyers, though rarely as many as twenty partners. Then the Depression, which generated many lawsuits, made the big firms rich at the same time it bankrupted much of the profession.

What really ballooned the law firms, of course, was the New Deal, a splendid irony after most of the nation's eminent lawyers had joined together to denounce the economics, the philosophy, and the constitutionality of Franklin Roosevelt's program. In Roosevelt's first term, they had a high order of success in securing Supreme Court decisions killing off New Deal legislation. But the securities acts and the banking acts and the labor relations acts survived—and in 1936 Congress passed the Robinson-Patman Act, which empowered the Federal Trade Commission to punish manufacturers because they had failed to fix their resale prices—the minimum prices at which stores had to sell the public what the manufacturer sold them—or because they *had* fixed them, depending on the inclinations of the commissioners. The intent was to prevent both predatory pricing by firms hoping to achieve monopoly status by driving competitors out of business and exploitative pricing by firms that had already achieved a dominance permitting them to overcharge consumers. The dual purpose encouraged both lawyers and judges to make the law mean whatever they wanted it to mean on any given day.

Commenting on Robinson-Patman, a German observer of the American legal scene once observed that in his country businessmen would not tolerate such a "make-work program for lawyers." Lawyers were needed to advise clients as to what they could or could not do, and then again when the client misunderstood what he had been told. Robert Swaine, who was about as committed as a man could be to the illegitimacy of administrative agencies, told a little story about clients' "difficulty in understanding all the delicate nuances [of the Robinson-Patman amendments to the antitrust law]; as, for example, the distinction between refusing to do business with a price-cutter and taking agreements from customers not to cut prices. Some years ago, a Cravath partner had occasion to explain this distinction to a client whose business was being seriously affected by price-cutters. When, some months later, the Federal Trade Commission investigated the client for alleged resale price maintenance agreements, one of the first papers found in the files of the sales manager was a memorandum to his district managers: 'Cravath says we can refuse to sell to price-cutters, but can't take agreements to maintain prices. Accordingly, whenever you put a price-cutter back on our list on his agreement not to cut prices, do not send a copy of the agreement to the home office.'"[10]

Meanwhile, the tax code grew and grew and grew, to literally thousands of pages, and the profitability of an enterprise became in no small measure the result of the cleverness of its tax lawyers. And here, one notes, the accuracy of a lawyer's advice was subject to a quick reality check: The deduction was allowed or it wasn't—or a competitor benefited from a deduction that hadn't been taken by the lawyer's client. In the 1950s, there grew up a habit of "letter rulings," by which a tax lawyer could solicit from the IRS an opinion on whether something he wanted to do for his client would or would not stand up. The generalist legal adviser was at a loss to handle these situations because there was no way he could possibly keep up with these floods of letters and keep practicing any law that wasn't tax law.

The pervasiveness of government regulation and taxation meant that companies of any size could not be effectively managed without the advice of lawyers. And not just any lawyers; only experts in separate sections of the law coming out of Washington could keep up with the rulings, especially in the 1930s, when many of them were not even published. The government began publishing a Federal Register only after it was embarrassed by a 1935 Supreme Court decision pointing out that the parties, prosecuting authorities, and lower courts had all mistakenly relied on a section of the Petroleum Code that had been eliminated by an unpublicized Executive Order.[11] Even then, the agencies that heard cases came to require that lawyers practicing before them be separately admitted to that practice, as the courts in each state require that lawyers who wish to practice in that state acquire a separate license or some form of temporary permission. Laws and rules are no more the same from federal agency to federal agency than they are from state to state. And publishing ventures sprang up—a Bureau of National Affairs, a Commerce Clearing House—to keep the specialists up-to-date on what the government was doing, what cases had been decided to what purpose, and what rules had been handed down under the agencies' rule-making authority.

In the companies, CEOs—reluctantly, slowly, sometimes under duress (newspapers in 1944 had pictures of Montgomery Ward chairman Sewell Avery being carried out of his office on his swivel chair by federal marshals enforcing a ruling of the National Labor Relations Board)—had to change their orientation to government regulation. New generations of managers passed through business schools and learned that they could no longer assume that their disclosures to stockholders and the public, their labor relations, their marketing practices, and their financing plans were matters beyond the reach of scrutiny by officious bureaucrats. There were rules and regulations that would have to be obeyed and seen to have been obeyed. And only your lawyer could keep you safe.

The nature of business lawsuits changed when government became the adversary party. Losing a contract case to a private opponent meant money out of pocket to a company, but losing an antitrust case or a rate case or a labor relations case might well mean a permanent change in how the company would be organized or would do its business. In traditional law practice, the lawyer's function was to reach a settlement that allowed both parties to go about their business, especially in that large majority of cases where, once the trauma of the dispute had passed, the two companies would once again be doing business with each other. (When suing soda fountains that had adulterated its syrup when making their drinks, Coca-Cola rarely sought damages, just a guarantee that it would never happen again.) In my own work at the OPA, I tried to maintain such attitudes as the government's lawyer. But in many of these government cases, compromise was simply impossible. Defenses of great complexity had to be mounted, and large law firms that once had farmed out their litigation work to others developed litigating departments that became the largest parts of the firm. The trial lawyers' attitudes of today (called "scorched earth," symbolizing an insistence that the lawyer will do anything to "win") grew out of cases pitting government agencies against rich corporations. As Congress increasingly criminalized white-collar offenses, the ethics of the criminal law bar—always oriented toward giving the prosecution the hardest possible time—came to dominate these litigation departments and sometimes the firms themselves. Clients in any event expected no-holds-barred advocacy when the government was, from their point of view, at their throats.

As law became more complicated and more intrusive into daily operations, corporate chief executives became increasingly reluctant to let outsiders control what the company would do. Prior to World War II, the general counsel of a company was likely to be its outside law firm, and in those cases where there was a full-time in-house general counsel, he was likely to be in charge of a small staff that did the repetitive scutwork. Not infrequently, such an inside general counsel would do double duty, serving as corporate secretary, a cognate activity, or in some more remote function, such as personnel director.

As time passed, regulations proliferated, and the tax code grew, no single outside lawyer could answer the chief executives' questions about how some piece of law or regulation was going to affect the business. The lawyers who could answer the questions about regulations and specialized procedures at administrative agencies might well have the company's most feared competitors on their client roster. Many top executives were uncomfortable with the idea that they were getting advice on key decisions from the same people who were advising their rivals. Looking at the totality of his situation, the CEO came to feel that he wanted to control the information his outside counsel received. It would be best, he felt, to have his in-house general counsel become a mediator between management and the outside lawyers hired by the company to resolve particular problems. "The general counsel," as Bob Banks, then general counsel of Xerox, wrote in the *Harvard Business Review* in 1983, "has evolved from kept lawyer to chief legal officer."[12]

Though individuals could insist that they did not change their profession when they put on a company's uniform, the move from outside counsel to inside counsel brought an inescapable loss of autonomy. "If you're in-house counsel," says Stephen Bundy, a professor of legal ethics who came to academia from the Cravath firm, "and one person is paying your salary, and you're in the building every day—and you may get involved in the decision-making process and have an investment in the decision that was taken—you're not going to look for contrary arguments." Worse: The politics of the corporate situation could easily develop in ways that meant the outside counsel would be called in only after the inside counsel had given his boss his view of what could or could not be done— and if outside counsel wished to be hired again by inside counsel, it behooved him not to offer a contrary opinion. Jesse Choper, an accountant and lawyer who became dean of Boalt Hall, the University of California law school, remembers from his time at Price Waterhouse the gradual loss of accountants' status as the partnerships yielded to their clients' arguments against what the business community liked to call "rigid professionalism." Steve Bundy says, "The line between being a hero and being a sucker is a very fine line."

But the inside general counsel attending the board meeting is necessarily the CEO's man. Elihu Root could say to a client, "Don't do it, because it's a rotten thing to do"; house counsel simply can't say that. He may not even be able to say, "Do you *really* want to do this, knowing the trouble and expense it may entail?" Increasingly—and this became one of the least-considered wounds to the profession—CEOs want their general counsel to have the same exclusive loyalty to the company that they expect from employees who do not have professional responsibilities. The lawyer's fundamental contribution to the negotiations that are part of every legal dispute—his professionally developed sense of what is and is not important to his client's situation—was devalued by the client's insistence that the client knows best, that his priorities and his values are to control what the lawyer does. Too many lawyers then decided that they agreed with the client. In business, after all, the customer is always right.

Lawyers retained to work for a corporation at the pleasure of in-house counsel also know less than they used to know about their clients' personnel and activities. The outside lawyer is no longer expected to be well informed about what is going on in the company. His liaison with the company often is not with operating divisions but with the "legal department"—at some firms, in fact, outside counsel is asked to clear with house counsel before making an appointment to see anyone in management. The quality of judgment is a function of the quality of information, and when the outside lawyer is totally dependent on house counsel for information, his judgment is necessarily limited. Moreover, he will find it politic not to disagree with the views of inside counsel, whether in fact he agrees or not. Gary F. Torrell of the Los Angeles firm of Paul Hastings, who took five months away from his firm to serve as house counsel for the Bass interests' S&L and real estate group, offered read-

ers of *American Lawyer* two golden rules: "Make inside counsels' lives easier" and "Make inside counsels look good in front
of their clients, colleagues, superiors and subordinates."[13]
Where the client's interest fits into those golden rules is not entirely obvious.

Almost by definition, outside counsel will have a wider view
of the meaning of a company's decisions. I remember one occasion when I was approached by the CEO of a moderately large
company about helping to extricate his company from a deal in
which inside counsel had unwisely agreed to terms limiting the
company's future activities abroad. It took some difficult and
delicate negotiations, but I was able to work it out. The inside
counsel, as I recall, was not chastened by the experience.

The normal expectation now is that when a problem arises
where a law firm can be helpful, the general counsel will tell
his contact at the firm he uses most often, and perhaps other
contacts at other firms at the same time. There is a "job" to be
awarded. Some general counsel, working as purchasing agents
for their employers, seek first of all to get that job done at the
lowest price. Others are more concerned about exactly what
the outside firm is likely to do or not do and whether there are
values in long-standing relations with these firms. But the first
category is growing rapidly, and the second category is shrink-
ing. Not only are relationships hampered between the corporate leadership and the company's lawyers, they are greatly
diminished between counsel and the less senior personnel
whose education in the legal consequences of their action was
once to a large degree the responsibility of outside counsel. Indeed, the close relations between client and firm were often ce-
mented on these lower levels. "The relationship between
[junior partner and subordinate corporate officer]," Harrison
Tweed once wrote, "is almost precisely the same as that between the old-fashioned general practitioner and his client-
friend of long standing. . . . It generally happens that as the
corporate officer goes up in the hierarchy so does the lawyer.

Frequently, the close business and legal association and the personal intimacy exist for twenty-five years or more."[14]

Bob Banks thinks the instruction of a company's junior officers can be done better by in-house counsel because he knows who "the client" is within the company: "The great majority of the legal services provided to the corporation do not rise to [the] level of the corporation as a whole. The business decision maker is not usually the Chairman of the Board but, most often, a lower level businessman solving problems within his sphere of responsibility. These are the 'clients' of the OGC [Office of General Counsel] lawyers."[15]

Some lawyers feel that their work has benefited from assistance by in-house counsel, who know who's who and what's what in the client company and can save outside counsel a great deal of time in isolating a problem and finding a solution. Most older lawyers who have worked under both the relationship system and the transaction system feel that they were more valuable to the client—as well as more satisfied by their work—when they were close to the enterprise. I am one of them: I think complicated matters that require the attention of a lawyer are best handled by outside counsel who have the full trust of management. While I was both an officer and outside counsel of Xerox, the patent department became involved in a scrap with the research division. Because I was the firm's outside counsel, I could make recommendations for resolving the issue at a different level—a level that was indeed appropriate to the importance of the decision the company had to make and that could not have been reached by an inside counsel. When a lawyer is no more than the technical executant of corporate plans, he loses much of his societal function, because it is his influence on his clients' decision making that justifies his special status in society.

In recent years, government rules have inadvertently broken the previous ties of lawyer-client relationship in whole industries. One of them was investment banking. Prior to the 1940s, corporations negotiated the term of new securities issues with the investment bankers who would sell the bonds to the public. Each side was represented by its own counsel, who were intimately involved in planning the issues. Then the government mandated competitive bidding by underwriters for railroad and public utilities issues, which were the bulk of the bond business. There was no time for different counsel representing different bidders to do their own "due diligence," investigating the relationship of the documents to the condition of the company. Instead, it became the custom for the issuing corporation to choose not only its own lawyers but also the lawyers who would represent the winning bidder. These lawyers clearly represented and still represent not their ostensible client, whom they discover at the end of the auction, but the securities issue itself. When lawyers are hired to represent clients who don't yet exist, personal loyalties are impossible. In the typical merger-and-acquisition situation, then, it seems reasonable to all involved that the lawyers for all sides, their fees dependent largely on the successful completion of the transaction, represent neither sellers nor buyers but the deal itself. Junk bond deal after junk bond deal yielded giant fees to lawyers whose "due diligence" was very soon shown to be lacking by the bankruptcy of the company.

Milton Freeman of Arnold & Porter in Washington, a well-regarded lawyer of my generation, has written:

> [It is] inconceivable that the needs of great corporations for legal assistance should not be met. . . . There are many attorneys in firms who are glad to organize or reorganize their firms so that they, instead of some competing firm, will be chosen to serve some of the large corporations' legal needs. . . . [L]aw firms have done what is necessary to respond to the needs of their clients, particularly with respect to specialization. . . . [S]ervice to the

client permits no other option. . . . In all cases it is *clients* who govern what they need and the law of supply and demand that governs how much and what type of legal services are needed.[16]

Freeman agrees that lawyers, not clients, must decide what they will or will not do for the fees they are paid. It doesn't matter that if one law firm turns it down, another will pick it up. Once a client is told that the law firm will do whatever he wants done, he may decide that he'd rather have his own people to do it. They'll be cheaper.

John Coleman, general counsel of Campbell Soup, told a meeting of lawyers that his attitude and that of his peers is "not dominated by stuff about collegiality and professionalism and so forth, it's dominated by business principles, and especially value. My particular team—which is very good, but I'm not going to argue that it's absolutely the best in the whole world— has strong talent and it has a very good business feel, and we can beat you all to a pulp. We can do the same stuff just as well for half price, consistently."

Half price seems to be the most common target. Ellen Joan Pollock reports that when Edward Shaw gave up his partnership at Milbank Tweed and went to the Chase Bank as general counsel, "he found he could get Chase's legal work done at half the price if he used in-house lawyers instead of outside counsel from Milbank and the other firms he occasionally retained. He figured that in-house lawyers cost the bank about $100 an hour, including salary and other overhead costs. Outside lawyers billed the bank an average of $200 an hour. As he faced pressure from the corporation's senior officers to keep legal costs down, it was clear to Shaw that in-house was the way to go." Shaw told Pollock, "Obviously, [Milbank] would have had to grow an awful lot faster if we hadn't grown from fifteen attorneys in 1976 to seventy-three [in 1987]."[17]

"At our firm today," T. Neal McNamara of San Francisco's

Pillsbury Madison & Sutro (a firm with more than 630 lawyers) told an *American Lawyer* symposium in 1991, "it's safe to say our clients are among our major competitors. Not only were they one of the root causes of our recession, they're exacerbating it."[18]

In the 1980s, it became customary even for large firms that did not claim any right to participate in a deal to increase their hourly charges by a "premium" to reflect the success of the client's cause. Ultimately, the contingent fee moved upstairs, into the best office suites. In the 1990s, clients began to turn the tables—led by Aetna Insurance's Zoe Baird, the insurance companies tried to gear fees to results to give their outside counsel a stake in defeating plaintiffs or reducing estimated awards. The Resolution Trust Corporation, going after accountants (and lawyers) who had participated in planning the fraudulent activities that destroyed so many savings-and-loan associations, made a deal with Cravath, Swaine & Moore by which leading partners of the firm agreed to work for less than their normal hourly rates in return for payments that could run as high as $600 an hour per lawyer if the firm gained high recoveries for the government.

Ellen Miller-Wachtell, general counsel of NBC, feels that when dealing with outsiders it's important for the client to set all the parameters of the work: "Outside counsel expect to be able to take a case and manage it in the way they determine is best, from staffing through a strategic outcome determination. We don't believe that. Those decisions are ours, down to the basic issues of staffing—not only of how many lawyers, but who should be doing our work outside. Some of these conflicts are resolved to a greater or lesser extent during the course of the matter, but it will influence our decision for the next matter."[19]

Even at NBC, of course, the day may come when outside opinions are highly valued. After the network's news division was blasted by General Motors for having staged a fire for a "magazine" television show that featured the supposed dangers of a GM pickup truck design (and after the general counsel of GM and NBC's parent, GE, had without the intervention of any outside law firm worked out the wording of the apology NBC would make), NBC hired outside counsel to investigate the extent of the involvement of its own news staff as distinct from outside producers in the disastrous on-camera demonstration.

Today, it is hard to see a future for the sort of relationships I had with the CEOs of client corporations. The corporations are too big, and their legal needs are too various. Legal advice has become one part of what must be delivered through a management information system, and it is the essence of an MIS that the more abstract messages go furthest. The best law firms with the best relations will have to build links between senior, but probably not top, management at the client corporation and the firms' partners, because relations at the summit are going to be rare. But the CEO must understand that the corporation at all levels needs the counsel of outside lawyers, and those lawyers must recognize that their future lies in autonomy and not in telling the client what he wants to hear.

The truth is that a CEO who buys legal services instead of consulting his lawyer is the victim of a system he believes benefits him, a system that lets him pretend his problems can be solved by the machine. The law firm then becomes a gear in that machine; and the lawyer becomes a tooth in the gear, and a great profession loses its way.

CHAPTER 5

So the Law Firms Change

1

I never practiced as a solo practitioner, and sometimes I have to remind myself that when I first came to the bar most American lawyers had one-man offices. That was a different world, a world of men (there were virtually no women) who made their own way in a community, finding people who needed legal services, and doing their best to remember what they learned in law school. Sometimes they were locals with family connections, often they were just successful candidates at bar exams who "hung out a shingle" and hoped to find clients. They couldn't afford much in the line of law libraries or services to keep them current with the most recent decisions, and most of what they did was highly repetitive work—wills, estates, divorces, incorporations, bank loans, home sales and purchases, and personal injury—where law didn't really change that much from generation to generation. What you learned in law school (or in apprenticeship) was what you practiced, and if you kept on good terms with the judge's clerk he would help you make sure all your papers were filed in good order while you were learning what was meant by law school phrases such as "causes of action" or "estoppel." Some lawyers had clerks and sometimes the clerk stayed on, paid a little better once he had passed the bar exam, hoping to inherit the practice if his mentor was aging or to become a partner if he was working for a younger man. But usually when an apprenticeship was over the apprentice went out to try his luck.

These independent lawyers weren't necessarily popular—their "open-and-aboveboard business," the turn-of-the-century western writer Eugene Manlove Rhodes wrote bitterly, was "living off the unlucky"—but they were vital to the social cohesion of their communities. In many American towns, especially in the Midwest and the South, the courthouse was the central structure, standing in the middle of the main square. Judges rode circuit to service these courthouses; lawyers generally stayed in their own towns, where they were fixtures—presidents of the school board, chairmen of the library or the concert-and-lecture society, members of the board of the county hospital. At their best, the solo practitioners were the psychiatrists and social workers of the middle class, helping people solve their problems, able to do so because they had access to the courts and the processes that could impose solutions if the parties couldn't find their own. They also, of course, without even trying, built business for each other, because once one party to a dispute had a lawyer, the other party needed a lawyer of his own. The gag line told of a town that was too small to support a single lawyer, but once two of them hung out shingles there was more business than they could handle.

The image of the profession usually related to litigation. The popular heroes were the district attorneys and, sometimes, the defense lawyers. Even then, criminal cases loomed large in the public mind, and the flamboyant defense lawyers got the press attention. In fact, the number of criminal defense lawyers was small, because the number of criminal defendants who could afford lawyers was small, and to the extent that courts appointed lawyers for indigent defendants (there was no constitutional right to a lawyer until 1963), it was low-paid and dispiriting work, not really part of the average lawyer's experience or self-image. Still, that was the image: Lawyers were, and in a sense still are, preeminently the people who have access to the courts.

One entire class of litigators—the plaintiffs' personal injury bar—was compensated almost entirely by result. The case was taken on "contingent fee," which came out of the payment received by the plaintiff. No payment, no fee. These fees were heavy, in most instances a third or more of the settlement offered by the insurance company or the damages assessed by a jury. The court in effect collected the fee for the lawyer, directing that the money be paid by the insurance company to him rather than directly to the victim. (Thus, by these means, with the uncomfortable consent of the court, hundreds of millions of dollars were taken off the top of the money Johns Manville paid to get out of the bankruptcy into which it had been plunged by the claims of former workers suffering the lung disease asbestosis.[1]) And the lawyer's expenses on the case, which could be considerable, came over and above the fee.

Men like Melvin Belli in San Francisco, F. Lee Bailey in Miami, and James Jarmail in Dallas advertised their enormous earnings as lawyers and drew imitators. My fellow Cornell Law alumnus Arnold I. Burns was not entirely kidding when he quoted a definition of contingent fees for the edification of students at the Cornell Law School in 1990: "If I don't win your case, *I* get nothing. If I do win it, *you* get nothing."

For the lawyer who does it well, litigation is more fun than anything else. But traditionally—and it is a tradition that still held when I came to the bar—the best lawyers counseled their clients to avoid litigation whenever possible. Judge Learned Hand told a meeting of New York's City Association of the Bar that as a citizen he would fear litigation beyond anything but sickness and death; and most lawyers agreed with him. It was also in lawyers' self-interest to avoid litigation, because few clients could afford to pay for the time that would be consumed by a trial. Taking a personal injury case to trial risked leaving the lawyer out-of-pocket for preparation costs, expert witness fees, and the like, and with nothing for his time, if the jury didn't buy his case.

The lawyer as litigator was an individual in charge, and the assistants who came with him to the hearing rooms and courtrooms were very much his subalterns. Even the giant teams the big firms put together for the antitrust cases of the 1960s and 1970s were very much identified to themselves and to others as the soldiers in the army of the courtroom general. The young who were apprenticed to the profession through litigators acquired habits and mannerisms from their leader and became the repository of the traditions of the bar. By contrast, the lawyer as counselor increasingly became part of a group, much more flexible in orientation. The young apprenticed to the group were likely to have more independence, because they were exploring areas where their seniors were, frankly, not always up on the law or the rules. The variety of talents required by these teams changed the nature of law partnerships.

Most law firms probably started because two people liked each other, or an older man wanted a younger man to do some of the more tiring things. Office space for two cost less than twice as much as office space for one, and two could share the costs of a secretary or a clerk. Partners could fill in for each other when one was sick or overburdened with another matter. But functional specialization played a role early on. One man loved to go out and get clients; another was an "office lawyer," another had what Learned Hand called the "bathtub mind" of the litigator, loved to fill that mind with the facts of one case, then empty it and go on to the facts of another case.

Partners in most firms really *were* partners in the common-sense popular meaning of the word. Nobody could take fees for himself—all fees (including, in most firms, fees for service on a company's board of directors, whether or not the company was a client, and even payments for what the partner wrote and sold)—were put into a common pot, from which the partners drew by prearrangement in certain proportions. The theory was that the partnership should receive whatever any partner earned through the expenditure of his time.

In larger firms, the normal compensation process was one whereby a partner's share related to his age and the number of years he had been a partner in the firm; it was understood that some people generated more revenues in some years and others in other years, and that the partners who looked up the law and wrote the briefs and pinned down the clauses in the documents contributed to the revenues as much as the partners who met with the clients and tried the cases. At Cad wallader, Wickersham & Taft, the partnership agreement specified that a partner's compensation would be "measured by the extent he had enhanced the professional work and reputation of his partners."[2]

Clearly, firms had stars—called "name partners" in the days when firm names changed when partners retired—and their compensation might be extraordinary; even today, it's unlikely that the most successful business lawyers make as much in constant dollars as did William Nelson Cromwell or Paul Cravath or John Foster Dulles. But the firms were communitarian. If a man was sick, his partners picked up the slack, and when lawyers retired they generally continued to keep some share of the revenues of their old partnership, an arrangement usually acceptable to the younger people because they expected to be the beneficiaries of it when their time came. To prevent the retired partners from becoming too much of a drag on the active partners in bad years, the partnership agreement frequently specified (as ours does at Coudert) that the total pot for the retired could not be more than a certain percentage of the firm's net profit.

The first large law firms, in the last years of the nineteenth century, had dozens—even scores—of lawyers and grew up to serve clients with multiple involvements, usually railroads, public utility companies, and banks. In New York, the largest law firms were often identified by their banking clients: Milbank Tweed with Chase, Sherman & Sterling with National City, White & Case with Bankers Trust, Davis Polk with Morgan, Simpson Thacher with Manufacturers Hanover. Into the mid-1980s, even after its own law department had mushroomed, Chase paid Milbank $100,000 a month for routine contacts.[3] Such clients needed rather specialized services in connection with real estate transactions, loan contracts, and collections, and the firms grew in "departments" handling different aspects of client needs. The bar in big cities began to lose its old collegiality of a lawyer is a lawyer is a lawyer.

Few large firms handled clients' suits for personal injuries or for divorce, though most would take responsibility for referring such matters to other counsel (and some would take a referral fee from that counsel for their troubles, though the ethics of such fees was a matter of dispute). But in general both lawyers and clients believed as late as the 1930s that a man with a license to practice law was capable of handling his client's problems, that lawyers in firms confronted with a problem to which they did not know the answer would consult with partners who'd had recent experience in similar cases, but that they would in the end handle or at least be responsible for the matter themselves. There had always been "narrow" specialties—patent law and admiralty law, for example; the first considered a dull specialty and the second a grand one, both practiced before their own courts and agencies. But they were exceptions.

Partners consulted with each other all the time; doors were usually open, and it was the most natural thing in the world for a lawyer who had just learned of a problem from a client to wander down the hall and talk it over with his partner. Some of the happiest memories of law practice in the middle decades of the twentieth century are the recollections of impromptu conferences in a senior partner's office, talking over some odd problem the firm had just been handed, engaging in discussions that challenged one's intellect, knowledge, and judgment. No client was billed for that time or, as an ordinary matter, for the time the juniors took discussing the problems they couldn't handle. Such sessions were often conscious "mentoring." Arnold & Porter in Washington had an open bar in the library at six o'clock; Paul Porter called it "the children's hour," and partners felt it part of their duty to drop down to the library every so often and talk law and cases with the associates.

The work to be done for a business in those earlier days was almost entirely in response to a client's problem. He "retained" the firm on an annual basis to make sure that "his" lawyers would be available to him when he needed them. There were deals to complete and nail down, contracts to negotiate, loans to arrange, securities to issue, bills to collect. The law itself was relatively unchanging; the lawyer knew the law and could advise his client when called upon to do so. The law firm was a resource for strategy and battle, not a scouting party to find changes in laws and regulations that might affect the future conduct of the client's business. The terrain on which battles would be fought was familiar ground for the lawyers, and where they did not know the landmarks they "looked up the law" in the casebooks, guided by ingenious index systems written in the hieroglyphics that were the universally shared mysteries of the profession. Large firms operating on a retainer basis often did not even have a litigation department. Robert MacCrate of Sullivan & Cromwell, who has worked extensively on the history of his firm, says that large firms tended to develop litigation departments in response to the phased introduction of regulation associated with the Public Utilities Holding Company Act of 1935. Commercial and personal injury suits involving public utilities could be sloughed off to litigation firms, but the impositions of the holding company law struck at clients' vitals; they wanted their counsel to sue—and, indeed, Sullivan & Cromwell, under the leadership of John Foster Dulles, who vigorously opposed the New Deal, was eager to sue.

In the retainer model, the client retained the *firm*, under the auspices of "his" partner, who was, of course, an integral part of the firm. The profitability of the law firm was a function of the extent to which the retainer (plus whatever supplemental bills the firm could send) paid the costs of the work to be done. All firms were always to some degree dependent on getting work from the associates (formerly called "clerks") that was worth more than they were paid. Pressure was heavy on them, not to log hours but to get the job done and move on to the next job. Many worked very long hours in cramped quarters. The novelist Louis Auchincloss was an associate at Sullivan & Cromwell long enough to get his own private office, a closet with a tiny window that faced into a dark air shaft. A younger associate new at the firm idly asked him whether he worked much at night. "I don't know," Auchincloss said.[4] But the firm billed its clients for their work, not for their time.

"It was astounding," Nancy Lisagor and Frank Lipsius wrote in their history of the firm, "how few could do so much [at Sullivan & Cromwell]. Two lawyers put together the purchase of the Matador Land Company [the second-largest ranch in Texas; the year was 1951], one of the most complicated land deals ever devised. It took three days to close, because it ultimately required 2,200 signatures on 600 documents. One of the lawyers, Bob McDonald, later joked that only two lawyers did the work because 'to explain the transaction would take more time than to do the work.'"[5]

At Cravath, Swaine & Moore, by contrast, the tendency apparently was to overwhelm a case with personnel. Railroad reorganization cases, a specialty of the firm, were an enormous amount of work for lawyers because different firms were needed to represent the interests of the company being reorganized, the stockholders, the various classes of bondholders, and the bankers who would in the end create and sell the new securities of the reorganized company. In *The Cravath Firm*, Robert Swaine notes that when trying such matters out of town in the 1920s, his litigation partner Frederick Wood "was accompanied by numerous assistants, all with bulky files crammed into many suitcases. If the matter was to take more than a few days, he set up practically a branch office at his hotel, with desks, filing cabinets, stenographers and associates in adjoining rooms."[6] One could argue that the modern law firm, with its tendency to marshal great numbers of troops, was born in Fred Wood's hotel rooms. Certainly, Cravath followed the model, setting up what became a separate law firm, several dozens of lawyers, to work several years from an office in White Plains on the antitrust case the government brought against Cravath's client IBM. The ratcheting of salaries for beginning lawyers in the larger firms in the 1970s and early 1980s was in large part a result of Cravath's need to pay more to get anyone to work on this dreary stuff. More than one observer has cynically remarked that perhaps IBM's stockholders and management might have been better off if the company had lost rather than won this case, on which the legal fees ran into several tens of millions of dollars.

As government involvement with business became tighter and more pervasive, companies wanted the law firms they retained to be able to handle a new range of their legal problems. Law firms increasingly *did* become scouting parties, keeping track of the movements of a government that had become, from the point of view of many business clients, "the enemy." Training acquired in law school and bar exam courses—and even in experience in the courts—became much less valuable to the active business practitioner. The members of the existing law firm often enough could not cope with the rush of laws and rules in specialized areas of government regulation. Their choice was to expand the firm to acquire the expertise the client needed or to find outside counsel who could be engaged, usually through the law firm rather than by the client himself, to handle these problems.

In the patent and admiralty areas, and in the defense of personal injury suits (where the insurance company's counsel pulled the laboring oar, anyway) this was the normal procedure. Firms also normally referred to local counsel cases brought under the law of another state (though someone from the firm might well go out to organize and supervise the work). Into the 1950s, it was common practice for even the larger firms with the largest clients to send antitrust work, say, to a firm that specialized in antitrust, or Federal Communications Commission work to lawyers who practiced before that commission, or immigration cases to outside specialists, and even tax work to tax specialists. Not many law firms outside Washington felt themselves competent to maneuver through the labyrinths of government. As late as 1980, New York's Kelly Drye engaged Washington's Patton, Boggs & Blow to lobby Congress for the Chrysler bailout legislation. "Lobbyists may be lawyers," the lawyer-reporter James B. Stewart wrote two years later, discussing Kelly Drye's action, "their expertise valuable in drafting and examining legislation. But in the eyes of the corporate lawyers, they do not practice law."[7] In the 1980s, as though to illustrate their difference from law firms elsewhere, several large Washington firms established business subsidiaries that did consulting or lobbying work, run by people who might or might not be lawyers.

2

The progress of law firms after World War II was something to behold. From the 1940s to 1990, the large law firms grew rapidly and steadily, feeding on the ever-increasing intervention of the government in what had once been private business—complicated tax codes, aggressive antitrust enforcement, antidiscrimination laws, environmental requirements, questions of corporate governance, and securities issues. Every year, American business spent a larger share of its revenues for legal services, and the great firms seemed to grow greater simply by the motion of the clock. In 1983, when the Commerce Department started producing these figures, Americans spent $40 billion for legal services; by 1989, the number was $83 billion.[8] The Los Angeles–based firm of Gibson, Dunn & Crutcher grew from about 200 to about 700 lawyers between 1980 and 1991; the Cleveland-based firm of Jones Day grew from 239 lawyers to 1,221.

Lawyers in my generation could not even have imagined the incomes partners twenty years younger than ourselves now take home in dozens of the huge "businesslike" law firms, with their boxes of computer printout, their profit centers, their branches scattered through this country and other countries, their new-business presentations to other law firms' clients, their firm meetings where the partners wear name tags and strike up conversations with each other as though they were strangers, linked to each other by the common interests that tie together, say, manufacturers of plumbing fixtures, who also have conventions in some of these same hotels. *American Lawyer* reported that in 1989, which may turn out to have been the peak year for profits in large law firms, there were seven firms, all based in New York, at which the partners averaged better than $1 million each.

Right after World War II, there was one lawyer in the United States for every 790 people; in 1970, there was one for every 572 people; in 1990, there was one for every 320 Americans. Over the last quarter of a century, the number of lawyers in the United States has gone up by almost two and a half times, and the income of lawyers has multiplied more than six times, probably topping $100 billion in 1993. There is ever more for lawyers to do, whole categories of profitable specialty—environmental law, international law, antidiscrimination law. Mark Twain once observed that Congress was in session again and no

man's life or property were safe. For lawyers the relevant observation could be that Congress or the state legislatures are in
session again, and there's going to be new business for us: With
rare exceptions, our law-writing processes produce new work
for lawyers, year in, year out.

Once one large firm spread itself into new specialties or into
many cities across the country, other firms began to be concerned that they would lose clients to people who could offer
what a Federal Trade Commission report would later call "one-
stop shopping" for legal services. Cities such as Richmond and
Minneapolis, where a 30-lawyer firm would have been a giant
in the 1960s, became homes to 300-lawyer firms twenty-five
years later.

To get experts in taxes or the various branches of administrative law, mergers and acquisitions, then real estate, then bankruptcy, diversifying firms admitted people to partnership by
"lateral entry" from government and from other firms rather
than insisting that the new partners rise through the ranks of
associates within the firm. Soon it became an inescapable conclusion that some partners were more significant than others
for the prosperity of the firm. Their specialty was more important in drawing new clients to the firm; their ties with important clients were particularly close. The cynical term
"rainmaker" came into daily use. With specialization, inevitably, also came stratification. As recently as the 1960s, most
large firms ran with an egalitarian system of partner compensation that, except for a small bulge bracket of "name partners" or
"senior partners," gave an equal share of annual profits to all
those with the same seniority at the firm. At the few firms
where there might be major variations between what partners
of the same seniority were paid, efforts were made to keep it
quiet—at Sullivan & Cromwell, for example, shares in the profits were divided annually by a sort of Doge's council that met
in secrecy, and nobody was supposed to know what anybody
else got.

The system of equal shares had come under organized attack at other firms as early as 1940. In his history of his own firm of Cleary, Gottlieb, Steen & Hamilton, Leo Gottlieb traced the end of equal shares in the Wall Street firms to demands made that year upon what was then the firm of Root, Clark, Buckner & Ballantine by three mid-level partners: future Supreme Court Justice John M. Harlan, Willkie Bushby, and William P. Palmer. There were seven partners in the same bracket as the three who complained, and among them was Gottlieb himself. The protesters' argument, Gottlieb recalled, was that "serious inequities had developed in the productivity of the group of seven roughly contemporaneous partners of the firm who had equal shares in the firm's profits at the highest level below the senior partners and that fairness and the future welfare of the firm required a substantial upward revision of the profit shares of the three proposers and a downward revision of the shares of other members of the group of seven." (The group of three did not propose to increase Gottlieb's salary, "giving as the reason for this suggestion that I had said that I did not wish to have my share increased. However, after consulting with me and learning that, while I had said that I did not wish to join the group of proposers because I did not share their views, I had not said that I did not wish to have my share increased if the shares of the proposing group were increased, the senior partners modified the plan by increasing my profit share. . . .")[9]

Resentment of the muscle shown by the three Root Clark partners, Gottlieb wrote, was the reason he and several of his colleagues at the firm decided to leave and start their own firm, one of the few where, we are told, "lockstep" partnership shares are still the rule. Cravath still has a variant system in which partners receive increasing shares up to the age of fifty-five, then decreasing shares up to retirement to counsel status at age sixty. Sullivan & Cromwell in recent years, while retaining its secret council, has instituted a procedure by which partners cut back their shares at ages sixty-seven, sixty-eight, and

sixty-nine preliminary to retirement at age seventy. (In the trib-
al memory of the firm is the fact that old Cromwell lived to age
ninety-four, in a town house bordering Rockefeller Center, and
kept taking substantial pieces of the firm's income till the day
he died in 1948.) Milbank Tweed hung on to payment by seniority until 1984, and later suffered personnel losses reported-
ly because younger productive partners felt that the firm's
pension plan gave too high a proportion of the earnings to retired partners. But at most firms some partners are now definitely more equal than others, and the profit shares are
reallocated at a sensitive meeting every year.

Together with sheer size, these compensation arrangements
tolled heavily against collegiality. Meanwhile, the growth of
specialties, added originally for the needs of one client, forced
law firms into a marketing mold. The client in whose interests
the specialty was acquired was not likely to provide enough
business to employ a department. Other clients of this firm
might not need this specialty—or might be happy with the tax
specialists or antitrust specialists or real estate specialists in
other firms to whom they now gave their work in those areas.
To sell the time of the new partners, the firm would need a
strategy to reach out for new business. And the Supreme Court
decided that the First Amendment protected the commercial
speech of law firms that wished to sell their services.

When I was a young lawyer, it was considered shockingly
bad behavior to solicit legal business; the young lawyer was
supposed to conduct himself in such a way that his telephone
would ring. If the telephone rang with a call from a company
known to be a client of another law firm, he called that firm
first to make sure its partners understood that he had not in any
way tried to take the business away. Trying to take clients away
from other law firms might even constitute barratry if it involved the stirring up of litigation. By 1990, the attitude had
turned completely around. Jonathan Green, vice president and
general counsel of the Rockefeller Group, which had been represented for more than a generation by Milbank Tweed, told a

reporter that he always had "the feeling that Milbank has our best interests in mind. But," he added, "any service provider should feel they have to compete for your business."[10] Large, spread out geographically and intellectually, needing to cover an enormous fixed cost every year, the modern "mega" law firm also found itself in a fiercely competitive business that pushed out of the ring those with genteel professional habits.

Time has shown that specialization also has a frightening downside: Unlike the law degree of old, which was good for a lifetime, specialist training retains its value only as long as the specialty is in demand. Great firms were built in the 1960s and 1970s—Kaye Scholer, Cahill Gordon, an enlarged Cravath—on the defense of corporations against antitrust prosecutions. When Ronald Reagan came into office and the Justice Department decided antitrust was at best a low priority and at worst a hangover from old-fashioned liberalism, the antitrust partners were—literally—out of work. The 1986 tax act devastated the tax bar. Many of them moved to real estate law, only to see the real estate practice crater in the early 1990s. Bankruptcy became the specialty of choice in 1991 and 1992, and will someday, inevitably, go the way of the others. Much of the hunger to make top dollar now, which has been so damaging to the reputation of the bar, can be traced to this new insecurity, to the possibility that a lawyer, like an athlete, will have only a few years to maximize his reward and must get what he can get while his talents are in demand.

3

A young partner in what is now a midsize (110-lawyer) firm says that "the practice of law changed forever when lawyers decided they should be making as much money as their clients." There were three ways to do that.

One was the contingent fee, where immense rewards could come out of the client's award.

The second, the Wall Street variant of the first, was Wachtell Lipton's system of charging large flat fees, like the investment bankers' fees, for the successful completion of a deal.

The third was the "leveraging" of associates' time. Lawyers were never students of Karl Marx, but in the years of the Cold War they took a leaf from Marx's book. For Marx, who did not understand the allocation of capital or the role of innovation, all profit was the result of the exploitation of labor. It was the "surplus value" generated by the workers over and above what they were paid that allowed the capitalists to live atop the hill while their employees were down in the mud. Restructuring the law firms in the 1960s and 1970s—in large part as a response to corporate clients whose bookkeepers wanted specific invoices for what their money was buying—the large law firms designed a system reminiscent of Marx's vision. They would pay their associates a fixed salary and bill the clients per unit of time during which the associate worked on that client's business. Then, by requiring the associates to work very long hours, they would generate profits the partners could take home. There was no secret about this: In mid-1990, Jack Nussbaum of Willkie Farr & Gallagher told *American Lawyer* that "his partners' hope was to get associate hours back up to the 2,200-a-year pace that was the norm during the 1988 boom year. That way," he explained, "Willkie Farr would restore most of the profitability that had given the partners average profits of $785,999 in 1988, as compared to a projection of about $600,000 in 1990."[11]

If the firms were "mentoring" their young associates, preparing them for careers at the bar, the exploitation would be defensible as a payment for indispensable help. After all, the law clerks of a hundred years ago were paid nothing at all and contributed to the profits of their masters. For years, major firms tried to cycle their recent law school graduates through the different departments of the firm and to give them some say in which kind of law they wanted to practice. Now, increasingly, young lawyers go where there is an opening for them. As their beginning salaries rise, the firms focus less on acculturating them to their new profession and more on slotting them rapidly into a specialty where their work can earn fees. Apart from professional sports and the entertainment industry, these are the best-paying jobs young people can get—in 1992, the brightest graduates of the best law schools were paid as much as $85,000 a year to work in the fifty largest metropolitan law firms. But it's not clear what they get for their time except the money.

Moreover, everyone involved sees the early years of employment at a big law firm as what law professors Marc Galanter and Thomas Palay have called a "tournament of lawyers."[12] The winners of the tournament become partners in the firm. Even the losers, historically, have done remarkably well. When Lisagor and Lipsius wrote their book about Sullivan & Cromwell in 1988, they found a hundred former associates of the firm in good jobs at client companies—seven of them as CEOs. Today, however, the chances of winning the tournament are much diminished, both because the firms are no longer expanding and because the increased specialization of the training gives it a lesser surrender value outside the firm. It's not unknown for young lawyers to work on one aspect of one case, and nothing else, for months and even years at a time. When that case is over, their value on the job market has not been greatly improved from what it was before they joined this firm.

Almost everyone agrees that the burdens on the associates have grown much too great—and the *purpose* of the work has become intolerably confused. At the large firms, associates are now expected to "fill the book" (show time sheets involving two thousand hours a year of work for clients). If the lawyer takes the normal ten holidays and a minimal two weeks' vacation, this demand works out to forty-two *billable* hours a week, which implies fifty or even sixty hours a week *at the office*. The associates in the large firms cannot play the piano or paint a picture or act in a church play because they simply don't have the time. The tragedy is that, in the end, the single-minded drive toward winning the competitions at the firm will make these young lawyers not only less useful citizens, less interesting human beings, and less successful parents but also less good as lawyers, less sympathetic to other people's troubles, and less valuable to their clients.

The pressure extends to the partners, who are expected not only to keep up their own totals of billable hours but also to keep the associates busy. Blair Perry of Hale and Dorr in Boston reported that one of the sins of which he had been accused by his partners when they fired him was that he did his own work and failed to "leverage" (use associates and paralegals) on his cases.[13]

Trapped by this compensation system for partners and associates, the large law firms had an inexorable need to grow. The salaried associates could be persuaded to work the extraordinary number of billable hours required of them because there was a pot of gold at the other end in the form of a partnership. But additional partners could be created only by growing firms, and each new partner the firm made would then require for his support the employment of additional associates.[14] Growth became exponential in the big law firms in the 1980s. Meanwhile, articles in magazines spoke of a "Bermuda Triangle" of thirty- to fifty-lawyer firms, which disappeared because they couldn't offer clients or associates the benefits promised by the giants.

4

This exponentiating growth process was made possible by a cost-plus fee structure under which clients were charged by the hour for the time the lawyers devoted to their matters. Like the defense industry in World War II and the hospital industry after the passage of Medicare and Medicaid (with their requirement that the government pay doctors "reasonable and customary" fees for their procedures), the law "industry" found it only natural to expand at an accelerating rate.

Like any other service, legal work has a value to its purchaser, and the payment for it should reflect that value. But the value is hard to determine. Waving away concerns that cost-plus arrangements were inflating the number of hours for which law firms billed their clients, Abraham Karsh of Arnold & Porter told the *ABA Journal* that "quality work takes time."[15] If law is a business like plumbing, however (and lawyers, in denying their obligation to do pro bono work, like to argue that nobody asks plumbers to work for nothing), then clients will in the long run refuse to allow lawyers to decide what level of quality a case requires, just as they refuse to allow plumbers to decide that the bathroom would look better with solid gold fixtures. The plumber and the painter and the automobile repair shop also charge by the hour, but they will give you an estimate first—and in many cases will guarantee that estimate. They may even offer a choice of quality standards to which the job can be done. If the customer can make do with something utilitarian, he pays less; if the job has to be gold-plated, he pays more. And the customer, knowing at least the approximate price, also has the chance to change his mind about whether he wants the job done at all.

Every good lawyer wastes part of each week telling clients for heaven's sake not to do something that would, in fact, generate fees for his law firm, but it's easier to give such advice when the lawyer's time is limited. Once time becomes in effect unlimited—because new associates can always be hired or existing associates worked even harder and more profitably as the load expands—the temptation arises to do as the client asks, whether or not the lawyer thinks it's the right thing for him to do. Many resist the temptation, but some—especially associates who have been informed that their own chance of making partner rests to some extent on their business-development skills—cannot.

Often a law firm can do no more than guess at what a case

will cost, if only because there is an opponent, and each side's costs will be heavily influenced by the other side's tactics. In law, the most routine matters, even registration statements for a securities issue, where the computer has been taught to do the work by itself, can turn out to be more complicated than expected. Whatever the reason, however, the disconnection of the cost of the work from its value to the client creates a problem more serious than the ethical dilemmas the professors learnedly dissect and the bar associations agonize over.

And this conflict, unfortunately, is most prevalent in the great metropolitan firms that are presumably the leaders of the profession. They have an enormous nut to crack every year, with operating expenses well into the tens (at a few firms, into the hundreds) of millions of dollars. And although their condition is not so perilous as that of the solo practitioner, who does not know what business may walk through the door next month, the fact is that their future income is far less certain than that of a businessman. Billing by the hour necessarily means that a firm's income grows according to the man-hours devoted to the client's concerns. Seth Rosner, who has taught law at NYU and chaired the General Practice Section of the American Bar Association, points out that such an arrangement "makes the client and the lawyer adversaries."[16]

Making the situation even worse at some firms is the recent custom of billing the client for every disbursement, with a markup for the firm over its out-of-pocket costs: copying of documents, secretarial work, meals in the office while working on the client's business, travel, telephone calls, messenger services. Almost every issue of *American Lawyer* contains another example of billing for disbursements that makes old-fashioned lawyers cringe. It is hard to think of anything more likely to sow distrust between client and lawyer than the discovery that the law firm has been charging the client ten times as much per page for making Xerox copies of documents as the client pays when he does such things himself.

Law firms feel that such criticisms are unfair. The system of billing by the hour and by specific disbursement is what the clients have asked for because their accounts payable systems run on itemized bills, which their accountants demand. No lawyer likes filling out time sheets or having his work judged by the computer's report on how many hours he has billed. But it can't be avoided, they say: We live in a market system.

In markets, people haggle; they do not trust. Implicit in a professional relationship also is a lawyer's understanding that he is not supposed to make money on everything he does. The old solo practitioner wrote wills for very little money—clients definitely did not want to spend a lot of money on wills—on the well-founded assumption that he would have profitable fees from the administration of the estate. The retainer would be profitable some years and not others. The client understood that, in years when very much more work had to be done than could be covered by the retainer, he might get a supplemental bill, but in the ordinary run of events he knew he would pay a little too much in some years and a little too little in others.

The present situation is unstable. Corporations are used to dealing with vendors of services. Accountants have been competing on a price basis for some years, not very happily. If current trends continue, the corporate counsel's job increasingly is going to be the purchase of legal services from what management considers more or less a commodity market of large law firms. Only about a tenth of American lawyers work in these firms, but they set the tone of the profession. In the small towns, solo practitioners or two-partner firms may still practice law much the way their grandfathers did. But in cities where the big firms have branches and there are local firms with twenty-five lawyers and more, traditional lawyers can be squeezed between the commodity services corporate management wants to buy and the commodity services that are what is offered by most of the lawyer-advertisers who urge New Yorkers to dial 1-800-WHY-HURT for "the law offices of Seth Benson" or tell people in Washington, "If you have a phone, you have a lawyer."

This plague has already infected the relations between

lawyers and a rather more upscale group of possible clients. Financial services companies as significant as American Express and Chase Manhattan have offered their credit card holders fixed-price legal services—with "free consultations" and restricted hourly rates—to be paid, of course, through the credit card company. There is indeed some handwriting on this wall. If law firms are willing to remake themselves in whatever shape they consider most pleasing to clients, they may find that clients don't want the traditional law firm at all.

CHAPTER 6

THE LAW SCHOOLS: MISSING THE TARGET?

An old story tells of a farm boy whose father, ambitious for his future, sent him off to town five hours' ride away to be apprenticed to a lawyer in the county seat in hopes that the boy himself could someday be called to the bar. Three weeks passed before the youngster had a chance to return home and have Sunday dinner with his family. The father asked his son how he liked the law. The boy thought seriously for a while, then said, "Pa, I don't like the law. I'm sorry I learned it."

1

"In 1834 Judge Thomas Lacy of the Superior Court of Arkansas Territory admitted to the bar brash young Albert Pike . . . who had merely been reading lawbooks on his own, without examination, on the ground that after all, it wasn't like issuing a diploma to practice medicine; he couldn't kill anybody by poor practice of law."[1]

2

In the last two decades, Americans have had a fascination with law schools. A book about the first-year experience at Harvard Law, *The Paper Chase*, became a popular movie and television series, and made a star of a curmudgeonly theater and movie director who had never acted before. Real law school professors became public television celebrities, as a future president of Yale demonstrated the Socratic method for the cameras, using as his victims panels of a dozen or so well-known (mostly) nonlawyers discussing the Constitution and its relation to their work. The excitement, the huge work loads, and the competitiveness of law school became something all kinds of people knew and talked about. First-year law school enrollment, which had been in the 10,000 to 15,000 range in the early 1960s, shot up to over 50,000 by the middle 1980s. In 1991, there were 171 law schools accredited by the American Bar Association, with an enrollment of almost 130,000. There were almost 5,600 full-time teachers, with 1,365 "deans and administrators."[2]

Expanding law schools was easy for the universities because the job required virtually no capital investment—no laboratories, and by liberal arts standards not a very great library, because a high proportion of the work was in the casebooks, which students bought for themselves. Law instruction almost everywhere was given primarily before large classes in amphitheaters, and student tuition paid the salaries of the professors with considerable left over. Law school tuitions rose at the same exponential rate as tuitions in other parts of the university, and many universities actually made money on their growing law schools. Talbot d'Alemberte, president of the ABA in 1990–91 and formerly dean of the law school at Florida State University, told the *ABA Journal* that a community college nursing school or dental hygienist program would not be accredited with the pupil–teacher ratio of the average American law school. He suggested that the reason for the high pupil–teacher ratio at law schools is that "we run legal educa-tion in a way that is least burdensome to professors, and most advantageous to the university systems."[3]

The expansion of law school enrollment in numbers and prosperity did not, however, produce much analysis of the methods and purposes of legal education. In 1871, Christopher Columbus Langdell introduced the case-study method of in-struction at Harvard Law School, and nobody has ever found anything better. Even those schools that in the 1960s made publicized decisions to turn themselves into schools of "policy studies" rather than mere law (Yale, Chicago, USC) never really abandoned reliance on cases as the raw meat of instruction. Cases are what the law is about; in Justice Holmes's famous phrase, the life of the law has not been logic but experience. Though most of what is taught in law school is appellate cases, to understand what the judges are saying students must learn the facts as well as the law that can be applied to them—and every experienced lawyer knows that the facts are the heart of the matter in at least four fifths of the disputes that wind up as cases at law. Meanwhile, the Socratic method absolutely guar-antees that the student will have prepared the case, because nobody can possibly wing it when a law professor is asking questions. By never telling the students what the professor thinks, pushing the student off her initial certainties about how this case should be resolved by asking her to answer questions she has not considered, the Socratic method forces students to think on their feet in an embarrassing situation, with all their classmates watching and listening. (In this case the gender pro-noun *she* is particularly appropriate, because historically it was believed that women would not stand up well to this kind of pressure and were therefore unsuited for law school—but once the bars were down, the female members of the law student population rose dramatically, until in 1992 they passed the 40 percent level.)

The purpose of law school most commonly enunciated is to

teach young college graduates to "think like a lawyer." Lawyers must be masters of relevance: They must be able to see quickly which pieces of information are "evidence" and which are irrelevant or tangential to a client's cause. Whether in negotiation or on trial (or in conference with clients), lawyers must be quick on their feet, able to handle even the questions they cannot answer in a confidence-inspiring way. Most important of all, they must have the ability to suspend judgment, to see both sides of a case that is presented to them, for they may be called on to argue either side. The task of the law professor is often to change a student's mind, and then change it back again, until the student and the class understand that in many situations that will come before them professionally they can with a whole heart devote their skills to either side. Then they have to block out much of that part of their mind that saw the other side, finding ways to diminish and combat what they once considered the strong points of the opponent's argument. In the public forum, they are expected to be *aggressive* for their client: The system rests on the assumption that judges and juries will select the better cause when both sides have been forcefully presented. In the wonderfully precise language of Judge Charles Wyzanski, the study of law gives its masters "clarity of expression, precision of definition, organization of thought, and more generally the capacity to deal argumentatively."[4] But not—note well—the ability to deal effectively with other people.

Spouses of entering law students are given psychological counseling at many schools to warn them that their husbands or wives are about to change, to become incredibly absorbed in the mountains of work they must accomplish, more assertive in family disputes, and more sensitive to little annoyances they would once have brushed off. These personality changes are not good for their home life, and are often not good for their future relations with clients, either. Focus groups of businessmen queried by the Case Western Reserve University Law School in Cleveland elicited "authoritative," "insensitive," "arrogant," "intimidating," and "know-it-all" as the responses to the word *lawyer*. The businessmen also complained that lawyers never admit it when they make a mistake.[5] And it is a common observation that law school experience tends to beat the idealism out of law students. As Richard D. Kahlenberg wrote in his book about being a student at Harvard Law School: "We came to law school talking about using the law as a vehicle for social change, but when it was time to decide what we would do with our lives, we fell over each other to work for those law firms most resistant to change."[6]

But what happens here is worse than changes in manners or in political attitude, which are likely to happen anyway. (Clemenceau once said that he would disown any son who was not a socialist at the age of twenty or remained one at the age of thirty.) As the bumptiousness of judgment is knocked out of these youngsters, it may be replaced not by tolerance of ambiguity (which is arguably the goal of all education) but by cynicism. If you can argue either side, why should you worry about your client's goals, his reasons for hiring a lawyer? "We sever all sense of 'I know what I think about this and I know what my responsibility is,'" says Margery Schultz, who teaches ethics at both the medical school and the law school of the University of California (Berkeley). "We make them face the limits of their assumptions and their viewpoints. And then we leave them there. And we *can't* do that."

Law school education deals not with people but with abstractions—because, as NYU's Stephen Gillers puts it, "[t]he law school classroom . . . is a place of ideas . . . a place that celebrates the life of the mind and rewards intellectual achievement."[7] But nobody would think of teaching future doctors just from books and pictures; mechanical as much modern medicine has become, medical students are never allowed to forget that patients are people. There is a good deal of cleverness for its own sake in law school instruction, and too little willingness to look at the program to find and, if feasible, slaughter both the sacred cow and the sacred bull. "Too often," the ABA Task Force on Law Schools and the Profession concluded, "the Socratic method of teaching emphasizes qualities that have little to do with justice, fairness, and morality in daily practice. Students too easily gain the impression that wit, sharp responses, and dazzling performance are more important than the personal moral values that lawyers must possess and that the profession must espouse. The promotion of these values requires no resources and no institutional changes. It does require commitment."[8]

Anthony Amsterdam of NYU Law School gave a talk in 1984 about how twentieth-century legal education looked from the perspective of the twenty-first century. The worst weakness, he argued, had been the restriction in the modes of thinking inculcated in students, which handicapped rather than helped them to learn from their later experience as lawyers. Among missing modes had been "ends-means thinking," defined as

> the process by which one starts with a factual situation presenting a problem or an opportunity and figures out the ways in which the problem might be solved or the opportunity might be realized. What is involved is making a thorough, systematic, and creative canvass of all the possible goals or objectives in the situation—the "end points" to which movement from the present state of affairs might be made—then making an equally systematic and creative inventory of the possible means or routes to each goal, then analyzing the ways in which and the extent to which the various means and goals are compatible or incompatible with one another, seeking means to reconcile them or to prioritize them to the extent that they are irreconcilable.[9]

The definition is elaborate and ornate, but its content when digested is as good a brief statement of the function of the lawyer as counselor as one could hope to find; and the fact that we do not seek to develop such modes of thought in law students is a profoundly important criticism of the education now offered in the law schools.

Because litigation produces the cases the students study, the model is one of conflict, which troubles the older members of the practicing bar. Justin Stanley's ABA Commission on Professionalism noted that "experienced litigators know that litigation should be approached on a basis short of all-out war, yet the way zealous advocacy is apparently discussed in some law school courses might make it hard to recognize this fact."[10] The political battles that occur in many law schools and in the law faculties are even more abstract, not about the practice of law and what students will do and will be asked to do when they emerge into the great world, but about such things as whether law itself is a millstone on which the government grinds up blacks and women, a system by which the well-to-do oppress the oppressed. Are there enough blacks or women or gays on the faculty and in the student body? Should the placement department permit the U.S. Attorney's office or the CIA to recruit at the law school? Cultivation of the qualities of mind and soul that might make a student a better lawyer take a place far back from the charge to reshape society.

The Critical Legal Studies movement is commonly described as an attempt to expose "the gap between law on the books and law in actual practice"[11]; but, in fact, the CLS professors deal with what they consider the hidden agenda and the outcomes of law, not with the practice of law. (Even the great abstraction that does occasionally enable practicing lawyers to make a difference in the behavior of society is scorned. "The use of rights in contemporary discourse," one of the CLS advocates writes solemnly, "impedes advances by progressive social forces."[12] Presumably this means that the right of a speaker at a law school to be heard impedes those who want to shout him down.) On both left and right, the attitude inevitably grows that ethical behavior is far less important than political belief. In a group of second- and third-year students at George Washington University Law School with whom I met to discuss their experience and expectations, it was the most politically active on both left and right who said that their observation at their summer jobs had been that successful lawyers were out for the buck and cared for little else.

Neither the doctrines of Natural Law nor the analyses of Critical Legal Studies have much to do with anything a practicing lawyer encounters in his work. But even when the law professors do deal with the decisions a lawyer must face, their taste for abstraction (and for defining the social role of the lawyer) may overwhelm their good sense. In a 1989 discussion of a case in which a lawyer in Arizona was forbidden to tell a court that his (deceased) client rather than the defendant was guilty of a murder, because such testimony would violate the sanctity of attorney-client privilege, Yale's Geoffrey Hazard observed that by letting the lawyer testify "one can do justice in this case. However the consequence is, in some degree, to instill anxiety on the part of others. Therefore the detriment is visited on some other defendants who would like to be more confident that whatever they say will be held in confidence. . . . It's not simply a question of whether we would let justice triumph over law but the question of what tragic choice is the law to make." One of the participants in this discussion (which occurred at a session of the American Law Institute, where they debate what the law *is*—and sometimes what it should be) noted that the case, which he had studied, really raised the question of whether a little group of criminal lawyers in Phoenix might be trying a new tactic of getting their client off by blaming a dead man who couldn't be examined by the court.[13]

There is an enduring explanation for the growth of ethics courses at the law schools in the last twenty years: Watergate. Students who were barely born at the time will spontaneously say, because they read it in their textbooks, that the shame of the profession was the predominance of lawyers in the shady group that bugged the Democratic National Committee head-quarters at the Watergate office complex and then tried to help a president who himself was a lawyer (and a brilliant one) cover up what he and they had done. There was indeed, as Lloyd Cutler has pointed out, more disgrace to lawyers in the larger Watergate story than these students realize, for the subsequent investigation of what the Nixon campaign had been doing turned up "not only illicit and sometimes illegal corporate be-havior, but also a good deal of legal laxness and ethical blind-ness among corporate lawyers . . . [who] actually participated in drafting false papers that cloaked these illicit payments with a cover of propriety."[14]

A number of the courses in legal ethics were first offered in 1974, usually in the third year of the three-year program, as part of the often rather feeble course about what it's like to practice law that most law schools felt themselves obliged to of-fer. Law professors were asked to sensitize themselves to ethi-cal problems and include discussions of ethics in their presentation of contracts or torts or corporations or whatever. (It was not universally admitted that such instruction should be part of the law school program: "I never thought it was the pro-fessional responsibility of law schools to teach people not to lie or steal," Supreme Court Justice Antonin Scalia told a reporter for the *ABA Journal*. "That is a public misconception of the role of the law.")[15] By general agreement, simply asking professors to help was not a very effective approach. Reporting in fall 1992 on a new emphasis on ethics to be introduced in fall 1993, Columbia University Law School Vice Dean Harriet S. Rabb announced a mandatory eight-day course for third-year stu-dents to be taught by practicing attorneys using real-life cases. She admitted the failure of what she called "the pervasive method," by which all faculty members got periodic memos asking them to include ethical questions in their usual courses. This process, she said, "told the students that it wasn't worth their attention."[16]

The teaching of ethics at law schools has been largely in the hands of people for whom the law is a succession of hypotheticals—for whom the life of the law has been logic, not experience. The result has been that when it comes to ethics questions most law school graduates have little sense of what is expected of them.

Michael S. Josephson, who taught legal ethics at various law schools before establishing an institute dealing with the subject, says he decided to get away from law school teaching after his child was born, finding "inconsistencies between my role as a law teacher and as a parent. When you're teaching law, you seem to abdicate responsibility for moral judgment. It's almost professionally unacceptable. But when you're raising a child, you can't just say, 'Do what works.'" The inexcusable outcome of our present teaching, Josephson argues, is that "a lot of lawyers equate 'ethical' with 'legal,' and that's one of the most destructive attitudes we have."[17]

One of the problems is that much of what has been presented as legal ethics goes back to the old prohibitions against advertising and soliciting, which the Supreme Court has negated. There are still excellent reasons to look askance at much solicitation, especially in class-action cases too often brought primarily for the benefit of the lawyer—to the disadvantage of third parties, who may have to hire their own lawyers, appear at depositions, and produce documents at immense expense. The old code of ethics that recognized stirring up lawsuits as an evil expressed a considerable truth.

Teaching from that perspective alone, however, would be a great mistake. Some kinds of solicitation actually fulfill a public need. Monroe Freedman has offered a convincing hypothetical. His tale is of a solo practitioner to whom he has given the name "Laura Eagle," who learned from a friend who was a social worker about an abominable nursing home where old people were being mistreated. The social worker signed them up as clients for her lawyer friend, who brought a class action on their behalf, gaining money damages (of which she took the usual one third) and a court order requiring the owner of the nursing home to clean up his act. The local bar association prosecuted her for soliciting. "Eagle was suspended from practice for one year, while the lawyer who represented the nursing home spent the same year serving as president of the state bar association." Freedman reports that when he used this hypothetical at an ABA Conference on Professionalism in 1987, a fellow panelist thought the result was proper: Though Eagle "achieved the sort of good the legal profession aims at," said the panelist, "she *is* guilty of unprofessional conduct."[18] The study of ethics is interesting in part because the subject says different things to different people.

Bernard L. Diamond, a medical doctor who teaches at the University of California, wrote in a book for college students contemplating law school that the young lawyer emerging from school soon "discovers that the professional practice of law often requires nonlegal answers to human problems whose very existence seems not to be recognized by the legal curriculum."[19] Ethical teaching that focuses narrowly on "professional" issues such as solicitation or conflict of interest between clients, then, tends to reinforce rather than reduce the cynicism left over from the student's other courses. Legal ethics can be understood only in the context of the relations among people. Even the most elaborate of the ethics courses deals only in passing, if at all, with the crucial decision the practicing lawyer must make: Do I want to represent this client?

Monroe Freedman, the most ardent of all celebrants of unrestricted advocacy and total loyalty to a client's cause, does recognize the problem. He writes that "implicit in the exercise of the lawyer's moral autonomy is the lawyer's moral responsibility for the choices she makes. . . . [T]he lawyer's choice of client can properly be subjected to the moral scrutiny and criticism of others."[20] But this is only one page in several hundred in his ethics textbook.

Few law professors even raise the question of whether a lawyer with time to sell should accept any client who can afford his fees: "Everybody is entitled to a lawyer." The really important thing young lawyers are taught in this context is that it is always unfair for people to hold the sins of the client against his lawyer—even when the client is Baby Doc Duvalier. From the law school's point of view, of course, it is also true that instruction on the moral significance of accepting a client may not have practical relevance for the student setting out into the real world. Only a very small fraction of the graduates of the better law schools will go off to hang up their own shingles. The graduate who goes out to work in a big firm is far removed from the decision to take or refuse a client, and nobody consults him about whether or not he *wants* to work on something. Senior partners will not welcome instruction from recently hired associates about the ethics of taking on a client, fighting to keep a dangerous product on the market, or attacking a client's opponents because he wants them attacked.

Stephen Gillers of NYU bridles at any thought that the law schools are to blame for the relatively low level of ethical concern that so many younger members of the bar seem to display. "What students learn in law school," he says, "is the tip of the tail that is supposed to be wagging the dog. If young lawyers lack ethical concerns, it's because they go to work in law firms where the senior partners are interested in nothing but making money, where they may be explicitly told that they are not to let ethical concerns get in the way of making money for the firm."

Gary Bellow of Harvard Law would put more of the burden and the blame on the law school. He writes:

> It is of course true that all lawyers learn to practice from practice. What is not true is that what they learn will be uniform or necessarily consistent with what one would consider even minimally adequate professional practice. The bulk of law school

graduates do not get jobs with institutions or firms which have the time, resources, talent, or inclination to develop systematically their knowledge and skills. In most instances, the new lawyer is simply introduced to "the way we do things here" and is expected to act accordingly. If "the way we do things here" incorporates high standards, systematic consideration of alternatives, adequate models, and appropriate ethical norms, the young lawyer may well learn what is worth learning. If the opposite is the case, the young lawyer will learn the opposite. . . . Legal scholarship and teaching should be much more concerned than it now is with the actual functioning of the legal system and its institutions, particularly the institution of counsel as a law-making, law-enforcing, law-nullifying activity.[21]

It is worth pointing out that being a law school dean does not seem to be habit forming. In 1993, there were 176 law schools in the United States recognized by the American Bar Association. No fewer than 43 of them had new deans. Relatively few law school deans serve in their posts for as long as five years, and it's hard to convince a tenured faculty to try anything new when they know the dean asking it is likely to be gone before the project matures.

3

The failure to teach the human aspect of practice is a subsection of the larger failure to relate law school education to any aspect of practice. From the point of view of the law student, the most practical thing to do in law school is to take the courses in taxes or securities law or environmental law, and be up to the minute on the most recent legislation and court decisions in a field that he can offer to a prospective employer as his "specialty." Dean Ronald A. Cass of Boston University Law School has said of his students: "Every one of them increasingly needs a specialty." Across the continent, Dean Paul Brest of Stanford Law School agreed that lawyers in the twenty-first century will need "more specialization." Stanford's first three "concentrations"—encouraged but not required—are in business, environmental law, and poverty law.[22] The student looking for a job with the big firms knows he is far more likely to be hired if he can demonstrate that he can beef up the firm's capacity in a specialization.

In an ABA symposium on legal education in 1990, Robert MacCrate of Sullivan & Cromwell said the large firms "do not complain about law schools." Roberta Ramo, from a smaller firm in Albuquerque, noted that even if the law schools were doing an acceptable job of training youngsters to work in firms like Sullivan & Cromwell, that did not mean they were doing an adequate job for anybody else: "The economics of large firms have forced them to make their young lawyers productive very quickly. . . . So associates get trained very narrowly so they can be productive very quickly. As a managing partner, I see a lot of lawyers who want to come to New Mexico after they've been at very large firms for three or four years. . . . I find their skills often are not useful because, while they're excellent in a very narrow area, they have truly not learned how to be lawyers. Because of that kind of specialization, we're seeing people who do not look at problems or their own behavior as lawyers used to, but see things very narrowly. They have never gotten a feeling that they are officers of the court."[23]

Historically, of course, people did not learn to be lawyers in law schools. Abraham Lincoln never went to law school, and would have been astonished at the thought that such a thing might be required. So would Algernon Sullivan, who founded Sullivan & Cromwell. Until well into this century, most American lawyers achieved that status via apprenticeship in a law firm or to a single experienced lawyer rather than via academic training. Some of these people were very distinguished lawyers. Robert H. Jackson, Franklin Roosevelt's attorney general, the U.S. prosecutor in the Nuremberg trials, and eventually a Supreme Court justice, became a lawyer originally through the apprenticeship method. One of the earliest female partners at Sullivan & Cromwell took the bar examination after working as a secretary in that office and studying on her own. The American Bar Association recognized early on that success in law school and the ability to practice were not necessarily correlated: As early as 1892, when law schools were still relatively uncommon, the association's annual convention called for the elimination of what were then common provisions in states with prominent law schools that graduates be admitted to the bar on presentation of their diploma. Everybody, the ABA insisted, should pass a bar exam before he (the "she" is, of course, more recent) was permitted to hold himself out to the universe of clients as a lawyer.

There were advantages to the apprenticeship model, as I saw for myself when I was in effect an apprentice at Sutherland and Sutherland even though a law school graduate. Watching one's elders and betters deal with clients, negotiate contracts, and try cases provided templates to try out for oneself. Apprentices learned to return telephone calls the same day. And service as an apprentice was, if one was lucky enough to have seniors like the Sutherlands, an unending lesson in the ethics of the law.

David Link, dean of the Notre Dame Law School and formerly a partner in the Chicago firm that became Winston & Strawn, opened a panel discussion of legal education for the 1990s by telling his fellow panelists:

> When I graduated from law school twenty-nine years ago, people learned to practice law at the feet of a master. Lawyers would take you under their wing, either within your firm or, in my case, at a government agency and later at a law firm. Even if you went into solo practice, there was someone in town to men-

tor you and teach the practice of law. Inevitably, what also was taught was professionalism. . . . Somewhere along the line in the last thirty years, however, lawyering became more expensive. Overhead skyrocketed, reflecting huge increases in the costs of associates' salaries and training, office space, libraries, computers, and so on. Efficiency became a priority, and the mentoring system broke down. The seniors were pressured to increase their billable hours and could no longer afford to spend time with the young people coming in. In the meantime, no one was teaching practice or, incidentally, professionalism. . . .[24]

Some of this effort to find a substitute for mentoring within the law school has gone to "role-playing" sessions, where law students encounter clients, witnesses, antagonists, and tribunals, all played by other law students, with a professor in the room to critique everybody's performance. The College of William and Mary's Marshall-Wythe School of Law in Williamsburg, Virginia, sets up mock law firms in the first year, with students acting as clients. In a two-year cycle, the mock law firms simulate client contact, actual cases, and appeals of the cases. "Students playing clients," Milo Geyelin of *The Wall Street Journal* writes, "have reported deep anger and frustration in their relations with their lawyers." At the University of Pennsylvania, students view videotapes of lawyers in action in a required first-year "professional responsibility" course.[25]

New York University Law School, which was among the first to have a program in which students worked with real clients for real ends (in landlord-and-tenant court), has built an expanded preprofessional program around a required first-year course called "Lawyering." Dean John Sexton described it as a way to use "situations" rather than cases for law instruction. "Langdell and his followers either missed or disregarded a simple point: Real people don't find themselves in cases; they find themselves in situations. Lawyers don't encounter their clients in cases; they encounter them in situations. Or, at another level, even the closest reading of an appellate opinion misses the human element of the lawyer's job. How, for example, does a lawyer interact with a client? How does a lawyer provide guidance, both legal and moral? When and how should a lawyer say no to a client? How does a lawyer confront the possibility of taking action that does not violate any law but does offend the underlying spirit of the law—for example, using discovery to exhaust an adversary? . . . We can use [the situation method of instruction] to examine the lawyer's role—to teach that a lawyer is a counselor, investigator, negotiator, advocate, and even moral authority. . . .

"The core of the 'Lawyering' course is a series of exercises based on fact patterns that simulate traditional lawyer's work: conferring with clients, negotiating with adversaries, preparing informal advocacy, and examining a witness at trial. Many of the exercises involve doctrinal material the students are covering simultaneously in their traditional classes; thus, the students see from the outset how legal doctrine actually works in practice, and how it affects lives."[26]

Among the changes Dean Sexton hopes to make in this program in the years ahead are a great expansion in the proportion of their time that law students spend in small classes and an increase in their production of written work. "To pursue this program," Dean Sexton notes, "we ultimately would have to add several more faculty."

Most law schools rely primarily on "clinical" programs, giving law students a chance to work on real cases involving real clients, to fill some part of the gap between law school and practice. The first such programs were at the University of Tennessee Law School in the 1940s, and the Ford Foundation has vigorously promoted them since the late 1950s. The attempt is to find something in law comparable to what the medical schools do for future doctors. But the professors who teach future doctors are themselves medical practitioners, and most of the professors who teach future lawyers are academicians, a number of whom tend to defend themselves against calls for clinical education by denigrating its intellectual value and calling on its practitioners to publish more than they do. "These pressures," Gary Bellow of Harvard Law School writes, "are often inconsistent with the work styles and time demands faced by clinical teachers and are unlikely to tap the academic potential of the field. They have not only deterred new entrants into clinical teaching but have embroiled clinicians in a complex debate over the nuances of status, security, and responsibility in law teaching, which drains energy and attention from the programs themselves." Bellow looks skeptically on simulation as a substitute: "[I]t tends to oversimplify the psychological and interpersonal dimensions of lawyer work and to screen out important aspects of the impact of race, gender, and class on the functioning of law and lawyers. Used uncritically, it again heralds skill and craft as the solution to many of the value conflicts lawyers confront and to present idealized versions of the sort of relationships in which law is inevitably embedded."[27]

Two generations have passed since Judge Jerome Frank urged that the courtroom should be part of the classroom, that law students spend some ponderable part of one year actually observing trials. This proposal has now been made easy by the creation of a cable television channel that presents actual courtroom proceedings. Produced by *American Lawyer* and sponsored by Time Warner, one of the nation's largest cable operators, "Court TV" is widely available, but still not very widely used by law schools.

Roberta Ramo has argued that the great value of clinical work, which she thinks should be required, is that it gives "the students at the very best law schools who will go to the very best law firms in the country . . . their only chance to really see the law from the other side. . . . I think it's very important to the whole justice system that the very best lawyers know what it is like to work in a clinic setting and to represent someone with no resources. I have a strong feeling that when the dean of

Harvard Law School says that we don't need to worry about clinical programs so much because he's training corporate lawyers, that we are missing the point—which is not just to train corporate lawyers, but to give a whole professional group an insight into how the justice system works."[28]

Norman Redlich, Sexton's predecessor as dean at the NYU law school, noted wryly that despite all the talk, there had been no demand from the field that the law schools undertake the expense of clinical courses: "The law firms and the practicing bar generally cannot be taken seriously in their constant criticism that law schools aren't doing enough in skills training and professionalism if, in the process of evaluating law students, they continue to care only about grades on first-year exams. And they don't even try to pressure law students, in their second and third years, to take the very courses they are urging law schools to adopt into their curriculum."[29]

The value of the clinical experience as a promoter of ethical behavior is a little less clear. In many cases, clinical work seems simply to move back in time Stephen Gillers's biting observation that young lawyers lack ethical standards not because they've been poorly taught in law school but because their experience on their first job tells them nobody cares. Professor Lawrence Hellman of Georgetown Law School ran a clinical program that put third-year students into Washington law offices to help and observe. Geoffrey Hazard notes:

> Feedback reports from the students gave Professor Hellman a reading on what the young were being taught by their older professional peers. The students were indeed learning ethical lessons, but often very bad ones. . . . A substantial fraction of the students directly observed significant ethical violations. These included instances of conflict of interest, withholding of vital information to clients, refusal to communicate with clients and apparent mishandling of client funds. . . . Many of the practitioner-mentors shrugged off student initiatives to discuss ethical

issues and exhibited extreme discomfort if pressed to address the issues seriously. The message many students received was that the lawyers generally don't know their ethical responsibilities and don't want to know them.[30]

4

The British political philosopher T. H. Weldon thought the world of policy could be divided into three parts: puzzles you solve, problems you work at, and difficulties you avoid. The puzzle part of legal education has indeed been solved: Most students do learn to think like lawyers. The problems are mostly being worked at, through combinations of clinical programs and specializations. There remain the difficulties, one of which is also an opportunity.

The difficulty that can become an opportunity is the cost. In his report on the future of the NYU law school, Dean Sexton estimated that in 1992 his students had to spend $30,700 a year to study law at NYU and live. The school's policy is that no grants will be given to anyone until after the student has arranged to borrow $15,700 a year. This means that many— perhaps most—NYU students leave law school owing $47,000, even if interest does not begin accruing on their loans until after graduation, *on top of* what debts they may have from their years as undergraduates and before they have to pay for the courses that prepare them for the bar. New York is a more expensive place than most, but a frighteningly high fraction of our new lawyers start work dragging a debt burden of tens of thousands of dollars. With few exceptions, the third-year students who met with me at George Washington Law School in Washington were constricted in the jobs they could choose after graduation by the need to make repayments approaching a thousand dollars a month *immediately*, from post-tax income. It is hard to blame them if they go hunting for the biggest salary they can find, regardless of the quality of life or training offered by the firm that will employ them.

It has been estimated that only 2 or 3 percent of the graduates of the nation's fifty most respected law schools take public service jobs (other than judicial clerkships, which normally lead to private practice). We have a tradition in this country of paying for the college education of members of R.O.T.C., who promise four years of service in the military after graduation. Since the days of President Carter, we have had a National Teacher Corps, which repays the debts of newly licensed teachers who start their careers in hard-to-staff schools. President Clinton has launched a National Service Corps that would repay the debts of college graduates who serve in a police department or teach school in low-income districts or help the homeless.

Surely we could have a similar program that would make it financially feasible, even financially desirable, for recent graduates of law schools to work in legal aid, for public defender or prosecutor offices, as legislative assistants, or in the counsel's offices of state and municipal government. If they could afford it, a number of our best and brightest law students would rather work with public policy implications than in a private law office that serves private interests. Meanwhile, the public prosecutor and defender offices and the legal aid societies are limited in the people they can recruit because they can't pay the salaries the best young lawyers command in the job market. A Lawyers' Service Corps should not require a federal bureaucracy, as the participants would be hired locally. As their contribution to the program, localities that wish to participate might be required to add slots in those offices that help poor people. The costs would be modest: If ten thousand graduates a year went to work for public agencies and legal services programs and claimed forgiveness for $20,000 of their debt to the student loan programs, the price would be $200 million of the $7 billion the service corps program is expected to cost when up and running toward the end of the decade. And there would be great benefits in the provision of legal services to ordinary people, to the profession, and within the law schools.

The greater difficulty is in the educational background of law students. There is much talk about how the legal systems in the Western world are part of the "superstructure" of capitalist economies. This may or may not be true. What is unquestionably true is that the legal systems in the Western world rest on a large body of philosophical, social, literary, and religious history. The English novelist Evelyn Waugh liked to say that if children stopped reading the Bible and studying Latin we would lose the capacity to write good English prose. If the community of lawyers is severed from the cultural tradition that produced Coke and Mansfield, Marshall and Holmes, Learned Hand and Benjamin Cardozo and Henry Stimson, we will lose our capacity to understand why law must be a profession and not a business. We are already far along on this path, and our children will be sorry for it.

We of the older generation like to think that the younger generation is less well educated than we were, which is obviously untrue. They know Chinese and quantum mechanics, they empathize with computers, they really understand about chlorofluorocarbons and the ozone layer, and they can manipulate derivative securities. We can't do any of that. But the people who wrote the laws and designed the legal profession couldn't do any of that, either. They knew Plato (who wrote: "A city which has no regular courts of law ceases to be a city"); the history of the Roman Republic, the Glorious Revolution, the American Revolution, and the French Revolution; the origins of the Constitution; and the Bill of Rights.

The leaders of the bar used to be men who read in the classical languages for pleasure, who quoted the Bible and Shakespeare in their briefs as a matter of course, relying on clerks sometimes for their law but never for their literary analogies.

They were people who agreed with Thomas Jefferson that "history, politics, ethics, physics, oratory, poetry, criticism, etc., [are] as necessary as law to form an accomplished lawyer." They believed that a lawyer should know accounting but *needs* philosophy; that for understanding the idea of a contract, acquaintance with anthropology and psychology is apt to be more valuable than case law; that you can often learn more about people from great novels than you can from studying the law books. They recognized that a good lawyer almost by definition should be a person of breadth, who has a grasp of what yesterday teaches us about today and tomorrow, who knows that the real meaning of words such as *freedom* and *justice* can be found only in the tapestry of history.

This cuts against today's grain, but the cut must be made. Our system of law and lawyers grows out of our country's past—which was a Eurocentric past. The glory of America was that it made no judgments about the origins of its citizens: In our mythology, and often in reality, they became Americans, equal sharers of their country's past. Our past is not other countries' past, our institutions are not other countries' institutions. We are custodians, not owners, of our laws and institutions. We will be bad custodians if we cannot find a way to share the traditions and beliefs of the people who designed and developed them. This does not mean that we are bound by a cultural form of what the lawyers have long referred to as *stare decisis* ("it stands decided"). Many things are not decided, and as Justice Holmes wrote: "It is revolting to have no better reason for a rule than that it was so laid down in the time of Henry IV."[31] But it does mean that law schools should require and supplement what has for almost seven hundred years been called a liberal arts education.

For some of us, the best thing the law schools could do to improve the legal profession would be a crusade to improve the liberal arts education of lawyers. If they are going to be subjected to the Socratic method, they should at least have read

Plato's remembrances of Socrates. Many years ago, law school students were encouraged to take courses elsewhere in a university; many law professors at Harvard, for example, thought it was a good idea for their students to take the philosophy courses offered by William James and Josiah Royce.[32] What survives from those days is mostly courses taught jointly with the business school, plus courses taught *at* the law school by sociologists or economists trying to associate their discipline with what lawyers are taught. When Milton Katz, the organizer of the Marshall Plan in Europe, taught at the Harvard Law School, he was trying to show law students how the "legal order" has an impact on economic activity; today's economics-and-law movement that grows out of work at Yale, the University of Chicago, and the University of Rochester in the 1970s tries to convince lawyers that economic consequences should control their thinking about the role and the rule of law. *"Fiat justitia ruat caelum!"** thundered Lord Mansfield; how many contemporary economists—or lawyers—would know what that means? And Mansfield was no theorist; his specialty was commercial law, and when he heard business cases, he often summoned two respected businessmen to sit on the bench with him and help him understand what the witnesses were saying.

Lawyers who are going to be counselors, as the best lawyers will be, should have at least an introduction to the insights that can be provided by psychology, psychiatry, and sociology. Such courses are available elsewhere in the universities, and the law schools should arrange entry to them for their students and give credit for strong accomplishment in them. The best teachers can kill both birds with the same stone. Herma Hill Kay, who became dean in 1992 at Boalt Hall, the University of California (Berkeley) law school, reports that her students can get eight hours of credit at the law school for courses taken in other parts of the university. From her own career she remembers most happily a course on law and anthropology she taught in

***"Let justice be done though the heavens fall!"

the 1960s with Laura Nader, and the struggle to get it listed in both the arts-and-sciences catalog and the law school catalog under the same number: "They kept saying, 'But then people will think it's the same course,' and we kept saying, 'But it *is* the same course.'"

NYU ethics professor Stephen Gillers says:

> Once it may have paid to be an intellectual and a professional. Now it pays to be technically proficient. When I was in law school I was dumbfounded; I'd had no idea there was all this wonderful intellectual excitement in the law. When I went into practice I was astonished at how much a lawyer even at the highest levels is occupied with the minute and tendentious aspects of cases. Questions of right and wrong, I found, questions of what the rules *should be*, played no role. It was all finding the facts that supported your client and trying to keep the facts that harmed him away from your opponents. I felt a discontinuity. I must tell you that knowing what I know now, knowing how low are the chances of finding a place in the law worthy of the energies of an intelligent and selfless college graduate, I would not go to law school.

Part of this disillusionment is the result of inadequate preparation for thinking about law. In 1954, Justice Felix Frankfurter wrote a letter to a twelve-year-old boy who had asked him for advice on becoming a lawyer:

> My dear Paul:
> No one can be a truly competent lawyer unless he is a cultivated man. If I were you I would forget all about any technical preparation for the law. The best way to prepare for the law is to come to the study of the law as a well-read person. Thus alone can one acquire the capacity to use the English language on paper and in speech and with the habits of clear thinking which only a truly liberal education can give. No less important for a lawyer is the cultivation of the imaginative faculties by

reading poetry, seeing great paintings, in the original or in easily available reproductions, and listening to great music. Stock your mind with the deposit of much good reading, and widen and deepen your feelings by experiencing vicariously as much as possible the wonderful mysteries of the universe, and forget all about your future career.[33]

Even after such preparation, there would be much danger of disappointment for the young person come to the bar. For we are not rewarding or encouraging the habits of mind that make law a great profession and lawyers great men. Justice Holmes spoke of living "nobly" in the law, and surely the majority of law students, starting into the paths of practice, would hope to live nobly. The question is whether they will have the opportunity. Law schools cannot create such opportunities by themselves. The challenge is to everyone—but first to the bar itself.

CHAPTER 7

THE JOB FOR THE BAR ASSOCIATIONS

1

W here does the responsibility lie for safeguarding the integrity and reputation of the bar? Obviously, with the bar associations, which have long held themselves out as far more than mere social organizations for those "called to the bar." Lawyers are a diverse group, performing an immense variety of tasks in a society that lives within a legal order, and the pollsters will find lawyers on all sides of virtually all issues. Few economic developments or government actions are harmful or helpful to all lawyers, and some things (changes in the Securities and Exchange Commission rules on the registration of new securities, for example, which created jobs for in-house corporate lawyers and did away with jobs at law firms representing investment banks) may be good for one group of lawyers and bad for another. But anything that harms the reputation of the bar harms all lawyers; anything that helps the reputation of the bar helps all lawyers.

Thus, bar associations should, of course, be urgently concerned about what clients and the general public think of lawyers. When bar associations began to become important in the early years of this century, they organized "grievance committees" to hear complaints against lawyers, and many of them claimed responsibility for policing the profession. They drew up codes (more ambitiously, "canons") of ethics, exhorted all lawyers to obey them, and sometimes got legislatures or courts to write them into law. The American Bar Association, early in this century, created its own "canons of ethics" as a guide to its state and local affiliates.

These codes covered a number of bases. They included provisions to establish minimum fee schedules, restrict entry to the profession, and prohibit solicitation, many of which worked to benefit lawyers who already had practices and against lawyers starting out in the world. Other sections prohibited lawyers from cooperating with laymen and members of other professions in providing services (title searches, tax advice, claims settlement) that were considered "unauthorized practice of law." It is as true in the definition of legal codes as it is in politics that where you stand very often depends on where you sit. And it is difficult for any group of people joined by a professional bond to avoid the temptation of creating a trade association promoting their own interests rather than a professional association dedicated to improving the services they render the public. But the authors of the codes of ethics were men of noble intention, and to the extent that the canons truly governed the performance of the bar, clients and the courts were protected.

One of the hallmarks of professional status is that professionals discipline themselves: People not inducted into the mystery of the profession are assumed not to know enough to judge professional performance. In some states, the law that set up licensing procedures for lawyers required them to become members of an "integrated" or "unified" bar association and pay dues, much of which went to the associations' procedures for disciplining members. In most states, where membership in such associations was voluntary, the courts nevertheless delegated to the bar associations the task of investigating charges against lawyers and either imposing punishments on those who violated the codes or bringing cases against them before judges assigned to hear such matters.

Unfortunately, zealous prosecution of such cases has an uncollegial look to it, and over the years the bar associations did not have a very good record for fulfilling their responsibility to protect the public and the courts. When disciplinary matters were transferred by the Illinois courts out of the Chicago Bar Association and into an independent Attorney Regulation and Disciplinary Commission, the proportion of complaints against lawyers that were actually investigated rose from 17 percent to 43 percent, and the proportion carried through to formal hearings rose from 3.5 percent to 13.5 percent.[1] Most states have now turned over to the courts the function of disciplining lawyers. Only a few states, however, give the discipline boards the kind of resources they would need to make their policing function truly effective. Moreover, especially in states where judges are elected, and thus worry about the opposition they may create to their reelection, the bench has been kinder than the bar in devising light punishments.

And the bar associations have not educated their members well in what their canons of ethics say. Professor Richard Abel of UCLA reports that forty-six of the fifty states prohibit fee splitting (paying another lawyer for forwarding a case), but a random sample of 600 lawyers practicing in those states in 1984 produced a vote of 40 percent who thought the practice was permitted and 27 percent who didn't know one way or the other. Of the one third who knew it was illegal, almost half thought it was okay anyway if the forwarding fee was "reasonable."[2] What Professor Abel describes as a "careful investigation of litigators" in Michigan found that only 57 percent of them felt obliged to correct "a clearly false statement regarding a material issue in a deposition." "When I served as a member of the New York City and New York State bar association ethics committees," Judge Judith Kaye wrote in 1988, "it was a constant surprise to me that so many lawyers who sought advice were unaware even of the existence of the Code of Professional Responsibility or the compilations of ethics opinions, or where to find either. It was also my impression that our service—while unquestionably valuable—more often succeeded in furnishing guidance about how far a lawyer could go in a situation without incurring sanctions, rather than instilling—or exhibiting—an appreciation of ethical standards."[3]

The canons of ethics in virtually all the states and in all the years in which they have been adopted include a call for a lawyer to report other lawyers for misconduct; but to say the least, the canon has not been enforced. Like other professions, the practice of law tends to create an us-versus-them attitude that makes it uncomfortable for people to report their colleagues. Doctors tend to be charitable to other doctors, policemen don't report other policemen much, and lawyers consider excuses when contemplating bad things other lawyers have done. Despite the canons of ethics and rules of procedure, nobody is really surprised that they do not do more. "At present," the ABA's Commission on Professionalism reported in 1986, "hardly any such reporting occurs. . . . [F]ew lawyers, if any, are ever disciplined for even knowingly failing to report the misconduct of a fellow lawyer." The commission noted that though many lawyers and judges must have known about the sinkhole of bribery in the Chicago courts that was exposed under the name Operation Greylord, virtually none of the complaints that led to the investigations had come from lawyers. "Ironically," the commission added, "judicial figures who merely refused to accept bribes, but did not report the criminal solicitations— as they were ethically required to do—have been widely praised."[4]

In December 1992 the New York Court of Appeals, the

highest court in the state, held that reporting unethical behavior by other lawyers or judges was a duty, and ordered a trial for a lawyer who had been dismissed by his firm after he insisted that the firm report dishonest behavior by one of its own associates and who claimed that the reason for his dismissal had been his whistle-blowing. This was not a very attractive case—the dishonest behavior was a cover-up of the associate's failure to process the lawyer's own co-op purchase correctly—and its use by the court as the occasion for asserting a duty to report seems to send a signal.

State courts and state bar associations are responsible for fining or suspending or disbarring lawyers, and not all of them notify the American Bar Association, which has no official role in such matters. Nevertheless, the computer file of names of lawyers whose censure or punishment *has* been registered with the ABA contains more than 40,000 names.[5] In this day and age, there would be virtually no cost to making a search of that file, available via telephone to anyone with a computer and a modem. Clients and opponents have a right to know whether a lawyer has been censured. Made national and computerized, such a service could be structured to eliminate a name after some years without additional offense, and even to contain the lawyer's explanation of how his name got on the list.

Since 1987, attorneys in California have had to inform the State Bar if there are three malpractice complaints against them in any twelve-month period, and the *California Bar Journal* each month prints page after page of the names of lawyers who have been punished or have consented to discipline. The State Bar also maintains a "hot line" for clients who wish to call and see if their lawyer has had a malpractice claim against him or has been subject to disciplinary proceedings. Professor Leonard Gross of Southern Illinois University, urging his state to adopt similar procedures, notes: "Such a system would enhance both the client's ability to make informed decisions and the deterrent effect of malpractice lawsuits."[6]

The argument for publicizing complaints is most often made when the complaint is one of excessive fees, which the canons of ethics also condemn. In 1986, when the new immigration law gave certain previously barred aliens a chance to become citizens, the ABA found private attorneys charging up to $3,000 for filling out forms that nonprofit organizations would complete for $100. In New Jersey, the courts have established an arbitration panel to decide disputes on fees, but it has not been widely publicized, and in the absence of publicity hardly anyone knows the service is available. Bar associations should create and publicize such arbitration panels across the country in the interest of that overwhelming majority of lawyers who *don't* overcharge.

Admission to the bar and continuation at the bar are privileges, not rights, and years of experience certainly should not protect a lawyer who has violated the ethics of his profession. The purpose of disciplinary actions against misbehaving lawyers, Lord Mansfield wrote in 1778, in an often quoted opinion, "is *not* by way of punishment, but the court on such cases, exercise their discretion, whether a man whom they have formerly admitted, is a proper person to be continued on the roll or not." But the principle should be tough: The profession owes itself and its clients an incessant care for reputation. The people elected to leadership positions in the bar associations should, of course, be the lawyers with the highest reputation among their fellows, whether or not they have come through the chairs of the lower levels of office in such associations. And they should also be tough-minded people who are strong enough to bear the unpleasantness of enforcing ethical standards for the good of the community as a whole. It is not enough for the ABA to vote as it did to spend $1 million for a public relations and advertising campaign designed to assure the public and the bar itself that everything is really okay.

2

The feeling that lawyers are not trustworthy is the most debilitating aspect of public (and client) attitudes today, but most lawyers feel themselves directly affected by it only on rare occasions. Their own clients trust them—and should—and in their own work they stay easily within the envelope of the rules. But there is one area where few lawyers can avoid discomfort when looking at their profession. The rhetoric of the profession has long insisted that our system is one of "justice for all," that our courts must not "ration justice," but the visible truth is that we are not living up to our professed beliefs.

Most local bar associations do accept some level of responsibility for making legal services more available. They manage the annual fund-raising drives for the local Legal Aid Society and they promote pro bono activities by their members. They often participate in political action on the local and state levels to increase the funding of the public defenders' offices, and on the national level to enhance the capacity of the Legal Services Corporation that was part of President Lyndon Johnson's antipoverty program—the most unpopular part for the Reagan and Bush administrations, which tried to kill it every year.

The bar's claim of a concern for justice for all is the central justification of its demand for public respect, and the best of its reputation comes from the tradition of lawyers working on behalf of those who cannot afford representation. *Pro bono publico* ("for public good," usually abbreviated to just pro bono) is the term for such altruism. Perhaps the most famous pro bono case in American history was *Gideon* v. *Wainwright*, in 1963, when Abe Fortas, of the firm then called Arnold, Fortas & Porter, argued through the Supreme Court the appeals of a drifter who had been convicted of a crime in a trial where he was not represented by a lawyer. The Court threw out the conviction and established a rule that anyone the state wishes to try for a felony is constitutionally entitled to counsel, and if he can't afford it himself the state has to pay. Fortas was not paid for his time working on this case, and his firm was not paid its expenses in connection with it. The recollection of *Gideon* v. *Wainwright* made it almost unbearably sad when Fortas, having been elevated to the Supreme Court himself by President Johnson (and nominated for chief justice), had to step down after the revelation of his financial dealings with a Wall Street operator.

Pro bono is the glory of the bar, and we shall discuss it further when we look at the contributions to improved behavior in the profession that have been made by the law firms. Still, what has been done in the past will not be nearly enough for the future. Too many people who need lawyers still go unrepresented because the bar has not organized itself to provide them with the services they need at a price they can afford. To improve the reputation of the bar sustainably, the bar associations must find ways to deliver on the profession's promise that justice will not be rationed by price. Erwin Griswold, formerly dean of the Harvard Law School and solicitor general of the United States, now a partner in the Washington office of the large firm Jones Day, says that some of his most depressing moments are when he has to tell people he knows who need the services of a lawyer that, except for truly pro bono work, of which his firm does a good deal, its managing committee can't even consider matters where the amount involved is less than $25,000.

In the 1970s, the inability of the traditional profession to find ways to serve middle-class clients became the trigger for two Supreme Court decisions that turned the bar upside down. The first was *Goldfarb* v. *Virginia State Bar* in 1975. The Virginia bar had established a minimum fee schedule for legal services, and Goldfarb found that every lawyer he approached demanded the same fee—1 percent of the value of the property—to work on the closing of a commercial real estate deal. The property had changed hands not long before, and there was relatively little legal work to be done on this resale, but nobody was willing to shave the price. Goldfarb sued, and the Supreme

Court ruled that such minimum fee schedules constituted restraint of trade under the antitrust laws. At a distance of almost twenty years, it is hard to disagree with the Court, or to remember why the bar associations insisted that in an age of rapidly changing technology affecting routine legal work it was acceptable behavior to arrogate to lawyers rather than to clients all the profits from improved efficiency.

Even before the *Goldfarb* case, lawyers had begun to organize themselves into "legal clinics," like medical clinics, to serve groups of clients. And some affinity groups, most notably labor unions, had attempted to contract with such clinics, or with individual lawyers, to provide legal services of a relatively routine nature at an annual price for the entire group. To bring their services to the attention of the public, these legal clinics wanted to advertise their existence. A pair of Arizona lawyers, John R. Bates and Van O. Steen, put an ad in the local paper announcing "legal services at very reasonable rates," and the Arizona bar association moved against them. The state courts censured them, and they appealed to the U.S. Supreme Court, which, in 1977, in *Bates v. Arizona*, established a First Amendment right for lawyers to advertise.

In retrospect, again, it is difficult to see how the organized bar could have hoped to prevent that sort of advertising, especially after the *Goldfarb* case had declared minimum fee schedules a violation of the antitrust laws. What is the use of a right to entice clients by charging lower fees if the clients cannot be told about it? Moreover, as the ABA Commission on Professionalism reports: "The effects of the decision have been positive in many ways. Surveys suggest that many people who were formerly fearful or uncertain about consulting a lawyer have now received legal services and been satisfied with both the services and the fees."[7] The 1993 survey by *The National Law Journal* showed that 68 percent of Americans had "made professional contact" with a lawyer at least once in the preceeding five years—up from 52 percent in 1986.

Most commentators find that the growth of competition

among lawyers following the Supreme Court's *Bates* decision has made it easier to find lawyers and has cut the fees people have to pay lawyers for our inescapable wills, for divorces, for adoptions, for bankruptcies, for defenses against charges of reckless or drunk driving, for making the landlord repair the boiler or renew the lease. Prepaid legal service plans of one sort of another, some organized by unions or employers and some operated as lawyer co-ops with a common marketing agent, may cover in at least some minimal way as many as 71 million people.[8] Just having a lawyer to make a phone call on a poor person's behalf represents a real value. And it's by no means clear that the advertised storefront law firms, which are paying to project a brand image, are less competent or more rushed by other people's business than the solo practitioners they are in part displacing.

Service to moderate-income Americans probably improved during the 1980s, especially by comparison with what was available before. But this is a period when the number of lawyers had risen by roughly 60 percent and expenditures on legal services had more than doubled. By simple arithmetic, legal services *should have* become more available. And an increasing proportion of the services delivered in an age of computers and "clinics" comes off an assembly line. How many of the people who now have "access" to a lawyer really have a lawyer to whom they can turn when they're in trouble? It makes a difference to the quality of justice whether the lawyer represents a person, a purse, or a principle.

Moreover, awareness of the need for legal services may have outrun the improved provision of them. The recent ABA/ALS (Association of Law Schools) Task Force on Law Schools and the Profession quotes J. A. Dooley, speaking at a Tulane University conference called "Access to Justice in the 1990s": "Service creates demand. Some of that demand widens the understanding of what service should be given. New notions of legal need emerge. Thus, as service increases, perceived need increases."

And it adds a more specific comment from B. F. Christensen of the American Bar Association that "the more legally savvy clients become, the more likely they are to utilize the legal services available to them—before signing a contract to buy a house, or becoming mired in debt, or trusting to dumb luck that the intestacy laws will provide for their families and estate what they would themselves."[9] Perceived need is, of course, central to the delivery of legal services to people who cannot afford a continuing relationship with a lawyer. The advertised storefront firms necessarily provide "transactional" help, doing what the drop-in client wants them to do, on an assembly line basis. And many of them, as revealed in their advertising, seem more interested in getting lucrative personal injury lawsuits than in serving the daily legal needs of poor and moderate-income people.

Further evidence that a still-unsatisfied market exists out there for moderately priced legal services can be found in the aggressive promotions of prepaid legal services plans, especially by the credit card companies, which will take their usual percentage of the sale—perhaps we should say "fees." American Express, as noted earlier, offers its cardholders membership in one of these plans, with a multipiece junk mail brochure suggesting that for a "retainer" of $7.95 a month they could get a free consultation from a lawyer (including a free update of a will and review of existing leases and contracts) plus a "diamond dial watch." Follow-ups to take care of the problems identified in the consultation would come at a fee of $59 an hour (charged, of course, to the American Express card). American Express card services receive their income from annual fees paid by the cardholders and "merchant fees" by those who permit their goods and services to be purchased with the card. Because they are not in the business of charging high interest rates to cardholders on extensions of credit, as the banks are, they have a relatively upscale clientele. Even in this community, the mailing piece suggests: "[F]inding and retaining an attorney you can rely on to help you with your personal legal problems can be a time-consuming, expensive undertaking."

"Even prudent and responsible citizens may not have an adequate will," the Amex letter continues; "they may sign unfair leases, or mortgage agreements, or employment contracts. They may even fail to pursue important cases of real merit such as insurance benefits, warranty claims, and IRS appeals because they do not have access to affordable legal counsel. Many of our Cardmembers report that this is their reality. . . ."

Prepaid legal service plans for employees have been growing since 1976, when the tax laws were amended to give them full standing as employee benefits, tax-free to the recipient but tax-deductible to the employer. The United Auto Workers plan, which covers nearly all the legal services a middle-aged married auto worker is likely to want, covers two million people; the AT&T plan covers 275,000. In most cases, these plans offer panels of local lawyers paid by the plan administrator as the doctors of a health maintenance organization are paid by the insurance company.

Through such programs, more than 20,000 law firms receive small monthly payments from more than 50 million Americans, most of them through their union or as a benefit from their employers. The monthly fee to the law firm runs from $7 to $15 per employee in the program. Among those including prepaid legal services in their benefit package since the late 1980s is the New York law firm of Skadden Arps, which gives access to other (non-Skadden) lawyers to its entire nonprofessional staff.

In summer 1991, *The Wall Street Journal* published a noncommittal article on these plans, reporting: "Clients with recurring but relatively minor problems, such as landlord-tenant disputes, say they love having an attorney on-call to intervene. Those with major but routine legal problems, ranging from personal bankruptcy to divorce, also praise prepaid services as a low-cost way to get advice. But subscribers seeking quick answers to one-time problems often express frustration, complaining that lawyers don't return phone calls and seem unwilling to spend time on the free consultations." The article also hints at more sinister matters, suggesting that the lawyers who accept the customers of these services may play bait-and-switch, pushing the members of the plans into signing up for expensive work not covered by their contract.[10]

In recent years, fewer companies have added employer-sponsored prepaid legal services to their employee benefits roster, though many "cafeteria" plans include legal services among the choices offered. Perhaps because the rewards from working with these plans are less than can be hoped for from contingent-fee clients, few of the solo practitioners and small firms that should be most eager for stable sources of revenue have proselytized for such programs. Some lawyers undoubtedly share the worries doctors feel when contemplating health maintenance organizations, which may in effect dictate the treatment the patient/client can be given.

And there is an alternative already in place: a bar association referral service. There are about 350 of them in the United States, handling as many as five or six million requests a year.[11] These are in the process of rapid improvement, having learned from the Hyatts and Jacoby & Meyerses. The referral service run jointly by the New York County Lawyers and the City Association of the Bar interviews lawyers who wish to be listed and verifies their claim to a specialty; in 1992, the New York City service answered 110,000 queries, twice as many as in 1987. In early 1993, the Los Angeles County Bar Association had a staff of eighteen, who screened the callers before referring them to the lawyers on the panel.[12] The charge for the referral service is nothing; the charge for the first half hour's consultation with a lawyer is $25 in New York, less in some other places. Some referral services have pro bono panels that will see people without charge. A number of the referral services are timid and reflexive, and many bar associations still take little responsibility for them. Only about 5 percent of Americans even know that their state or local bar association has a referral service to which they can turn when they need a lawyer, and an American Bar Foundation study found that only 1 percent of the people who had used a lawyer in the previous three years had found him or her through a referral service.[13] Tomorrow's referral service should be quite different: a vigorous, well-promoted alternative to the advertised legal clinics, with the needs of the client computer-matched to the competencies of the lawyers who have signed up for the panel.

Ideally, a bar association referral service should maintain a panel of lawyers who have agreed to take clients from the association at or below fixed rates for specific tasks (real estate closings, uncontested divorces, minor court appearances, wills, and so forth) and fixed fees per hour for nonstandard or specialized services. The best system would probably be one in which fees and lawyers' expenses would be paid through the association rather than directly to the lawyers, providing its administrators with an information stream as well as commissions of perhaps 2 or 3 percent to pay the bills of the service itself. In return, the bar association could provide the participants with verified statements of their income and reimbursed expenses. Commissions would pay for the salaries of the people who work for the service and for advertising campaigns urging people with legal problems to get the name of a lawyer from the bar association, rather than relying on television commercials. The association should also maintain a small staff of inspectors who would continually sample the work done by the lawyers in the panel and the fees charged for it. Lawyers working for the legal clinics could be included on the panel as individuals. While the bar association could not and would not guarantee the competence of the lawyers in the panel, it should keep an eye on their work, counsel them about inadequacies, and be ready to remove them from the panel as required.

Meanwhile, the bar associations could encourage rather than discourage the establishment of group legal service plans by employers for their employees, labor unions, trade associations, or other affinity groups. Such plans could themselves be users of the bar association's panels. The quest should be to spread affordable legal services through the community, to reduce the uncertainty and unfairness in people's lives. The goal should be the return of the lawyer's counseling function to the center of professional life, and if possible a decline in litigiousness. Many large firms could visit this problem within their own organizations, for their clerical and other nonlegal employees often have legal problems of their own and find the firm unresponsive to their needs. One young partner in a large law firm who has been an associate in two other large firms reports losing arguments with his partners that before going out to the great world with pro bono programs the firm should help its own moderate-income people with their housing, financial, and marital problems. At the least, firms should be shepherds through the bar referral programs for their own legally needful employees.

Bar association referral services probably should not stress the personal injury, product liability, and malpractice cases that the advertised law offices offer, because contingent fees have made this the one kind of case affecting ordinary people that the profession is now well organized to process. In their drive to improve the reputation of the profession, moreover, bar associations should support rather than oppose efforts to substitute social insurance for litigation as a system for compensating victims of either carelessness or bad luck. Very few people other than the trial lawyers and the insurance companies who benefit by the present system still believe the theory that tort law—liability for "wrongs"—promotes more careful behavior by those at risk of being sued. Speed limits prevent many more accidents than the fear of being sued, and tough-minded peer review committees do more to make doctors careful than malpractice cases. The "defensive medicine" doctors now practice to provide defense against lawsuits when something goes wrong adds substantially to medical costs and only trivially, if at all, to the safety of medical procedures. Every year brings disheartening new evidence that the danger of lawsuits does not deter automobile companies from persisting in the use of risky designs or fragile parts. The bar itself does not put much faith in tort law to control misbehavior. When the government began suing lawyers for collaborating in the looting of S&Ls and banks, the response of a number of bar associations was not to welcome this addition to the limited resources available for policing the behavior of the profession but to seek legislation that would exempt lawyers from liability for actions they had approved and helped carry forward.

An air of belligerence, of all-out "advocacy," pervades the theory and practice of law today. Such attitudes are relatively new to the profession and by no means essential to it—even to its function as what the personal injury trial lawyer Stuart Speizer aggressively calls "the Equalizer" in the contest between the powerful and the powerless.[14] The purpose of the claim entered on behalf of the victim of an automobile accident or a defective gas stove or human error in a hospital is not to punish the miscreant who did the damage but to help the victim. Until the 1980s, worker's compensation was an insurance system of this kind. The discipline on employers came in part from inspection under the occupational safety laws, and in part from experience ratings of the insurance premiums. The role of lawyers was minimized because the facts were usually not a source of dispute (if the band saw cut off the worker's finger, the employer paid whether or not the worker had been careless in using the band saw), and the fees paid to lawyers were controlled. Because the compensation related to losses of income and not to pain and suffering, some workers undoubtedly did less well than they might have done under a full-blown tort liability system, but many others received—and received quickly—benefits they well might not have received at all if their only route had been litigation. But the worker's compensation system in many states, under pressure by lawyers, has been changed by expanding the size of the award and by increasing the fraction that can be taken in legal fees.

In private conversation, almost nobody inside the profession speaks well of the lawyers who descend upon the relatives of those killed in an airplane accident, or Vietnam veterans exposed to Agent Orange, or former miners or shipyard workers dying of asbestosis. As already pointed out, the fact that victims have received only about a third of the hundreds of millions paid out by Johns Mansville in connection with the asbestos cases in the first six years of that litigation has outraged most lawyers (including President Bill Clinton) as much as it outraged the public. The lawyers who are suing the tobacco companies and the lawyers who are defending the tobacco companies are both engaged in an exercise at public expense (for the defense of such suits is an expense the tobacco companies can deduct from their taxable income). Agitation by the medical profession, accelerating tax increases on tobacco products, and laws prohibiting tobacco advertising on the airwaves have made smoking profoundly unfashionable among educated people in the United States and left little public purpose for litigation on behalf of smokers who acquired their habit before the government demanded warnings in the print advertising and on the pack. (The Environmental Protection Agency, however, by giving nonsmokers a possible action against their employers for damages due to smoking by others in their presence, may have opened a fruitful field for lawyers to force corporate policies against smoking in any public room or workplace.)

At their worst, however, the vagaries of tort law are better than nothing at all. On the European continent, and even to a degree in England, the tradition has long been that the state through insurance schemes provides the funds for medical treatment of injuries people receive through their own carelessness or the carelessness of others. Other state-provided insurance, or social benefits packages, take care of replacing the income workers lose after accidents. The principle is that victims of accidents should be made whole (or as close to whole as makes sense) by the society in its entirety, rather than according to whether someone who has insurance to cover such mistakes can be held accountable for the accident in a court of law. Under these circumstances, the social need for giving poor people access to lawyers who can sue on their behalf is far less significant than it is in the United States, where medical care is still often at the expense of the patient and income replacement is available only for work-related accidents, if then.

We would have much less need for contingent fee arrangements in the United States if we had a plan of unified national medical insurance and an enhanced Social Security system to replace income lost because of accidents anywhere. This would also take the monkey off the back of employers in states such as Maine and California, where the courts have been willing to qualify dubious injuries and psychological stress as work-related. Serious policing of the safety of the work force should be done by government inspectors, and a very moderate reduction of the money that now goes to personal injury lawyers in the worker's compensation field would permit major expansion of such inspections.

We have taken modest steps in this direction. A person injured in an automobile accident collects from his insurance company if he is insured, although the courts have forbidden juries to consider the question of whether someone else has already paid the bills when considering the extent of the damages the insurer for the other party in the accident should pay. (One section of President Clinton's health care reform package would eliminate double-dipping on medical costs.) Bills have been introduced in the California state legislature to eliminate insurance premiums entirely by putting a surcharge on gasoline at the pump to pay the costs of automobile accidents. These bills do restrict awards for pain and suffering, and thus strike directly at the profitability of the contingent fee—but by eliminating the uninsured, who now constitute almost two fifths of California drivers because rates are so high, they may on balance make the system more fair. They also promise, convincingly, a reduction of more than a third in the total Californians spend for auto insurance.

We already have provisions in the Social Security system to help support the spouse and children of a breadwinner who dies from an accident (or from any other cause). Though it is by no means clear that people who die in accidents should leave their family greater benefits than people who die from pneumonia, our expectations now are that "wrongful death" should yield dependents a recompense, and the Social Security Act could be modified to provide something like the "double indemnity" clause in a life insurance policy. In the absence of such social insurance programs, it is simply special pleading for insurance companies and their policyholders to propose rules that will make it more difficult for injured people to sue those who can be claimed to have some responsibility for their injuries.

It may be too much to ask bar associations to become leaders in the search for social insurance systems that might cost less and yield greater benefits to victims than tort law as we know it. But surely they should not employ their political weight and skills to keep this issue off the legislative table. Those of us who criticize the "we-can-get-you-money" advertising on television have a special obligation to help legislators craft remedies for those to whom the advertising is directed.

Other matters could also be taken off lawyers' plates. Most divorce actions where there is little or no property to contest could—and maybe should—be handled by specially trained social workers rather than by lawyers, whose training, after all, gives them no special insight into the problems of broken families. Paralegals are all that is needed in most landlord-and-tenant cases, and brokers who have passed specified courses and perhaps exams could handle most purchases of homes without pay-

ing lawyers to draw up boilerplate documents. Professor Roger
C. Cramton of Cornell Law School argues: "The prohibition on
the unauthorized practice of law should be limited to representation in contested court proceedings. . . . Provision of a greater
variety of service alternatives, many of them at substantially lower cost, to all Americans may be the most important step in improving access to justice for the poor."[15] One is embarrassed in
retrospect to remember the fight some bar associations put up
against the preparation of individual tax returns by accountants,
whose expertise in these matters, after all, is likely to exceed a
lawyer's unless the lawyer is also an accountant. What all this
comes down to is that a bar association that sees its job as that of
a trade association can be of only limited help in repairing and
maintaining the reputation of the profession.

3

Really poor people will still lack necessary legal services after
all these reforms are completed, and the indications are that
this condition will worsen, despite the improvement in the last
twenty years. A study by the Maine Commission on Legal
Needs found that only 23 percent of the legal problems of
Maine residents whose income put them below the poverty
line had in fact received any attention from a lawyer[16]—and
Maine, with 56 percent participation, boasts the second-highest
proportion in the country of lawyers participating in pro bono
activities (Idaho, with 59 percent, is first). These are the people
who have the least understanding of what their rights may be
under the contracts they sign when they rent an apartment or
take a job or sign for a charge account or a credit card. The idea
that they are priced out of the market for the legal services they
need should be repugnant to all lawyers.

The District of Columbia "Rules of Professional Conduct,"
which are not unusual, proclaim in capital letters:

A LAWYER SHOULD PARTICIPATE IN SERVING THOSE PERSONS OR
GROUPS OF PERSONS WHO ARE UNABLE TO PAY ALL OR A PORTION
OF REASONABLE ATTORNEYS' FEES OR WHO ARE OTHERWISE UN-
ABLE TO OBTAIN COUNSEL. A LAWYER MAY DISCHARGE THIS RE-
SPONSIBILITY BY PROVIDING PROFESSIONAL SERVICES AT NO FEE,
OR AT A SUBSTANTIALLY REDUCED FEE, TO PERSONS AND GROUPS
WHO ARE UNABLE TO AFFORD OR OBTAIN COUNSEL OR BY ACTIVE
PARTICIPATION IN THE WORK OF ORGANIZATIONS THAT PROVIDE
LEGAL REPRESENTATION TO THOSE UNABLE TO OBTAIN COUNSEL.

In smaller type, however, the "Comment" on this rule notes
that it "expresses the profession's traditional commitment to
make legal counsel available, but it is not intended that the
Rule be enforced through disciplinary process."

A committee appointed by New York State's highest court to
investigate the state of legal services to poorer people reported
back: "A crisis now exists which jeopardizes both the welfare of
poor persons and the legitimacy of the legal system itself. . . . It
is grotesque to have a system in which the law guarantees to
the poor that their basic human needs will be met but which
provides no realistic means with which to enforce that right."[17]

Federal appropriations for neighborhood legal services,
which had reached $321 million in 1981, fell by 25 percent in
the Reagan years, and only gradually recovered to the previous
peak (which, of course, represented much less purchasing power) in the Bush administration. Through both administrations,
the White House every year tried to do away with the program
entirely and appointed as its board members people known to
be out of sympathy with its goals. Still, some of this adversity
may have been good for the cause. By "privatizing" some legal
services to poor people, stimulating pro bono efforts, and subsi-
dizing practitioners and small firms to take on the business
rather than doing it through government offices, the Legal Services Corporation helped create a network of more than 2,300
offices that "provide civil legal assistance to persons unable to
retain private counsel."[18]

Donations to private legal aid offices are up, but not nearly as much as would be required to keep the salaries of legal aid lawyers at a steady fraction of the salaries paid to lawyers in the larger firms; the sacrifice required to do legal work for poor people has, if anything, grown as the profession has become richer. More pro bono work is done than the public realizes, especially by the large law firms, many of which credit their associates' "book" for as much as 500 unbillable pro bono hours every year. The American Bar Association Private Bar Involvement Project claimed that 123,808 lawyers gave time to pro bono work in 1990, which was about a quarter of all non-salaried practicing lawyers. The number is impressive, even gratifying, but it falls far short of meeting the ABA's 1988 resolution urging "*all* attorneys to devote a reasonable amount of time, but in no event less than 50 hours a year, to *pro bono* and other public service activities that serve those in need or improve the law, the legal system, or the legal profession." The recession at the larger firms, moreover, cut heavily into pro bono work, and there have been no signs that the firms are going to make sacrifices elsewhere to save the pro bono programs.

The blue-ribbon committee of lawyers appointed by the chief judge of the New York Court of Appeals urged in 1989 that the New York courts "adopt rules compelling lawyers to donate twenty hours a year to advance the legal needs of the eligible poor."[19] But the mismatch between the skills of a tax lawyer and the needs of the eligible poor may be too great to make such principles workable. Indeed, the Supreme Court in 1989 agreed that a lawyer could refuse an assignment from an Iowa court to defend indigent prisoners suing prison officials for damages from their brutality. The lawyer involved said he couldn't comply because he had no competence in such matters, as his securities and bankruptcy practice never gave him the opportunity to depose or cross-examine a witness, and Yale's Geoffrey Hazard thought he had a point. The Iowa rule, Hazard argued, had an old-fashioned "vision [which] contemplates practitioners com-

petent to handle practically whatever matter may come through
the door, whether it be a will, a deed, the replevin of a cow, or a
criminal charge such as horse stealing."[20]

Relatively few city lawyers have much practice in the kinds
of law most needed by poor people. Most surveys show that
half the profession does no pro bono work at all (even including
pro bono work helping churches and charities with legal problems), and only a quarter of the nation's lawyers devote more
than twenty hours a year to such causes. As we shall see in
chapter 9, imaginative firms that care deeply about their responsibilities in this area can and do organize themselves to do
pro bono work effectively, but most of the meaningful representation of poor people is going to have to be done by lawyers
who have learned to relate to such clients.

From its introduction in the law school curriculum to its execution by experienced lawyers, pro bono should concentrate on
the rights and remedies of individuals, not on a social agenda to
be created by poverty lawyers. If the result of winning a case
for a homeless family is to compel the construction of more
housing for the poor, that is a source of great satisfaction for
their lawyer as citizen—but his aim in bringing a case must be
the benefit of the individuals on whose behalf he speaks. Poor
people as well as rich people have the right to be clients whose
interests are paramount for their attorneys. Professor Jonathan
R. Macey of Cornell Law School has argued that such efforts on
behalf of the poor are economically inefficient. "Given a choice
between (a) 20 billable hours of legal services provided by a
partner in a Wall Street firm (valued at around $7,000) and (b)
$2,500 in cash, most people—middle class or poor—would take
the $2,500 in cash," Macey writes.[21] Though Macey's intention
is to disparage all pro bono work, he plants the seed of a useful
idea—the substitution of cash for time by those who do not
wish to do pro bono work. If we assume that a partner in a
large firm bills two thousand hours a year, and that twenty
hours of her time is worth $7,000, the partner can be assessed a

tithe of a tithe, or 1 percent of her billings, to support legal aid provided by others. That $7,000 probably pays for a hundred hours of the time of the less eminent lawyers who work in such offices. Rather than demand time and effort from the more successful lawyers, mandatory pro bono could offer a choice: twenty hours or 1 percent of billings.

In recent years, there has grown up among lawyers at least some degree of willingness to pay a tax for the benefit of legal services rather than giving time to the cause. The New York State committee that recommended compulsory pro bono offered to let lawyers off the hook for a price of $1,000 a year (twenty hours' mandatory pro bono at $50 an hour). NYU's Stephen Gillers is even more modest, proposing an annual license fee of a dollar or two per working day for every member of the bar, whether practicing or not.

Ideally, some of the money taxed from the law firms to support legal services for the poor could be spent through the bar association referral service. For applicants who meet an income criterion, the bar association itself should have the opportunity to tap into these funds for the poor to pay the standard fees of lawyers who are not dedicated poverty lawyers but handle the legal problems of ordinary people. But most of the money from this special tax on lawyers' fees should pay the salaries of the lawyers at the legal aid and legal services offices who have made helping the less fortunate the center of their professional careers. What is important for the self-respect of the bar is that *every* lawyer make some contribution, of time or money, to the costs of approaching the goal of equal justice for all. Trade associations can't call for new taxes on their members, but professional associations can.

Professor Gillers is a skeptic. "We'd rather wave the flag of professionalism, and insist that everyone else salute it," he wrote in the *ABA Journal*, "than dig into our pockets and help realize the promise of equal access to justice as our institutional responsibility."[22] But perhaps he's wrong.

4

One of the informing issues for the bar in the next few years will be the final decision on the legitimacy of nonlegal enterprises owned by law firms. Arnold & Porter in Washington were the pioneers of such subsidiaries, beginning in 1984 with a lobbying firm later sold to Grey Advertising. (The very idea that a law firm should own and operate a business later considered a suitable activity for an advertising agency is the sort of thing that once would have sent shivers up the spines of most lawyers.) Arnold & Porter's collection of owned subsidiaries includes the Secura Group, one of the largest bank consulting organizations in the country, headed by a former chairman of the Federal Deposit Insurance Corporation. And the firm is not alone. A survey by the *National Law Journal* late in 1992 showed that 33 of the nation's 250 largest law firms had a total of 48 "ancillary businesses." Some were quite imaginative, including a company that arranged celebrity endorsements by sports figures.

The drive toward such enterprises slowed in the 1990s—only two new nonlegal subsidiaries of large law firms were formed in 1991, three in 1992. What may have slowed down the process is that in 1991, by eleven votes, the House of Delegates of the American Bar Association passed Model Rule 5.7, condemning such subsidiaries. Then, in 1992, by seven votes, the association reversed itself. Even if the association reversed itself again, of course, law firms could continue to launch such ventures. The Model Rules are not binding on practitioners unless they are adopted by local authorities, and the few that have acted—most notably those in Washington itself—have provided approval rather than prohibition.

The leader of the fight against ancillary businesses has been Justin Stanley, a former president of the ABA, who chaired the association's Commission on Professionalism in 1985. In a letter he sent to every delegate to the 1992 convention in a vain attempt to preserve the previous opinion, he noted that in 1986 his commission had reported that "the greater the participation by lawyers in activities other than the practice of law, the less likely it is that the lawyer can capably discharge the obligation which our profession demands."

The problem with the 1992 vote, Stanley said later, was that in various parts of the country there were traditions that lawyers provided services other than law to some of their clients. They were, of course, trustees, but also financial advisers, sometimes through the agency of a counseling group that included nonlawyers. They were title insurers and sometimes co-venturers in real estate matters. These lawyers were concerned that rules forbidding law firms to operate subsidiaries might force them to divest themselves of activities that were not merely profitable to themselves but services the clients in their part of the country expected from them. Stanley, though disapproving of lawyers who went into real estate development with their clients, thought it relatively easy to grandfather such old-fashioned couplings while preventing lawyers from following in the footsteps of doctors and using their influence over their clients to persuade them to use consulting and other service companies the lawyers owned. In the end, lawyers who didn't care about fancy "diversification" but wished to guard their own inherited work voted against restrictions.

It is not simple to draw the lines between a lawyer's practice and certain service businesses that are clearly not professional. The ABA's Standing Committee on Ethics and Professional Responsibility decided in late 1990 that

> lawyers' ancillary business activities should be regulated rather than prohibited altogether. . . . First, [because] the provision of ancillary services by lawyers could be beneficial for both clients and the general public. . . . Second, [because] the Committee was not aware of any history or evidence of abuse or harm to the public or the profession arising from lawyers' participation

in ancillary business activities. . . . Third, [because] for a very
long time, lawyers in this country, particularly sole practitioners, have provided to clients and non-clients services that are
generally understood as included in the phenomenon of ancillary activities.[23]

In a rather disingenuous way, the committee tried to duck the
question of confidentiality in the lawyer-customer relationship
by extending to customers of lawyers' business operations the
same duty of confidentiality that exists between lawyer and
client. This would give such business ventures quite a competitive advantage over similar activities conducted by nonlawyers.

The truth is that when it comes to ethics the rule must be severe: What's not white is black. This need for stark judgment is
among the elements that distinguishes a profession from a business. When it is breached, the results can be horrendous.
Those results have long been known, and feared, in the context
of referral fees. Clients often are not told that when a lawyer
refers them to another lawyer for a piece of work, some part of
the fee they pay that lawyer may come back to their original
counsel. Ancillary activities where the law firm refers clients to
its own subsidiary are clearly in this box. "It's like the doctor
who gets a cut on every prescription," said Judge Edward
Lumbard, the almost-retired former chief judge of the Second
Circuit Court of Appeals. If the lawyer recommends the services of his subsidiary firm (if the doctor orders up tests performed by the lab in which he is a stockholder), there is
something in it for him, and there will always be reason for sus-
picion that he is not driven by the client's interest alone.

In counseling their clients as to their needs for specialized
consulting services and as to what they should expect to get for
their money from consultants, lawyers should be free of self-interest. There are and will continue to be problems of confidentiality in the attorney-client context, for the subsidiaries of the
law firm can be called to testify against the client, and the divi-

sion of information between the privileged material given to the lawyer and the unprivileged material in the hands of the consultant may be very difficult to make.

The more practical question returns again to the more philosophical question: When we say "we lawyers," what do we mean? Specialization has blurred many lines, but the profession must maintain the fence that separates "client" from "customer." Keeping that fence in good repair should be a major task of the bar associations.

CHAPTER 8

WHAT THE JUDGES CAN DO

1

In an unguarded moment, Chief Justice Charles Evans
Hughes, who was neither a radical nor a "legal realist,"
once admitted that the Constitution was whatever the
Supreme Court said it was. In England, which does not have a
written constitution, much of the law as it affects individuals
was actually created by judges in the course of deciding cases.
In the United States, a nation created by a revolution against
England, it was always understood that the legislature was the
primary fount of the law. But what the laws *mean* is in the
hands of judges, and lawyers' power to interfere in the lives of
other people derives entirely from their status as officers of the
court. Until a lawsuit is properly begun, the lawyer has no
more right than anyone else to command a reply to a claim, or
subpoena some company's papers, or demand someone's testimony. In many important areas of estates, bankruptcies—even,
in some states, personal injury matters—the fees lawyers receive for their work are subject to approval by a judge and may
be paid through the court. As a realistic matter, no effort to im-

prove the conduct of the legal profession is going to succeed without the help—ideally, the enthusiastic help—of the judges.

"People think of lawyers as fixers," said Judge Edward Lumbard. "And a lot of lawyers are willing to be thought of that way. To some degree, I think the courts are responsible. We don't have the judges who have the stomach for being tough. These people practice mostly in the state courts. So the federal judges are inclined to leave these things to the state courts."

Former ABA president Justin Stanley feels that this is the area where the American habit of electing state judges does the most harm. The electorate as a whole does not know enough about the candidates or care enough about the issues to exercise discretion when voting for judges. It's the lawyers who care, who contribute to the judges' reelection campaigns, who influence the party leaders when they make the selection of candidates. And one of the oldest traditions of politics is that you get even with those you feel have done you damage. A judge, like anyone else who runs for office, wants to be reelected. It's difficult to persuade him to police the lawyers who come before him when those lawyers are or easily can become active in political clubs. (This is not to say that there is no value in a political regime where judges, like other lawgivers, are subject to periodic approval by the public they rule; just that there is a serious question about the system as we now operate it.) Any reform movement that relies on the cooperation of judges must start, then, in the federal courts, where judges are appointed for life and owe no favors to the lawyers who appear before them.

Simon Rifkind joins right-wing critics in putting some of the blame for what has gone wrong in the profession on Charles Elias Clark, who was dean of the Yale Law School in the 1930s and judge on the Federal Court of Appeals for the Second Circuit in the following decade. It was Clark who spearheaded the drive to "reform" the federal Rules of Civil Procedure, make it easier for lawyers to get their cases into court, and reduce the element of "surprise" at trials. The obvious way to reduce surprise is to compel lawyers to tell their opponents what witnesses and what evidence they expect to produce when the case comes before the judge or the jury, and to allow the lawyers for both sides to conduct examinations and cross-examinations before the trial even opens.

"In criminal law," Judge Rifkind told an interviewer for *Litigation Journal*, "you can't arrest a person without probable cause. Yet in civil law, all you have to do is serve a notice, sign your name, and you can inquire about anything and everything. It is quite a startling discrepancy, no Fifth Amendment on the civil side. So I think a higher threshold for the commencement of discovery would serve a useful purpose."[1]

These "discovery" proceedings can themselves become extremely expensive, even punitive, and often compel the parties to try their cases twice, once without and then once with a judge in the room. The ABA Committee on Professionalism commented sourly on "double, triple or quadruple teaming on depositions" as an example of "wasteful, wholly inappropriate tactics…. Whenever such practices occur, they must be condemned and stopped because they are inconsistent with the lawyer's responsibility toward both the client and the system of justice."[2] In 1984, Chief Justice Warren E. Burger singled out discovery as a source of abusive advocacy—and exaggerated billing. He told the American Law Institute:

> [I]t has become trial by annihilation before the litigants ever reach the courthouse. The abuse factor is epitomized in the story of a young associate who was given the assignment to prepare massive interrogatories to wear down the opposition, to make it as costly a venture as possible so that a settlement might be coerced. Another episode tells of a young associate assigned to a case. After extensive study and preparation, he negotiated a settlement favorable to the client only to be criticized by his superiors because he "did not let the meter run" up a larger figure of billable hours through discovery. The courts and the judicial system of this country were not established by our forefathers as the private preserve of the legal profession.[3]

The worst aspect of discovery, however, is the fact that lawyers conduct it away from the courtroom and away from the direct supervision of the judge. Every wrong instinct of adversarial advocacy is thereby brought into play. The record of the testimony in the discovery proceedings will be available for use at the trial. There is gold to be mined in lines of questioning that elicit an apparent "admission" of something that will look embarrassing in the context of the evidence to be introduced at the trial—or a statement that could be construed, even twisted, to appear to contradict the testimony this witness can be expected to give at the trial. Some lawyers bully witnesses at discovery proceedings in ways a judge would never permit; others wheedle in a way jurors would find distasteful. In cases where there are multiple interests involved, all are entitled to take their turn questioning a witness on discovery, and some shamefully waste the witness's time by going over again, and yet again, material to which he has already testified. It is not unknown for a lawyer who has not been present in the previous days of discovery to start by asking a witness all the identification questions—What is your name? Where do you work? What is your title?—without the slightest concern that he is taking (without compensation) the witness's valuable time. "The transcripts of depositions," Judge Richard Posner of the Court of Appeals for the Seventh Circuit wrote in 1988, "are often very ugly documents."[4]

Justice William Rehnquist urged in 1973 that discovery be reserved for matters where the money in dispute was greater than $50,000.[5] Bringing that number up-to-date, accounting for inflation, would take the hurdle to about $150,000—probably too low, but a good first step.

The first abuser of discovery proceedings was, of course, the federal government, especially but not exclusively in antitrust cases. The separate office Cravath opened in White Plains, New York, to defend IBM against antitrust charges was required because the truckloads of documents the government demanded could not be housed in the existing offices. Corporations learned from their desperate experience in fighting the deep pockets of the Justice Department that when they had a case against another company, they could make the defense of that case fearfully expensive by employing the tactics the government had used against them. Judge Clark had said that his new rules promoting discovery were congruent with the existing rules of civil procedure, with their announced purpose to "secure the just, speedy and inexpensive outcome of an action." He certainly did not mean that discovery should become one of the most violent and sometimes vicious weapons in the battle between lawyers.

If they wished, judges could make lawyers use the discovery process only as Judge Clark intended. It is the responsibility of the judge to schedule the course of a lawsuit. Judges can and should make lawyers prove why they need the testimony or documents they demand for discovery and could narrowly restrict their imposition of cost and time on their opponents. When I was young at the bar, judges ruled scornfully against lawyers who wished to conduct what were called "fishing expeditions" among their opponents' employees or paper. The rules of evidence, requiring a demonstration that what is to be elicited is relevant to the cause of action, should be enforced in discovery proceedings just as they are in the courtroom. Judges could be receptive to complaints by witnesses or opposing lawyers that the discovery process was being abused, and could refuse to permit the use at the trial of statements drawn by an abusive discovery. It was in the context of a discussion of discovery that Chief Justice Burger made the comment noted earlier, adding that, in his time, "a lawyer's signature on a pleading or motion was something like a signature on a check; there was supposed to be something to back it up. . . . This is another area where a few well-placed sanctions will have a salutary effect."[6]

Unfortunately, in the more than fifty years since Judge Clark won his fight to loosen up the rules of procedure, acade-

mic theories of a lawyer's role have swung around to supporting a diminished role for judges. Where once the judge had
been the arbiter, resolving the dispute between the litigants,
now the judge has become more the bystander who holds the
coats while the other fellows fight. Once there had been general agreement that an actual lawsuit is a defeat for the
lawyers, as war is a defeat for the diplomats. Thus the highest
function of the judge was to get the dispute settled before trial—indeed, many jurisdictions required a "pretrial conference" in the judge's chambers as the last clear chance to avoid
actual litigation. Now the prevailing view is that judges should
rule only on questions of law; if there is a factual dispute between the parties, the judge should turn the matter over to a
jury.

There is some tradition for this view in the United States.
The Constitution requires a trial by jury for claims exceeding
$20 that fall within federal jurisdiction. Many lawyers fear that
judges may be biased by their own social status or by their political connections. Or they may just have quirky views about
some element of expert testimony one side of a case wishes to
introduce. There is not much that can be done about a biased
or quirky judge, while the biases of the members of a jury can
be tested in the process of jury selection and in any event tend
to cancel out. Still, the fact is that in Britain, whence the American tradition of jury trials derives, trial by jury in civil matters
no longer exists. And it is not uncommon in this country for the
opposing sides to waive their right to a trial by jury and to ask
the judge to rule on both the facts and the law. The costs to litigants from the loss of a right to demand trial by jury are probably overbalanced by the costs to the society at large from the
lost working days of jurors, the less efficient trial procedures in
situations where the information must be evaluated by amateurs, and injustice from the weight juries may give to extraneous arguments cleverly presented.

The theory that judges are not supposed to influence jury

findings also works to reduce the power of the judges to influence the behavior of lawyers. Chief Justice Burger likes to quote a report from a British lawyer named Odgers regarding the judge's influence on manners in British courts over the course of the nineteenth century:

> The moral tone of the Bar is wholly different from what it was . . . they no longer seek to obtain a temporary victory by unfair means; they remember that it is their duty to assist the Court in eliciting the truth. This is due partly to the improved education of the Bar, partly no doubt to the influence of an omnipresent press, but still more to Her Majesty's judges. If counsel for the prosecution presses the case too vehemently against a prisoner; if counsel cross-examining in a civil case pries unnecessarily into the private concerns of the witness, a word, or even a look, from the presiding judge will at once check such indiscretion.[7]

Judges acquire such influence because they can decide cases, and outside the big cities their influence is multiplied because lawyers must expect that they will have to appear again, even frequently, before this same judge. But increasingly, these days, the judge has come under instruction to avoid any statements or actions that might affect the factual findings in the case (and is subject to overrulings by the appellate courts should he do so). And the larger judicial districts in the metropolitan areas are so heavily populated and lawyered that the courthouse has dozens of judges working inside it, which means that this judge is not likely to hear another case from this lawyer for many months or even years. The end result is inevitably to erode the respect that lawyers show the courts and to encourage lawyers to play to the gallery in their dealings with each other. Judge Edward Lumbard tells his clerks that if their ambition in life is to practice law as it should be practiced, they should go south or west to small cities, where the members of the bar know each other and the judge knows all of them and a lawyer's reputation and ability to function are to no small degree a function of his character.

But the metropolitan problems have been spreading. In general, the ABA Committee on Professionalism urged:

> Trial judges should take a more active role in the conduct of litigation. They should see that cases advance promptly, fairly and without abuse. . . . Courts should play a more decisive role earlier in the litigation process. . . . Case management techniques must be employed by judges to move matters along. Sadly, litigation today frequently resembles the dance marathons of the 1930s, where the partners or, in this case the adversaries, move as slowly as possible to the music without actually stopping. . . . Parties do not bear all the costs of their own delay. There is a public interest in not clogging the courts with stale cases. Unfortunately, the responsibility for the efficient movement of cases must fall upon the shoulders of the judges largely by default.[8]

In recent years, people seeking to give judges a stronger voice in how lawyers behave have stressed greater use of Rule 11, which allows the court to make the losing side of a frivolous or abusive lawsuit pay the costs of the winning side. Adopted in 1983 as an amendment to the Federal Rules of Civil Procedure, the rule was intended to increase the risks to both clients and lawyers who abused their right to sue. "Lawyers," wrote Judith S. Kaye, later to be chief judge of the Court of Appeals in New York, commenting on the adoption of Rule 11, "must make their own inquiry into the facts and the law before filing papers; good-faith reliance on the client's word is not enough. . . . Rule 11 reinforces lawyers' obligations as officers of the court and their responsibility, *even above their client responsibility*, to the justice system, and Rule 11 reinforces those obligations in the most tangible possible way—by money sanctions."[9]

This has been advertised to the profession as the "English

rule," because it is routine procedure in England (and elsewhere in Europe) to assess the winner's costs against the loser. Settlements before trial are not in the form of a lump sum payment but are typically divided into two parts, one of which is calculated to pay the plaintiff's costs. Such a rule also, obviously, adds to the willingness of even a rich and angry plaintiff to withdraw an action if it looks likely to fail badly enough so that he will have to pick up the defendant's costs. It may indeed be true that the existence of liability for the other side's costs improves the civility of British law practice by making it risky for British lawyers to scorch the other man's earth. And it should be recognized that a rule forcing losers to pay winners' costs is in part a substitute for our system of the contingent fee, which is illegal in England. Under the English rule, plaintiff's counsel is assured that even if a judge finds his client has suffered less harm than the client thought, the lawyer will still get paid for his disbursements and his time.

The imposition of the winners' costs on all losers clearly acts as a deterrent to possible plaintiffs (and their lawyers, who might have to bear part of the burden). The deterrence is minimized in England by the existence of more extensive tax-supported legal assistance programs, by union-sponsored litigation funds, and by insurance policies that pay legal bills. American plaintiffs and their lawyers do not have such support networks beneath them. British procedure does seem, however, to set up separate categories of plaintiffs—"privately funded" as against funded by legal assistance or unions. And in the negotiating process that precedes a trial, such distinctions can be invidious. Professor Herbert M. Kritzer of the University of Wisconsin cites a study of 220 High Court cases in England in the mid-1980s, which showed that defendants offered to settle 90 percent of the cases where the plaintiff was funded by a union, 66 percent of the cases where the plaintiff's bills would be paid by legal aid, but only 53 percent of the cases where the plaintiff and his lawyer were on their own.[10] This may mean merely that the unions and the legal assistance institutions screen cases in ways that solicitors being paid by their clients do not, but the numbers do raise questions.

Many of the objections to the English Rule do not apply to Rule 11, which kicks in, not against mere losers, but against plaintiffs and lawyers who have abused the system—sued for libel as a way to intimidate publications, badgered business competitors, sued a manufacturer for a defective product when there was in fact no defect, entered motions before trial for the sole purpose of creating delays. To date, the record of Rule 11 penalties looks like very reasonable judicial behavior; for example, punishing an over-the-counter drug company for repeatedly suing *Barron's* because its front-page columnist Alan Abelson had written negatively about the stock, and a lawyer with a class-action suit who filed against every mortgage lender in Chicago (making lenders that did not do the business he sued about pay lawyers to defend them), and a lady who sued fourteen times to compel Loyola University to admit her to its medical school.

There do remain reasons to worry about the expansion of Rule 11 penalties. Innovative approaches to the law, and efforts to overturn existing law, can easily seem frivolous or abusive in the eyes of hostile judges. As Professor Kritzer notes: "A striking characteristic of the American bar is its entrepreneurial spirit. There is nothing comparable in the English legal profession, which historically has been reluctant to seek out or develop new areas of practice or causes of action." Judicial decision in the 1920s, not legislative action, made it possible for injured people to sue the manufacturers of defective products. Prior to that decision, any plaintiff bringing a case demanding compensation from a manufacturer (rather than the storekeeper who had sold the product) would have risked Rule 11 penalties had the rule then been part of the code. Not infrequently, the first cases to allege damage from, say, a defective automobile transmission are thrown out by the court, and it is not until a certain weight of documentation is built up that judges begin to take the claims seriously. The losers of the first cases are punished enough by the need to pick up their own expenses, without burdening them also with the need to pick up Ford's or GM's expenses.

Like any reliance on judges, greater use of Rule 11 carries the risk of judicial punishment based on individual bias—and perhaps even on political doctrine. This objection, however, can be overcome. John Marshall wrote in 1824, denying the state of Maryland the right to sue the then federally chartered Bank of the United States, that "the power to tax implies the power to destroy." Nearly a hundred years later, Justice Oliver Wendell Holmes, Jr., upheld a state tax on a federally chartered institution, noting that such power to destroy could not be exercised "while this court sits." Abusing Rule 11, a judge could in theory destroy a lawyer and his client, but the penalties could be stayed, reviewed, and removed; that's what appellate courts are for. It may be that the appellate courts might wish to establish a small bench of judges from different jurisdictions to meet on a monthly or an every-other-month schedule to hear appeals from Rule 11 penalties.

Among the ways that judges could regain their power over their courts (and their control of behavior by lawyers) would be an assertion of their right to police lawyers' fees. The ABA Committee on Professionalism wrote:

> No single issue between lawyer and client arises more frequently or generates more public resentment than fee problems. While distinctions can be raised between sophisticated and unsophisticated users of legal services, it is desirable to have open communications on fee matters with clients. This includes adequate explanation of the legal work to be performed in each case and why it needs to be done. . . . One particular approach warranting increased consideration is fee arbitration, to which clients could turn as a matter of right if they believe they have been overcharged. . . . Experience indicates that the issuance of pretrial orders by judges can be useful. The orders . . .

could, among other things, limit the number of lawyers participating in depositions and appearing before the court in oral arguments. Orders such as these will help minimize the size of
requested fee awards.[11]

The other route for judicial activism in policing the performance of lawyers is greater use of the judge's powers to deny
the sufficiency of a plaintiff's pleadings or give summary judgment, by which the judge can dismiss a case without a trial.
The effect is to raise the threshold for entry into the world
where lawyers can exert their "impositional powers," not only
on their client's antagonist and his filing system but also on a
whole world of witnesses. Judicial decision itself must be this
way or that way—the judge's agony is that he really must *decide*—but judges *can*, if they so choose, govern access to that
process with reference to probabilities. If a judge thinks it
highly unlikely that a plaintiff can prevail, he has an obligation
to the defendants, to the schedule of his court, and to other applicants for justice—and, indeed, to the plaintiff—not to permit
the waste of their time and money. A courtroom should not be a
casino where lawyers throw the dice in hopes that a jury will
read them wrong. As always, there must be worries about what
happens when judges are given discretion. In the end, we return to what Justice Felix Frankfurter said when asked whether
a man changed when he put on those robes. "By God," said
Frankfurter, "he'd better."

2

Judges at judicial conventions complain about the decline of civility in their courtrooms and swap stories of lawyers who obviously had coached their witnesses to lie before they put them

on the stand. Now a number of them have, however, gotten behind a volunteer "quiet crusade" called "The American Inns of Court," which attempts to extend to America its leaders' vision of the mentoring done by British barristers at the wonderful low-rise Georgian quadrangles behind the Law Courts in London, where many of them have their "chambers." This is by definition an alien phenomenon not likely to strike deep roots in the United States. Still, it is an impressive expression of dissatisfaction by the federal bench; today more than one in three federal judges is a member of an American Inn of Court, as are more than a thousand state judges.

This modest institution grew out of conversations between Chief Justice Burger and Judge J. Clifford Wallace of the Court of Appeals for the Ninth Circuit on a visit to London in 1977. Among those to whom the chief justice spoke on his return was Judge A. Sherman Christensen, a federal district judge in Utah. Rex E. Lee, formerly solicitor general, had returned home to be dean of the law school at Brigham Young University in Provo and was happy to give housing to the first American Inn of Court in 1980. It was set up with a relatively formal constitution, limiting membership to sixty-five and establishing a tripartite organization of "Benchers" (judges, law professors, and litigators with at least twelve years' experience), "Barristers" (lawyers with three to twelve years' experience), and "Pupils" (lawyers with less than one year in practice; some inns take Pupils in their third year at law school). The Benchers are members for life; the Barristers are members for three years; the Pupils are members for one year. Turnover is thus deliberately high, in hope that members will go out and serve as examples for others in their category. The Barristers and Pupils apply to become members, and the choices are made by the Benchers. When one inn fills up, its alumni can start another.

In 1993, there were more than 13,000 lawyers participating in American Inns of Court. They held monthly evening meetings, usually at law schools or at courthouses, at which "pupillage teams" of seniors and juniors staged demonstrations of court proceedings of a problematic kind. Joryn Jenkins, a law professor and editor of the AIC newsletter *The Bencher* reported:

> The pupillage demonstrations often lead to heated debate on questions of ethics. Many of the demonstrations focus solely on ethical issues. The programs remind experienced attorneys, as well as new practitioners, of their professionalism and ethical awareness. It instills in many the determination to live up to the standards expected by the judges, a strong sense of duty as an officer of the court, and an appreciation of the fact that each alone is responsible for the actions he or she takes, no matter whether a partner instructs him to pursue a specific course of action or a client requests that he do so.[12]

Refreshments (often including dinner), discussions, and critiques follow the demonstrations, providing opportunities for the kind of socializing known as networking. The advantages of these contacts to the younger participants are obvious, but the Benchers and Barristers also feel rewarded, because they have little opportunity otherwise to dip into the currents the young lawyers must battle as they swim upstream.

Professor Sherman L. Cohn of Georgetown University School of Law, president of the AIC, stresses "a second element of the Inn experience":

> Each pupil is assigned to a barrister in the pupillage team and the two of them to a master lawyer. The pupil is to spend two hours a month with the barrister, and the two of them with the master lawyer and the judge: in the courtroom, in deposition, in the office, at lunch—observing and discussing the practice of law. Much as the young pupil in the British Inn of Court does, following the old codger around, observing and discussing. And as much as the American medical model, where the med student and the intern go with the attending on grand rounds and discuss the cases together.

The purpose, Cohn continues, is to

> create an informal monitoring system where the young person,
> student or lawyer, has a more experienced lawyer and a judge
> outside of his or her law firm from whom he can learn skill,
> ethics, and civility—and with whom he or she can discuss the
> practice of law. We know that many young lawyers have doubts
> and questions about the practice of law. The last person to
> whom that lawyer would want to express those doubts is the
> partner in the firm to whom he or she reports. The American
> Inn gives the possibility of sitting down with a successful lawyer
> and judge outside of one's own firm and to discuss what the
> practice is all about.[13]

How seriously the Inns of Court phenomenon should be taken
is hard to say. It is clearly "elitist," but there are those of us for
whom that word carries a positive rather than a negative
charge. I like to think of the law as an elite profession. It is for
people who still have stars in their eyes about being lawyers,
and we need such people urgently. Ideally, such an institution
would encourage those in each locality who are most concerned about the future of the profession to learn to work together. It could help the judges, many of whom have not
practiced for years, understand the problems of the lawyers
who appear before them, and help the lawyers remember that
they are members of a profession. "When you are a member of
a profession," said Jesse Choper, dean of the University of California Law School, "playing hard ball is unthinkable."

3

Until this generation, just about every lawyer who cared about
the law wanted to be a judge. The county courthouse was mar-
ble and grand and elegant—and well-kept. The judge sat on a

raised bench and was the monarch of his courtroom, and he had attendants and clerks and the trappings of majesty. His car had a special license plate, and he could park in "no parking" zones. When he spoke in any gathering where lawyers were present, his words were heard. In the federal system, his appointment was for life, and he could keep his chambers, hear and decide cases, and collect his salary for just about as long as he wished.

There was a sharp decline in the respect felt by the public for the Supreme Court through the post–World War II period—from 83.4 percent expressing approval and trust in 1949 to 32.6 percent in 1973 ("more extensive than for any other institution in the United States," wrote sociologist Morris Janowitz[14])—and by 1993 the Court's ratings with the public, according to the Gallup Poll, had improved to only 44 percent. But all judges continue to benefit from an aura that still hovers over the nine definitive interpreters of the Constitution.

Finally, a judge has opportunities to *control* what happens in his courtroom that are virtually unique to his occupation. In its obituary of Judge Gerhard A. Gesell—who threw out the Washington abortion law four years before *Roe* v. *Wade* and ruled that President Nixon lacked authority to fire Archibald Cox, the special prosecutor he had appointed himself to investigate the Watergate scandal—*The Washington Post* wrote: "A tiger on the bench, he set schedules and insisted that they be kept. When he was presiding, he ran a trial with authority and complete control. . . . At 82 he was still one of the most vigorous and hardworking jurists at the courthouse, and his death was a surprise to many who admired him."[15]

Longevity, tiresome but better than the alternative for most people, seems to add to a judge's force. There is no other occupation where an eighty-five-year-old man like Judge Milton Pollack of the Southern District of New York could play anything like the role Judge Pollack played in the resolution of the collapse of the Wall Street house of Drexel Burnham. A matter of enormous complexity, involving all sorts of securities, gold, foreign exchange, and sophisticated options and swaps, with creditors all over the globe, which looked like a source of livelihood for literally scores of lawyers for at least a decade, was settled in eighteen months because Judge Pollack was in a hurry. When one of the attorneys objected that Judge Pollack was pressuring him unduly, the judge smiled in a kindly way and said, "I'm eighty-five years old, I've been a judge for twenty-five years, and *I* will tell *you* what is and what is not proper."

But for Judge Pollack, who had been one of New York's most highly paid litigators, service on the bench was a reward for years of practice before it. His successors at the bar seem much less interested in following his example. The judge's status even among lawyers has significantly diminished. The fact is that, with few exceptions, the judges live much less well than the leaders of the profession in the well of the court before them. Everyone is conscious of the fact that the judge takes home for his labors perhaps one tenth the income of a senior partner in a large firm or a successful personal injury litigator. The burden of work is up; the milk of human kindness has soured in the litigators; and lawyers and laymen alike feel little compunction about criticizing the performance of the judiciary.

In some ways most discouraging of all, because of the images it inescapably presents, the surroundings have shamefully deteriorated. Among the easy economies of state and municipal government is the maintenance of the courthouse. In the county seats, the courthouse is shabby now, and in some of the larger cities it is a disgrace. Even in the District of Columbia, the corridors of the federal courthouse are unappetizing. In spring 1993, the Judicial Conference, the administrative body of the federal courts throughout the nation, sent a memorandum to all the district courts telling them that, for budgetary reasons, no new civil jury trials could be started after May 12, until the new federal budget came into effect in October—there wasn't enough money left to pay the jurors. Judge Jack B. Weinstein said he would keep trying cases anyway but tell the jurors they would have to wait for their pay.[16] In New York, the then chief judge of the court of appeals (the state's highest court) got into an undignified slinging match with the governor of the state over the budget for the state's courts, to the point where he sued the governor to compel the allocation of additional funds. The suit was later withdrawn, having done nobody any good.

If the judges are to help police the bar, the legislatures have a lot of work to do. They must revisit the question of judicial selection to prevent the introduction of political hacks to the bench. In return for the judges' pledge to keep the cases moving and get the business done (for much of the apparent shortage of judges and courtrooms is the result of judicial failure to keep the lawyers moving), the legislators must appropriate enough money to set higher pay scales for judges and keep the courthouses shining as the beacons of law in their communities. From those to whom much is given, Queen Elizabeth told one of her Parliaments, anticipating a famous Franklin Roosevelt speech 350 years later, much is expected. To those from whom so much is expected, much should be given. We don't give our judges enough today—enough resources, enough support, enough respect.

CHAPTER 9

WHAT THE LAWYERS CAN DO

1

As the 1980s became the 1990s, to the shock and astonishment of the profession, the ever-expanding "law business" met its first postwar recession. Of the 500 largest law firms in January 1991, 193 were smaller in January 1992. The annual Price Waterhouse Law Firm Statistical Survey showed that 41 of the 373 large and midsize firms that participated were smaller in 1991 than they had been in 1987.[1] Profits per partner at New York's Skadden Arps fell in 1990 by more than 10 percent, at Boston's Hale and Dorr by 14 percent, at Gibson Dunn by 12 percent. New York's Milbank Tweed and Willkie Farr and Chicago's Winston & Strawn and a number of other firms got rid of partners. For 1991, not just profits but *income* went down at many of the larger firms, and 1992 was the worst of all. Those who suffered blamed extraneous factors: the government's cruelty in closing down Drexel Burnham (a huge source of business for law firms) and cracking down on lending for highly leveraged transactions; the decline in tax shelter work as the effects of the 1986 tax law played through the sys-

tem; the government's kinder, gentler approach toward enforcement of the antitrust laws; the reduction in new securities
issuance following the 1987 crash; and, of course, the recession
itself.

The assignment of causes was difficult, because law firms
had developed a habit of operating on borrowed money, with
long billing cycles and delayed payments, while clients verified
bills that might run into the dozens of pages, specifying hours
and disbursements. Managing partners were often uncertain as
to why receipts had stopped rising or had even declined, and
the most obvious way to make up the shortfall was to increase
the borrowings. In the boom years, as fee income rose into the
tens and even hundreds of millions of dollars, some of the larger firms had turned over their business management to nonlawyers with experience in running large enterprises. But when
income began to decline, these managers were often even more
confused than the lawyers, because the assumptions on which
they had been operating turned out to be wrong. The Boston
firm of Gaston & Snow, for example, one of the earliest to seek
"professional management," discovered itself to be insolvent
and dissolved.

In 1992, it became apparent to the most optimistic at the big
firms that the clock really had stopped—and might even be
running backward. This was the year the economist Ronald
Coase won a Nobel Prize for a paper he had written more than
half a century earlier, in which he had asserted that companies
that produced what they needed inside the firm, avoiding the
costs of ascertaining the market prices of their components,
would have an advantage over those that bought on the outside.
This argument was not, in fact, a strong one in 1992, when
General Motors was fighting its unions for the right to out-
source components and the collapse of the command
economies in Eastern Europe had revealed the extent to which
internal pricing schemes can be abused to create unresponsive
bureaucracies and monstrous inefficiency. But where the prices

of externally produced goods and services are determined on a cost-plus basis, which is true in the professional nexus, a company may indeed cut its costs and improve its efficiency by following the Coase model.

Over the period from 1960 to 1990, American corporations had, as earlier indicated, multiplied by *five* the fraction of their revenues paid for legal services. They became convinced that the only way they could get these costs under control was by moving the legal function in-house. Very large law firms, one hundred lawyers and more, sprouted *inside* the Fortune 500 companies, with ever-increasing reductions in the budgets for hiring outside counsel. According to a Price Waterhouse study of the legal expenditures of the Fortune 500, they reduced their payments to outside counsel by no less than 24 percent in 1991 alone. Companies such as General Electric and General Motors told *The Wall Street Journal* in December 1992 that they thought their expenses for outside counsel in that year had probably dropped "20 to 30 percent" in the case of GE, "15 to 20 percent" in the case of GM.[2]

Nor is there any assurance that the money from big corporations will come back to the law firms when good times return to the economy: An era has ended. Law and the other professions have lost much of the trust that Americans once placed in them. It is now clear that if they are to regain that trust they will have to show their patients and clients that they are committed not only to the delivery of the best professional services but also to the control of the costs those services impose on society.

Medical services cost Americans about six times as much as legal services, and the doctors were the first to come under cost pressure. They are beginning to change their ways in response. Where once doctors decided on treatments by their reactions to their trained observations, many in hospitals have now bound themselves to "protocols"—procedures developed by their peers and colleagues that must be followed before expensive operations, medications, and tests are prescribed.

Some of these protocols have probably been adopted as systemic defenses against charges of malpractice that lawyers brought in growing numbers in the first thirty years after World War II. They embody the habits, which doctors call "defensive medicine," that have added to the costs of medical services in a cost-plus system of reimbursement, where the introduction of new procedures automatically increases the doctor's income. Legislation in Maine has sought to prevent this by specifically giving physicians immunity from lawsuits if their work follows protocols established by medical specialty boards—but it must be admitted that lawyers are suing to have this commonsense arrangement declared unconstitutional. President Clinton, however, made the Maine legislation part of his proposed plan to reform American health care systems.

Other protocols are specifically directed at reducing the total bills for illness. And in this category, the doctors have found— to their surprise—lie not only some risks to the quality of care but some improvements. Studies show that sick people get better faster and more permanently if they get on their feet and out of the hospital sooner. Infections from surgical wounds, which keep a ponderable percentage of patients in the hospital longer after surgery, turn out to be less frequent if antibiotics are administered before rather than after the operation. The medical societies have begun to acknowledge that emphasis on keeping people well (which means rewarding the internist and the family physician more and the specialist less) would be the greatest economy as well as the greatest service the country could ask from its doctors.

Whatever new health care system results from the political turmoil, the costs today's system has created will almost certainly be based on competition between groups of health care providers for contracts to serve groups of patients. Like lawyers, doctors increasingly will be organized into large "firms" (health maintenance organizations) covering the range of expertise their large groups of patients require. We will then expect the medical profession itself to police the quality of the services the public receives. The political struggle that is getting the attention in the newspapers is the fight over who pays what and who gets what, but the political struggle that will matter most to future generations of both doctors and patients will be the fight within the profession over the quality monitors' obligation to enforce the standards inherent in the doctor's oath.

The analogies to legal practice are clear and should be compelling. Like doctors, lawyers are best employed keeping people out of trouble. The lawyer who wins the case in court is the publicized hero, but the lawyer who draws up the contract so carefully that the parties never wind up in court has performed a far greater service. Like the medical profession, unfortunately, the legal profession has organized itself to give the greatest rewards to the specialists, the people who handle the biggest troubles. And in the legal profession, great rewards are also allocated to those who *make* trouble. Perhaps this is one of the reasons doctors have a higher standing than lawyers when the pollsters make their polls.

The cost of legal services, like the cost of medical services, has been rising far more rapidly than the inflation rate for anything else people buy. In part, this is because both rights and wrongs have proliferated in an increasingly complicated world, in part simply because so much of the lawyer's income is earned today on a cost-plus basis. Modern technology makes the work lawyers do for clients less expensive. Searching out relevant cases was once enormously labor-intensive despite clever indexing systems, but the same thing can now be done with the push of a button through computer services (though the skill with which the lawyer manipulates the button, asking for the right words in the right way still determines the efficiency of the search). Forms that once had to be generated by hand through analogy to what was in the files can now be pulled out of a computer's memory. Because standards of relevance can be built into the computer programs, much drudge work that once required lawyer time can now be done by non-lawyers at lower rates. But just as technology has increased medical costs by making it possible to prolong lives that must be sustained by constant intervention, the power that office automation has given to lawyers has been focused not so much on reducing costs to clients as on expanding the definitions of the work that can and should be done for them.

As a result, society has begun to demand that lawyers, like doctors, make decisions not only on the basis of the excellence of the service to be provided but also on a basis of its cost. Lawyers will be watched especially carefully because their work can impose costs not only on their clients and the courts (the patients and the hospitals) but also on their clients' antagonists—and not infrequently, through "discovery," on innocent bystanders.

Peter Kreindler, general counsel for Allied-Signal, has urged law firms to get aboard the TQM (Total Quality Management) bandwagon, which is leaving without them. Developed in the Japanese automobile industry, TQM is a system for stopping error and inefficiency at the source, rather than waiting for the defective product to reach the end of the assembly line and then get fixed (more or less) in a separate operation. It requires attention to accuracy, cost, and quality at every step—and, of course, it requires feedback from consumers of the work. Kreindler said:

> I've been in my job five and a half months now and I've met with a lot of outside counsel who regularly do work for Allied-Signal. Never once have I heard an outside counsel say, "How are we doing? What are we doing wrong? What can we do better?" What I hear in these meetings, instead, is "We do this and we do that. We have people who have expertise in this area and in those other areas. . . ."
>
> Everyone complains about the costs of litigation. I daresay that there's not a firm in this room that has analyzed where those costs are generated. . . . Document production—tremendous cost. I would put together a team and look at your process-

es for how you do document services—how you number documents, how you produce the documents—and ask yourself, "Is there any way I could do that process less expensively?" Corporations in the future are only going to want to do business with firms that are going through this kind of exercise. . . ."[3]

The Chicago firm of Winston & Strawn developed its own TQM system—called ACE for "Above Client Expectations." Partner Gary Fairchild said that he sold it by telling associates "to put themselves in the shoes of the general counsel of the client, who gets a bill at the end of the month telling him or her that the firm provided this array of services for this much money. The associate has to think like the general counsel, who, on a macro basis, is going to say, 'Okay, I spent ten thousand dollars. Has my business benefited to the tune of ten thousand dollars?' On individual projects, associates need to think in terms of 'I spent eleven hours preparing a motion. Was there that kind of value, based on my billing rate, in this kind of activity?' By and large, associates are never made to focus on these activities. . . . They tend to think in terms of 'Did the motion succeed or did the motion fail, and was it filed on a timely basis?' These are all important considerations but are only a small element of the overall success qualifications that we need to meet in order for our clients to say, 'This was a quality job done on an efficient basis for a good price.'"[4]

It will not be that easy. Carrying out cost-reduction "protocols" in legal practice will require a change of lawyer attitudes. Reporter Richard B. Schmitt of *The Wall Street Journal* made the important, ignored, unsettling point: "Nowhere is any lawyer obligated, by law or by bar association ethical standards, to represent a client in the most cost-effective way."[5]

"Unstinting advocacy" is often praised as the highest tradition of the bar. Judge Learned Hand knew better: "Adult education," he said, "means we must give up inveterate advocacy." The lawyer has a responsibility not only to his client's cause but to helping the world get its work done. On a football field, Vince Lombardi said, winning was not the most important thing, it was the only thing. That is not true in the law office, and not even always in the courtroom, though once a case has gone to trial it may be necessary to fight to the death on all fronts. Clients *will* understand this. If the client has trust in his lawyer and respect for his lawyer's judgment, you don't have a problem: He knows you won't sell him out or persuade him to take a deal that isn't in his best interests—and he'll take the deal you recommend.

Sam Benson, a thirty-five-year-old Colorado lawyer, had an article in *Newsweek* recently titled "Why I Quit Practicing Law." He wrote: "I was tired of the deceit. I was tired of the chicanery. But most of all, I was tired of the misery my job caused other people. . . . Many attorneys believe that 'zealously representing their clients' means pushing all rules of ethics and decency to the limit."[6] Less violently, Theodore B. Lee, a California lawyer and former chairman of the University of California (Boalt Hall) law school alumni association, the son of Chinese immigrants who would not have dreamed before coming to America that their children would be lawyers, has, like young Benson and many others (an estimated 40,000 of them a year), dropped out of active practice and become a businessman. He said he made the change because "business is more fun. In law, there's always a feeling of a winner and a loser; in business, your attitude is, we can make money together." That's a sad observation. It's law that should be "more fun," because the lawyer not only helps his client make money, and through the negotiating process also helps those with whom his client does business to make money—he also offers his clients a panoply of assistance ranging from their marriages to their estates to their defense against government encroachments on their lives.

This was understood a generation ago. Rather than talking about winning, lawyers then would talk of the problem of getting the client to realize when he had really won the points in dispute that mattered most to him. Lawyers tried to be dispassionate, tried to prevent their clients from becoming overinvolved in their own cases. Much of the waste motion that now makes law so expensive comes from lawyers who find it emotionally satisfying or profitable—or even (for they have been mistaught) professionally correct—to make their clients' causes their own. "What's worse than the money wasted on the court system," said Howard V. Golub, general counsel of Pacific Gas & Electric, "is the lost opportunity to find solutions. Our energies should not be spent on recreational litigation."

Arbitration and conciliation procedures of various kinds have been available to lawyers and their clients for many years. The American Arbitration Association goes back to the beginning of the century. One of the most imaginative and extensively developed of such services today is called Alternative Dispute Resolution (ADR), a project by a group of lawyers, corporate executives, and law school professors known as the Center for Public Resources, in New York. Major cases have been settled under the auspices of ADR (a recent issue of the center's newsletter, *Alternatives*, for example, reports on a $30 million antitrust case in which a claimant against Honeywell, Inc. endured an imposed three years of discovery proceedings without getting to trial—and then agreed to an ADR "minitrial" that settled the case in two days, saving the parties an estimated $3 million in legal fees). And major ADR ventures have been launched: The same issue of the newsletter announces the establishment of a "Dispute Resolution Facility" in Oakland, California, jointly sponsored by insurance companies and a consumer advocacy group, to speed the settlement of claims against insurance companies by the victims of the firestorm that devastated the hillsides of that city in October 1991.[7]

What is needed, from all lawyers, is a change of attitude, simple but subtle and profound. Today, the assumption is that everybody needs a lawyer, someone who will fight for him in a hostile world. But that is not the way the lawyer saw himself in the past. When I came to the bar, clients who had a problem took it to a lawyer, who would listen to their stories and then say, "I think I can help you, and here's what I'd like you to do"—or, unhappily, "I'm sorry, but I can't help you." "We've moved," says Stephen Gillers, "from judgment to 'Can Do.'" Nothing in the "marketing" attitude has been more demoralizing to the practice of law than the self-promotion that suggests to prospective clients that lawyers can do more for them than lawyers can, in fact, accomplish. It should be possible to inform more people that legal services are available to them without selling them the idea that everybody needs a lawyer all the time.

Down in the trenches where the solo practitioners work, many lawyers have maintained the old traditions. The *ABA Journal* for December 1992 had a revealing report on seven lawyers around the country. One of them was from Tulsa, Oklahoma; Allen Smallwood, seventeen years a lawyer on his own, said:

> I consider myself to basically be a problem-solver for individuals who find themselves in the most stressful and taxing situation they've ever been in in their lives. . . . I have advised many of my clients in civil cases not to file a lawsuit, when a lawsuit was there, simply because I felt there was a better way to resolve the matter. . . . Lawyers are trained to think there is a legal solution to every problem. . . . [Changing the public perception of lawyers] starts with lawyers acknowledging that they are not omniscient, that there are not legal solutions to every problem. I also think we could greatly enhance our reputation if there were a law requiring a certain amount of pro bono work from every lawyer.[8]

He spoke for many others, including me.

2

The senior partners of the larger firms bear a special responsibility both for the public reputation of the bar and for the acculturation of the young lawyers who come to them, the cream of the law schools, the leaders of the future. These young people are also very vulnerable, most of them arriving with tens of thousands of dollars of debt from their years as students, needing the extravagant salaries they will receive. And their view of the practice of law will be determined in large part by their early experiences in their firm.

Many of them will already have had experiences, heady but not necessarily positive, in the big firms, which recruit students from the top law schools for summer jobs at salaries that range upward of $1,000 a week. While there, they are offered a sample of the big-time lawyer's life, taken to fancy restaurants for lunches and dinner, run around town in hired cars with drivers, given outings at country clubs—and worked to weariness on research into arcane aspects of clients' cases. Most "summer interns" come out of the experience liking the firm where they worked, according to *American Lawyer*, which surveys them every year and gives the firms report cards according to how highly the young people rate their months in the office. But others are always conscious of the fact that some of the interns will and some won't be promised jobs with this firm when they finish school. A judge's clerk who had worked in such a job the summer before his third year at Northwestern Law School said he had come to the law from a stint as a Navy officer and had been on the U.S.S. *Iowa* when it was shelling the hills above Beirut during America's brief involvement in Lebanon. "The tension at [ ]," he said, naming one of the very largest Chicago law firms, "was much worse than anything I experienced on the ship off Lebanon."

Sons and daughters of friends and clients have come to me asking about summer jobs at Coudert Brothers. They have been led to believe that if you come into an office for the summer and you help that office make more money you're fulfilling your responsibilities and assuring your future. I give them different advice. I urge them to do something they will never do the rest of their lives: work in summer stock, or backpack around Europe, or be a forest ranger, or play in a dance band at a summer hotel (which is what I did as a young man), refreshing themselves, broadening their vision of the world, adding to their life experience, and also, quite possibly, widening the choice of jobs they are likely to have thereafter—because each firm rather worries about new arrivals who spent their summers at another firm and "didn't learn the way we do things around here."

I like to think that Coudert Brothers is more humane than most (the firm seems to rank better than average in most of the *American Lawyer* surveys). Coudert doesn't drive the young lawyers to bill impossible hours, and since its founding 150 years ago, the firm has been involved in pro bono work and civic and community participation by partners. As an international law firm, Coudert Brothers finds a wide range of opportunities for such help, both at home and abroad. Of course, it isn't enough. I have done my share of public service over the years, chairing various Washington and other civic organizations and the nationwide Urban Coalition, negotiating the Panama Canal treaties for President Carter, serving as chairman of the President's Commission on World Hunger, and dealing with the Israeli-Arab peace negotiations of 1979–80. But among the younger people at Coudert Brothers, as elsewhere in the legal profession these days, public service does not seem to be a prime objective. Once you were more likely to find a lawyer on the boards of the museums, symphonies, operas, hospitals, and schools; today, the calls of civic duty seem less strong in the profession.

It is of critical importance that the most successful lawyers be generous with their time, accept the obligations of community service, and recognize a lawyer's responsibility as a *citizen*. The young lawyers need to see their elders in such roles. In 1988, I gave an interview to Linda Greenhouse of *The New York Times*, about what has happened to the practice of law: "We've created the impression that it's in the large law firms that the real 'there' is there," I said, "that it's where things happen, where you develop the leadership of the bar and get your own sense of personal fulfillment. I don't believe that's true. But a lawyer who may want to devote himself or herself to human problems finds that he or she will be paid far less to do that. The quid pro quo at large firms is dazzling. We attract them, we lure them, we bribe them, and in the process we don't tell them that they're going to be giving up a decent way of life. They are so busy racking up the hours, it becomes an obsession, not a life. Because a law firm today is such a massive enterprise, you need efficiency—you need to be sure that everybody accounts for his or her time. It gets to be the bottom-line perspective that dominates the thinking. They prepare themselves to justify the money that they expect to earn. They want to be able to hit the ground running, to be able to take on a big antitrust case without wasting time. We don't give them the encouragement to become broad-based people."[9]

We do them actual damage. In 1990, Emily Mandelstam reported in *The New York Observer*: "Making money has its price. And for many attorneys, that cost includes long hours, cramped personal lives and a stressful existence that, some sources say, is leading to increased abuse of alcohol and narcotics among lawyers. Also mentioned by many sources as a long-standing problem for high-powered attorneys is a high divorce rate."[10] People's family lives are beyond the reach of good example at the office, but firms should be sensitive to juniors'— and *seniors'*—needs to stretch themselves beyond their daily jobs and encourage them to do so. They don't now.

Reform of the way law firms charge for their services is thus essential not only in client relations but also in the career development of the younger lawyers. As long as every hour devoted to community service or pro bono work is considered money out-of-pocket for the firm, there will be a tendency at least for some partners to query why the firm's money should be "wasted" in this way. Just as relations between client and firm will be on a sounder footing if fees are negotiated for the job or for representation on retainer, relations between partners and associates will be better if, like other people, young lawyers can learn to work for a salary plus bonus on the understanding that the pay covers the skilled accomplishment of tasks mostly specified in advance.

A survey by the Maryland Bar Association found the hourly fee system a particular source of resentment for young lawyers:

> It appears to be the sense of nearly all young attorneys that their emerging value as professionals should simply not be measured by so linear a yardstick as that of hours billed. . . . The utilization of a time system was thought by nearly everyone to be wholly inconsistent with a sensitive evaluation of the worth of professional services provided. . . . It was our feeling that clients perceived attorneys in the terms in which they (the attorneys) defined themselves. Because those terms are all but wholly economic, the human dimensions of the relationship were felt to be minimized.[11]

Many alternatives to the cost-plus system of billing are now available. As David Boies of Cravath, Swaine & Moore told a 1992 conference cosponsored by *American Lawyer* and the American Corporate Counsel Association:

> The purchasers of legal services are more sophisticated and they realize that there ought to be alternatives to what is, in effect, a cost-plus contract. We all know that cost-plus contracts don't work very well in the defense industry or in many other industries. One of the things such an arrangement does is that

unless you have an enormously close tie between the supplier and the purchaser of the services, it becomes almost a conflict of interest where the more time that the supplier spends, the more money the supplier makes—where obviously the purchaser of that service has an interest in having the whole thing done quickly. . . . Contingent fee arrangements, flat fees, flat fees plus a bonus, discounted rates plus a bonus, or something that's renegotiated on a regular basis during the course of a long deal or litigation—all of those are real alternatives.[12]

Or, as Carl Leonard of Morrison & Foerster said at the same conference, "We've been paid to be inefficient. It's just kind of grown and grown over a generation."[13]

Zoe Baird, who was President Clinton's first nominee for attorney general, has been a pioneer of alternative compensation systems as general counsel of Aetna Life & Casualty. She told the *American Lawyer* conference that she was focused "very much on getting outside counsel to change their practice patterns and to focus upfront with me on what it is that I'm trying to achieve, and then to devise an economic relationship that will provide the incentives for the outside counsel to achieve what it is that we're after. . . . We have in our real estate area, for example, taken the 200-some firms that handle real estate and investment matters for us and we've negotiated a different fee arrangement with each firm.[14]

Kirkland & Ellis in Chicago has been taking commercial litigation on a contingent fee basis. "Clients," said litigation partner Fred Bartlit, "like a lawyer who has as much confidence in a case as they do. Before clients took all the risk. They could lose the case and still have to pay the bill. It's healthier if the client knows we're all in it together." General Motors has made different arrangements with law firms handling its different legal problems—environmental, energy, real estate, bankruptcy workouts, product liability. Among its most common legal matters is consumer claims under car warranties, and GM has made contracts with twelve law firms in twelve regions to handle that work, all of them on a flat-fee-per-case arrangement. GM wants the cases settled quickly to avoid bad publicity, and the flat fee encourages the law firm to settle fast. An hourly fee, a spokesman for GM's general counsel said, "motivates the law firm to overwork matters, and it forces the client to be a policeman." Handling GM's warranty work, said Richard Bowman of Bowman and Brooke in Minneapolis, is also good training for young lawyers.[15]

Another arrangement that has been tried at Bank of America, EDS, and Allied-Signal, among others, is one whereby the outside law firm lends associates or even partners to the client to work in-house when the burden of work grows too great for the general counsel's office. And sometimes the general counsel's office lends people to the law firm. All such arrangements are, of course, coupled with cost control. A unique arrangement between Continental Bank and the Chicago firm of Mayer, Brown & Platt has closed down Continental's in-house law firm of seventy-five lawyers and turned over all the bank's business to outside counsel; the law firm guaranteed that the total cost of Continental's fees would be less than it had spent the year before on its legal department—and the CEO of Continental promised to be kind if the law firm at the end of the year could show it was losing money on the deal.

In his *Fables for Our Time*, in the story about the man who was as abusive to his family after he stopped drinking as he had been before (just for different reasons), James Thurber noted that you might as well fall flat on your face as lean over too far backward. These fee arrangements are not, in fact, all that they seem to be. Zoe Baird said, "The plaintiff's bar has a very close alliance with the outcome for its client, and we need to get much more of that over on our side, too." But the objection to contingent fees is that it confuses the relationship by making the lawyer a partner in his client's action—and that objection is just as strong for an arrangement with a giant insurance company (or the Federal Deposit Insurance Corporation) as it is for an arrangement with the parents of a child crippled in an automobile accident.

The shift from hourly fee to fixed fee also is not a panacea. Cravath's David Boies noted that when you move in that direction the client's "attitude flip-flops as to how many people go to a meeting or a hearing or how many depositions we take. Before, they're always asking, 'Well, are you sure you really need that person at the hearing? Do you really need another partner on the case? Couldn't you get by with one or two less associates? Do you really need all those depositions?' As soon as we flip to the flat fee, then the same client says: 'Well, couldn't you use another partner? Are you sure you're taking all the depositions that need to be taken? Is there some more research that you could do?'"[16] Concern that the law firm is running up the bill shifts rapidly to concern that the law firm is skimping on service to profit by the fee. Moreover, the corporate accountant is happy with the itemized bill, which is the sort of thing he wants from other vendors, and tends to worry about the legitimacy of the fee that comes in "for services rendered."

"All of these kinds of things, ironically," Boies added, "tend to work best when you have the closest relationship with the client . . . these kinds of arrangements require a trust and confidence that is very hard to build up . . . unless [the client] knows very well that you have a long-term interest in it and are going to be there year after year." But there is nothing ironic about this statement. It is *the* meaningful statement in the practice of business law: The client has a right to expect that you have a long-term interest in his well-being, because you are his lawyer. It should be part of the mentoring to which the young associates in a firm are entitled that they come to understand that the relationship of lawyer and business client transcends money and advocacy. It is a counseling relationship. When that is lost, much else goes with it. When that is preserved, much else comes with it.

3

At most a third—and in many law schools, only a tenth—of the third-year students do the "legal clinic" that brings aspiring lawyers into contact with real clients—poor people who have trouble with the landlord, the bank, the welfare office. That could change tomorrow, if the hiring partners for the big firms let it be known that experience in the clinic would count significantly in their decision as to whether or not they want to hire someone as an associate. Big firms can and should organize themselves to take care of people in need, and they should play a part in the justice system. The senior partners themselves should set an example by taking some time every year to work on community causes or pro bono cases. This should not be seen as a bighearted firm display-ing its charity—it's something that goes with being a lawyer. The senior partners have to make it clear that time put into pro bono work, and the quality of that work, will be taken into full consid-eration in the ultimate decision as to whether or not someone will be made a partner in the firm.

The juniors in the large firms watch carefully to see whether or not the seniors are involved in public service. In the end, if we want our young lawyers to be better people (and most se-nior partners say they do, say they are shocked by how merce-nary the incoming classes are) we should make sure the seniors themselves are better people. My own feeling is that the young people still come out of law school wanting to be helpful, then go into the law firms and see how the "successful" lawyers op-erate. Their criteria become how many points did you score, how much money do you make, what sort of house do you live in. And because the firms want them to do so, they become "splinter specialists," putting their lives into a single corner of the law.

Large law firms can easily release half a dozen young associ-ates for several weeks at a time to work on the problems of peo-ple who couldn't hire any lawyer. They can maintain someone in the firm to handle the intake to this part of the practice, an important contribution because only a minor fraction of the people in a low-income neighborhood who walk in the door looking for a free lawyer can, in fact, be accepted as clients, and the choice of these potential clients requires expertise. In the absence of skilled assistance at the intake, the new young lawyers would need all their time to decide whether to take case A rather than case B.

There are, unquestionably, islands of light. In New York, more than forty of the city's larger law firms—firms such as Wachtell Lipton, Sherman & Sterling, and Weil, Gotshal & Manges—participate in the work of New York Lawyers for the Public Interest, dealing with employment discrimination cases, the treatment of the mentally ill, the legal problems of neighborhood charities, and the like.[17] In Washington, Hogan & Hartson has a branch of the firm devoted to pro bono work. Washington's Arnold & Porter reports that 203 of its 333 lawyers were involved in pro bono work in 1992, with a remarkable average of 220 hours per lawyer in pro bono work. Cleary Gottlieb and Willkie Farr in New York and Covington & Burling in Washington have contributed associates to man offices for the government's Legal Services Corporation; Bingham, Dana & Gould in Boston has been "lending" attorneys to Greater Boston Legal Services since the program was new, in 1969. From 1976 to 1988, Baltimore's Piper & Marbury had a joint program with the University of Maryland Law School to run a civil legal aid office from a building near the law school. In 1987, Latham & Watkins in Los Angeles got almost 200 of its 480 lawyers involved in one or another of 107 pro bono cases.[18] Perkins Coie, a Seattle firm with 300 attorneys, offers associates a six-month onetime "fellowship" to do pro bono work, and gives partners a four-month sabbatical every half-dozen years, expecting many of them to use the time for pro bono activities.[19]

In 1981, in remarks at a bar association seminar, Judge

Rifkind detailed the pro bono work at Paul Weiss in the preceding fourteen months:

> We undertook six cases in which we defended the City of New York in contract and tort claims. . . . We accepted three appeals under the District Attorney's voluntary appeals program. We handled three assignments for artists and performers, referred to us by the Volunteer Lawyers for the Arts. From the New York Lawyers for the Public Interest, we received two matters, including a class action, representing the inmates at Bedford Hills Correctional Facility for Women. We acted for indigent complainants in two Title VII actions. We served charitable institutions in twelve assorted controversies. On behalf of the NAACP, we represented two defendants sentenced to death by the courts of Texas. We prosecuted two criminal appeals in the same area. We represented Augusto Zimmerman, a jailed Peruvian journalist. We challenged the validity of the prisoner exchange treaty with Mexico on behalf of one Pedro Rogato, a U.S. citizen jailed in Danbury under that program. By an amicus brief, we supported the attorney-client privilege in the Upjohn case. Similarly, we participated in New York's challenge to the 1980 census and in the test of the constitutionality of the work requirement for welfare recipients.[20]

Sullivan & Cromwell has found that pro bono work on the civil side of legal aid cases is excellent training for young litigators, better than the warranties work for automobile companies it has replaced, the clients having taken such work in-house. Each year, moreover, the firm takes one of its most promising recruits, who has spent his first year out of law school as a judge's clerk, and assigns him to pro bono for his first year with the firm—at the full first-year salary, as a way *into* the firm, not as a way out of it. Robert MacCrate reports that the experiences the young pro bono lawyers bring back to Sullivan & Cromwell from their assignments have changed even senior partners' views of the practice of law and what it involves, to the benefit of all.

In 1989, Hunton & Williams of Richmond, Virginia, a law firm with more than 460 lawyers (formerly Supreme Court Justice Lewis Powell's firm), opened a separate office in a low-income neighborhood of the city, with 25 of its 460 lawyers volunteering to take turns helping those who lived in that neighborhood. The firm researched the maximum income Richmond's legal aid had set for its beneficiaries ($8,275 for a single person, up to $16,750 for a family of four), and defined its client constituency as those whose income ran from that figure up to about double that amount. Partner George H. Hettrick wrote in an article for the *ABA Journal*:

> We settled upon three areas of practice that many attorneys try to avoid, largely because these types of cases usually do not generate enough income:
>
> • Housing and real estate (landlord-tenant, simple deeds, and closings for first-time home buyers);
>
> • Family law (no-fault divorce, child custody, and child support); and
>
> • Guardianships for the elderly and minors.[21]

In the first year of the office, ten of the volunteer lawyers agreed to put in one hundred hours each working in the branch office in the slum, and the firm assigned a veteran partner to be in charge with a veteran secretary-receptionist who disposed of a high fraction of the cases that came in the door. By the third year, the firm had twenty-five enthusiastic volunteers from the group of younger associates. The office was open from 11:00 A.M. to 7:00 P.M. weekdays and 9:00 A.M. to noon on Saturdays. Anyone whose case was accepted was charged $50, by agreement with the lawyers already in the neighborhood, whose support Hunton & Williams sought and, somewhat surprisingly, received. "We now know," Hettrick concluded, "that [this office] should continue indefinitely. The office not only helps needy citizens get legal services and advice, but *it also enriches the professional experience and worth of the lawyers who give freely of their legal talent.*"[22]

Those who devote themselves full-time to legal work for poor people may gravitate to politically motivated lawsuits, which upsets their elders, sometimes correctly. But the young lawyers who take much lower incomes than they could make elsewhere to work for cause-oriented organizations such as the Lawyers Committee for Civil Rights Under Law should be and are admired even by their antagonists in the courtroom. The dimensions of the injustice to be fought is always a significant question. Arturo J. Gonzalez of the large San Francisco firm of Morrison & Foerster, for example, did a service for children throughout California when he put together a pro bono team of five in his firm to keep the state from closing the schools and punishing all the children in the lower-middle-income suburb of Richmond because the school district was bankrupt.

The reason pro bono is both the challenge and the test is not subtle in the least. If the legal profession does not stand for equal justice under law, then it is hard to see what it does stand for. And if the contention is that equal justice can be achieved without lawyers, it is hard to see why lawyers should enjoy the special rights and privileges and status that society awards them.

CHAPTER 10

WHAT SOCIETY CAN DO

1

In a real sense, law is what America is all about. In no other
system of government do the law and the courts play so
large a role, no other country has so many lawyers, and in
no other country have lawyers been so influential. Elsewhere
the totem of the society is a crown or a mausoleum or a spot of
sacred land; in the United States, it is a document under glass
at the National Archives. Alexis de Tocqueville wrote in the
1830s:

> In America . . . the lawyers form the political upper class and
> the most intellectual section of society. . . . If you ask me where
> the American aristocracy is found, I have no hesitation in an-
> swering that it is not among the rich, who have no common link
> uniting them. It is at the bar or the bench that the American
> aristocracy is found. . . . When the American people let them-
> selves get intoxicated by their passions or carried away by their
> ideas, the lawyers apply an almost invisible brake which slows
> them down. . . . Lawyers, forming the only enlightened class not

distrusted by the people, are naturally called on to fill most public functions.[1]

We have not relied on popular assemblies to vindicate the rights of the citizen; we have put our faith in documents and courts and lawyers.

The most frightening measure of what the legal profession has lost is that most Americans do not even remember the trust this society once placed in its lawyers. If a new Alexis de Tocqueville came to America today to study its laws and customs, he could never come up with the idea that the lawyers were the country's natural aristocracy. Lawyers blame the law schools, the law schools blame the lawyers, the judges blame the lawyers, the lawyers say the clients (or their sense that they must go the limit for their clients) made them do it. Others blame the culture: It's a jungle out there; ethical standards are down wherever you look. Wall Street brokers who hold themselves out as agents trade for their own account to their clients' disadvantage. Even the clergy seem more prone to scandal than they used to be. Why single out lawyers for the loss of ethical fiber at a time when ethical decline is so widespread?

Because lawyers are supposed to be the custodians of a community's legal and ethical sense. And if the source of our failures lies in the defects of our education, one of the causes must be our neglect of the law as a subject for study in our schools and colleges. The loss of self-respect in the profession and the loss of public respect both reflect the failure of the schools to convey to the young what law and lawyers have meant in the history of this country. Not enough is expected of today's lawyers by the lay public or within the profession itself, because not enough is known about how lawyers achieved their privileged position. Properly understood, law is *fundamental*. Archibald MacLeish, who was a lawyer as well as a poet, wrote that law tries "to impose *on* the disorder of experience the *kind* of order which enables us to live *with* the disorder of experience."[2] If the profession wishes to retain its privileges, lawyers above all others must understand why they have been granted exclusive access to the judicial processes of government and why the public has the right to expect that they will be vigilant not only in the interests of their client but also for the rule of law that protects us all.

Rich in humanity, controversy, and significance, the history of American law could be a bright, continuous thread through the sixteen years of elementary, secondary, and college education—if only we had the wit to pick it up. The danger in this course is that we will reduce our tapestries to threads only, teach homilies rather than history, and fail to convey the truth that the principles we are teaching are not in themselves the purpose of the legal enterprise. Humanity is not twisted to serve the goals of law; law grows out of the experience of man. The rules we cherish, while ultimately enshrined in documents, are rooted in the examination of cases, growing from lawyers' service to individual clients. "Let me speak feelingly as a lawyer," Charles Curtis wrote in 1959, "I hope the [Supreme] Court will never quite lose all interest in private litigation. Let it now and then burn a candle to the Goddess by deciding disputes that are important only to the parties. Let the Court never lose the judicial touch! Justice, as well as politics, has its grass roots."[3] We have a complicated story to tell, and we must tell it honestly.

2

History is not always pretty, and it does not teach just one lesson. Our goal must be that Americans come to understand the tone and climate of our legal rules of fair play, the reasons self-incrimination under oath is odious, the difference between evidence one may feel is good enough for deciding whether to buy this car rather than that one and evidence that is really good enough to place the weight of law on the side of one party to a dispute rather than the other: We wish a community devoted to justice, and we need citizens who know they need law to guide perception. This means we need an understanding of the forces that have shaped and nourished our legal system.

The danger of an overcommercialized law has been with us from the beginning. Law was a good living in the American colonies. In a letter in 1819 to his then and former friend Thomas Jefferson (they had written the Declaration of Independence together, with Benjamin Franklin), John Adams, nearing ninety, wrote that through a book he was reliving the 1760s, "when I was digging in the Mines, as a Barrister at Law, for Silver and gold, in the Town of Boston; and got as much of the shining dross for my labour as my Utmost Avarice at that time craved."[4] In Virginia in 1750, Richard Hofstadter noted, "the practice of law was a steady and valuable source of cash in itself, but, more important, led to personal connections and to knowledge of business trends and conditions, of the drift of the land market, all of which could be converted to speculative profits."[5]

In the early nineteenth century, under the intellectual leadership of Justice Joseph Story, the Supreme Court gave expression to Ralph Waldo Emerson's individualism and the supremacy of contract in human relations. David Brion Davis of Yale, describing the period from 1820 to 1860, wrote:

> The legal profession won prestige as America's dominant profession because it could make claim to disinterested reason and yet resolve disputes in ways that provided security and predictability to men who possessed or were acquiring power. . . . The growing emphasis on contracts became the key to promoting "modern" social relations built on individual responsibility. According to Theophilus Parsons [one of the earliest Harvard law professors], who helped to make contracts the cutting edge

of American jurisprudence, "out of contracts, expressed or implied, declared or understood, grow all rights, all duties, all
obligations, and all law. . . ." The American common law rein-
forced the one supreme social rule: promises freely made could
not be broken without legal penalty. . . . Each individual carried
an unmitigated burden of freedom, the burden of being responsible for his own fate.[6]

As the century moved toward its twilight, the doctrine of "liberty of contract" gave the courts reason to outlaw as unconstitutional many of the efforts by state and local governments to
redress the balance between large corporate organizations and
their employees or their consumers.

As noted earlier, the first "large" law firms served the corporate clients of the late nineteenth and earlier twentieth centuries by securing injunctions against labor unions and state
governments (the first labor injunction was not issued in the
United States until 1888, but by 1921 Chief Justice Taft was describing injunctions against striking workers as an employer's
"fundamental right").[7] The firms grew also by defending the
"trusts" the Rockefellers and Morgans, Gradys, Armours, In-
sulls, and Schweringens had created to eliminate competitors.
The distinguished historian Daniel Boorstin credits the first
trust to Samuel C. T. Dodd, a Pennsylvania lawyer from the
first oil state, who, after serving as a delegate to the Pennsylvania Constitutional Convention, became a lawyer for the Standard Oil Company and "the most ingenious legal metaphysi-
cian of the age." He was not, however, someone who found in
his income the measurement of his worth: "In order to give his
client Rockefeller the most detached and reliable legal advice,"
Boorstin reports, "he actually refused to accept stock in the
company."[8]

And there was always another strain to the emphasis on contract (and thus, necessarily, on lawyers): Contracts limited not
only the powers of purchaser and seller, landlord and tenant,

but also the authority of governments. In the eighteenth century, when the time came for the merchants of Boston to fight the Stamp Tax, they had on their side the argument that the Royal Charter establishing the Massachusetts Bay Colony, drawn up by the barrister John White in 1638, prevented Parliament from imposing a tax on the people of the colony.[9] The twentieth-century Scottish political scientist Charles McIlwain wrote that this commercial charter "approximated a popular constitution more closely than any other instrument of government in actual use up to that time in America or elsewhere in modern times."[10] Thus there was always a *document* between the American colonial and those who governed him. When the Sons of Liberty rose in New York, General Thomas Gage wrote to London: "The Lawyers are the Source from whence the Clamors have flowed in every Province. In this Province nothing Publick is transacted without them."[11] Adams may have made money in the mines of law, but he also saw a greater treasure there: "You and I," he wrote to a friend in 1776, "have been sent into life at a time when the greatest lawgivers of antiquity would have wished to live."[12]

Not the least of the objections to the Confederation that loosely linked the states that had won the Revolution was its inability to control the state legislatures that daily changed the law. "It will be of little avail to the people that the laws are made by men of their own choice," James Madison wrote in *Federalist* #62, "if the laws be so voluminous that they cannot be read, or so incoherent that they cannot be understood; if they be repealed or revised before they are promulged, or undergo such incessant changes that no man who knows what the law is today can guess what it will be tomorrow. . . . What prudent merchant will hazard his fortunes in any new branch of commerce, when he knows not but that his plans may be rendered unlawful before they can be executed?"[13] In Germantown, Pennsylvania, in 1787, as the Constitutional Convention met in nearby Philadelphia, a group of local businessmen announced they had banded together in an agreement to arbitrate all local disputes, "to prevent the people from wasting their property by the chicane of the law."[14] The people needed a contract with their government.

For Thomas Jefferson, who was a lawyer and a great drafter of documents, that contract could not be written by a cadre of judges who sustained the glories of the common law, but required stable codification to make sure that the will of the publicly elected legislatures remained in control. "Relieve the judges from the rigour of text law," he wrote in 1785, "and permit them, with pretorian discretion, to wander into its equity, and the whole legal system becomes uncertain."[15] The compromise, in the end, would be the Constitution, seen as a contract between the governors and the people themselves, which could not be changed by the legislatures or the courts but only through an elaborate consultative process.

Part of that Constitution asserted the gains in personal liberty that Englishmen had achieved from King John's Magna Carta to the settlement wrung from William and Mary when the Parliament evicted James II in the Glorious Revolution of 1688. The rebellious colonialists knew from John Locke and the historians of the Glorious Revolution about the horrors of the Elizabethan Star Chamber that had condemned Sir Walter Raleigh and the Earl of Essex without hearing any defense for them, and about the Bills of Attainder by which an unchecked Parliament had sent men to their death by legislative act—and they wanted to make sure the government they were forming could never have such powers. The writ of habeas corpus, which the widely read English commentator William Blackstone had called "the Bulwark of the [unwritten] British constitution" was enshrined in fundamental law, assuring that anyone arrested by the authorities would have his day in court, except at times of "rebellion or invasion." The government of the United States was constitutionally prohibited from passing a bill of attainder or any ex post facto law, making any past conduct illegal or any citizen a criminal by legislative action. No religious test could be "required as a qualification to any office or public trust." Treason could be charged and proved on the testimony of two witnesses to the same overt act or a confession in open court, but "no attainder of treason shall work corruption of blood"—that is, the children of the traitor could not be punished for his treason. Everyone accused of a federal crime was guaranteed a trial by jury in his own state.[16]

Even so, many found the Constitution as written in 1787 insufficient protection for the people and demanded a Bill of Rights. Alexander Hamilton fought back with the argument that the government to be established by the Constitution got all its powers only from that contract—and nothing in the Constitution empowered the government to interfere with the rights of speech, religion, assembly, access to counsel, freedom from search and from self-incrimination. "Why," Hamilton asked, "declare that things shall not be done which there is no power to do?"[17] Answering the objection that the very act of denying the government a power implied that it would have that power without the denial, the authors of the Bill of Rights added two amendments reserving to the states and to the people all powers not enumerated as those of the federal government.

As extended after the Civil War by amendments to the Constitution, the Bill of Rights covers virtually all governmental actions. Without sacrificing historical richness, the subject can be brought to date immediately in a classroom by focusing on the interests of today's students and helping them see how interpretations of the Bill of Rights by lawyers will determine students' freedom to write an uncensored article in their school newspaper or the validity of a requirement that a girl tell her parents before she can authorize a doctor to perform an abortion.

Most Americans—young and old alike—still do not understand, any more than their ancestors did, why such decisions are left to courts rather than to popular opinion, or by what mechanism they have come to reside in the courts. It is only through history that one learns how the creation of a constitution as a fundamental law invited a doctrine of judicial review to interpret that law, even to the point of overruling less fundamental law, and thus to a central role for lawyers. Madison, more than any other single person the author of the Constitution and the Bill of Rights, did not grasp any more than today's high school junior why the courts should have such power. To let judges "set aside the law," he said in 1788, "makes the Judiciary Department paramount in fact to the Legislature, which was never intended and can never be proper."[18] With a century's additional experience behind him, Judge Learned Hand (who agreed that the authors of the Constitution had never intended to give courts the power to overturn an Act of Congress) argued in response to Madison that a sovereign court was unavoidable in a government based on the separation of powers: "Without some arbiter whose decision should be final, the whole system would have collapsed."[19]

The man who made the history and placed law at the center of the American agenda was Chief Justice John Marshall, Thomas Jefferson's great enemy, who had led a jury to acquit Aaron Burr of treason and whom Jefferson suspected of wishing to read Christianity into a constitution that prohibited the establishment of religion. ("Our cunning Chief Justice would . . . find as many sophisms to twist [religion] out of the general terms of our Declarations of rights," Jefferson wrote bitterly, ". . . as he did to twist Burr's neck out of the halter of treason.")[20] Schoolchildren should know about John Marshall, for what he said and did has much to do with the lives they will lead. The occasion for Marshall's triumph, *Marbury* v. *Madison*, moreover, was interestingly ingenious, worthy of the highest order of legal imagination. Just before leaving office, President Adams and the lame-duck Federalist Congress passed the Judiciary Act of 1801, which permitted them to appoint a large number of their friends to new jobs. (A few years later, while president, Jefferson wrote to Abigail Adams in a correspondence begun with her condolence on the death of his daughter: "One act of Mr. Adams's life, and one only, ever gave me a moment's personal displeasure. I did consider his last appointments to office as personally unkind. They were from among my most ardent political enemies, from whom no faithful cooperation could ever be expected, and laid me under the embarrassment of acting throo' men whose views were to defeat mine; or to encounter the odium of putting others in their places.")[21]

Jefferson and his surging Republicans thereupon repealed the act and fired all the new appointees (including, though Jefferson did not know about it until some years later, the Adamses' son and future president, John Quincy). The displaced judges and marshals sued for their jobs, and the case came before John Marshall's Supreme Court, which ruled that sections of the Judiciary Act of 1798 were unconstitutional, thereby knocking out the 1801 Act, which was an amendment of existing law. Jefferson had the political victory—his people, not Adams's people, kept the jobs—but Marshall had the legal precedent that the Supreme Court could invalidate an Act of Congress. More than half a century passed before another federal law was invalidated—as it happened, by Chief Justice Roger Taney in the Dred Scott case of 1856, which greased the nation's path to Civil War by tossing out the thirty-six-year-old Missouri Compromise and pronouncing that anyone born a slave remained a slave for life unless manumitted by his owner, whether he lived in a "free" or a "slave" state.

Meanwhile, court systems and bodies of law grew up separately in the sovereign states, for the subjects of most lawsuits—personal injury caused by negligence, divorces, wills and estates, ownership of property, the rights and responsibilities of corporations, business loans and foreclosures, crimes—were determined by state rather than federal legislation and by state court decisions rather than the actions of federal courts. Here, too, much of the political life of the community revolved around lawyers and lawsuits, because in the United States only the courts *must* reach decisions; the president and the Congress can always blame each other and do nothing, but a judge is confronted with real people who have a real dispute he must resolve. As a result, Harvard law professor Henry Hart liked to point out, people necessarily go first to the courts when they feel that "there oughta be a law," and legislatures tend to act only after the courts have taken a crack at the problem.

State court judges such as Lemuel Shaw in Massachusetts, Benjamin Cardozo in New York, and Roger Traynor in California influenced the course of their times much more than many of the secretaries of state and congressmen and governors whose names are in the textbooks. *McPherson* v. *Buick*, the great case in which Judge Cardozo ruled that manufacturers could be liable for product defects even though the victim of the defect had never done business with them, ranks not far behind Social Security, deposit insurance, and FHA mortgages as a creator of the world we live in, but it is not even mentioned in, for example, *The Great Republic*, the most extensive of the college American history textbooks (about 1,300 pages long).

3

Twenty years ago, Daniel Boorstin, later to be Librarian of Congress, wrote: "American legal history, to the shame of the well-paid and luxuriously equipped American legal profession, remains one of the worst-chronicled of important American institutions."[22] Nothing has been published in the intervening two decades to change that judgment. Yet the tale is one of triumphs for the human spirit—the school desegregation cases, the decisions pronouncing "freedom for the thought we hate," the assurance of the right of counsel to defendants in criminal cases, the widening definitions of the "due process of law" governments must follow before seizing persons or property. And the tale is also one of disasters—judges assessing damages against striking workers who organized a consumer boycott of a hat manufacturer in Danbury, Connecticut; refusing to permit states to regulate the hours of employment, even of women and children; approving the wartime incarceration of native-born Americans of Japanese descent who had done nothing wrong. It is odd that a profession that rests so much of its work on already decided cases puts so little care and attention into cultivating a historical sense among its members—and cares not at all how the history of the law is perceived by the general public from which the courts especially derive their authority. "Law is probably the most neglected phase of our culture in the liberal arts curriculum," wrote Professor Paul Freund. "Yet the legal profession . . . functions in a lay society that does, and should, judge its performance. If this judgment is to be effective, it must be based on knowledge of the role of the profession and the character of its thinking."

There is much to be done here by historians, lawyers, and teachers working together. We teach American history in the fifth, eighth, and eleventh grades in our school systems, and most college students take a year's course in the subject. At each level, appropriate to the sophistication of the student, we could have pedagogical packages to be presented as a self-contained unit of work in a course—pamphlets, visual aids, suggested assignments that teach the role of law and lawyers in the political, economic, and social development of the country. The units should be lively, each built around important historical figures whose minds and contributions would be better understood in the light of this story, and they would illuminate a real issue significant in American history.

An obvious possible educational unit could be made from *Marbury* v. *Madison*, with the involvement of John Adams and

Thomas Jefferson, and the issue of the role of the courts in American governance. Another could start from *McPherson* v. *Buick*, for the Ralph Nader phenomenon, much product-safety legislation, and a good piece of our environmental law rest intellectually on Cardozo's always grave and prescient analysis.

There also springs to mind for purposes of teaching law with history the case of *Smith* v. *Allwright*, the case from the 1940s in which the Supreme Court invalidated the all-white primary that had become the significant election in the South. It should be taught for the importance of the issue (a majority of adult Americans, let alone schoolchildren, will be amazed to learn that within the memory of men still living the political parties in the Southern states were allowed to bar "colored people" from voting in their primaries), for the fact that it was one of the earliest cases argued before the Court by the future Justice Thurgood Marshall—acclaimed by Harvard Law professor Laurence Tribe as "the greatest lawyer in the 20th century"[23]— and for the extraordinary human document of Justice Robert Jackson's letter to Chief Justice Harlan Fiske Stone, urging that the writing of the opinion be assigned to Justice Stanley Reed rather than Justice Felix Frankfurter: "It is a delicate matter," Jackson wrote. "We must reverse a recent, well-considered and unanimous decision. We deny the entire South the right to a white primary, which is one of its most cherished rights. It seems to me very important that the strength which an all but unanimous decision would have may be greatly weakened if the voice that utters it is one that may grate on Southern sensibilities. Mr. Justice Frankfurter unites in a rare degree factors which unhappily excite prejudice. In the first place, he is a Jew. In the second place, he is from New England, the seat of the abolition movement. In the third place, he has not been thought of as a person particularly sympathetic with the Democratic party in the past. . . . With all humility I suggest that the Court's decision, bound to arouse bitter resentment, will be much less apt to stir ugly reactions if the news that the white primary is dead, is broken to it, if possible, by a Southerner who has been a Democrat and is not a member of one of the minorities which stir prejudices kindred to those against the Negro."[24] Chief Justice Stone reassigned the writing of the opinion of the Court to Justice Stanley Reed.

Schools now teach about the civil rights movement and touch on the role of law and lawyers and courts in improving the match between avowed American beliefs and American performance. But the teaching is shallow indeed next to what could be accomplished by real work on *Smith* v. *Allwright*.

The Pentagon Papers case from the 1970s contains no small part of the agony of the Vietnam War, a major statement of the right of the press to publish without prior censorship—and an unusual illustration of a lawyer refusing a case because of his disapproval of the client's wishes, the firm of Debevoise Plimpton having decided that *The New York Times* should *not* publish the documents and that therefore they did not wish to be involved in the case. It should not be disposed of in a sentence, as it is now in even the best of our textbooks; it should be part of what students take from their high school education.

Others will surely have other ideas for the historical legal material to be taught in our schools; certainly, the list of possibilities is enormous. This is, in any event, a task for a committee, not for an author, because legal, historical, and teaching perspectives are all required to develop teaching units. The aim should be to provide a menu for choice rather than a fixed curriculum, to supplement and deepen our existing history courses rather than to replace them. Different individuals would have different approaches to the subject: It is here, especially in the preparation of the college-level course, that the Critical Legal Studies group and the Natural Law professors would make their most useful input into education. In the end, schools and colleges would be offered a wide variety of teaching units and could make their own choice. It would not be expected that any school would teach all the units that would be developed or adopt one political point of view. Geographical variety should also be encouraged. State bar associations and local historical societies, working with local teacher groups, should develop separate units for the schools of their states.

The development of educational units in the law and legal history should not be done on the cheap. The nation's most accomplished lawyers should be involved, and the historians should seize the opportunity to steer some of their best graduate students to dissertation subjects in this area. Master teachers should be released from other teaching duties for substantial periods of time to develop and try out "cases" for the course. Teacher-training programs should give thousands of teachers monthlong summer courses at university-based law schools. Talented filmmakers should produce fifteen-minute tapes, perhaps dramatizing some aspect of a case or presenting a Socratic discussion of a major point about which reasonable people can disagree. Sophisticated testing should be done to find out what students actually learned from the units, not just whether they learned what the designers of the program hoped to teach.

Of all the projects to bolster our faltering legal system, this is one that could be put on the rails most quickly. Within three years, we could be introducing millions of students to effective educational materials that would make better citizens of all of them—and better lawyers of those who move on to study law. Before we can have respect for lawyers, we must first have respect for the law.

4

A community better educated in the law might also be willing to spend more money on it. Some of the disrespect into which the law has fallen results, as was noted in chapter 8, from the shabby surroundings of what was once described as "majesty." The court system—judges, prosecutors, public defenders, courthouse operation and maintenance—takes only three-fifths of 1 percent of all government expenditures in the United States. In 1991, 25 states actually reduced their budgets for the courts; in 1992, 35 states reduced their budgets. Judges still have perquisites, some of them highly valued. A judge is addressed as "Your Honor." In the courtroom everyone stands when the bailiff announces the entrance of the judge. But everyone professionally involved with the law knows that the docket she has been assigned by the court administrators and the chief judge leaves her fearfully little time for contemplation and analysis. A generation ago, J. Kenneth Galbraith wrote acidly of a society that coupled private affluence with public squalor. Much of his indictment was unfair: From 1950 to 1980, we spent immense amounts of money on schools, universities, hospitals, and parks—but not on courts and judges; with reference to the justice system, he was and is absolutely right. There has been money for jails and police, but not for courts and judges. And the caseload keeps growing every year.

Many of the reforms suggested in these pages will require additional public expenditure on the judiciary or something like the judiciary. Learned Hand said, "If we are to keep our democracy, there must be one commandment: Thou shall not ration justice."[25] A combination of pro bono work, pro bono levies, and government appropriation to public defender and legal services offices may assure that people get to tell their troubles to lawyers, and most of what those lawyers do—like most of what lawyers do for people who can pay their own bills—should take the form of counseling rather than litigating. But without appropriate fora where advocacy can be heard when necessary, the rationing remains: Justice delayed is justice denied. It may well be that the full panoply of judges and courtrooms will rarely be required to gain many of the rights the poor are now unable to assert, that administrative tribunals, mediators, and arbitrators in some form of alternative dispute resolution will serve us better than courts—and not only in cases involving the less-than-wealthy. But such mechanisms also need some housing, and some staffing, and some means of communicating the results.

If judges are to be asked to examine the complaints before they empower a lawyer to subpoena his client's foes, if they are to schedule and police discovery, the taxpayers will have to employ more judges, pay them better, and make their work surroundings more attractive. We must also reinforce professional perception of the role of the judge in doing justice. Learned Hand said a judge had "a delectable calling. For when the case is all in, and the turmoil stops, and after he is left alone, things begin to take form. From his pen or in his head, slowly or swiftly as his capacities admit, out of the murk the pattern emerges, his pattern, the expression of what he has seen and what he has therefore made, the impress of his self upon the not-self, upon the hitherto formless material of which he was once but a part and over which he has now become the master. That is a pleasure which nobody who has felt it will be likely to underrate."[26]

The quality of the judge's *job* has deteriorated in the forty years since Hand spoke that appreciation of his life. If the trial judge continues to be merely a bystander in the battle before him—and if the jury pool is picked over by legal psychologists looking not for truth-seekers but for people predisposed on one side or the other—there isn't much delectation left.

5

One of the most important favors the legislators who represent the public could do for the law lies in an area where the legal profession could launch the vessel and work the laboring oar. What President Clinton blasted lawyers for in his 1993 State of the Union message was the fact that more than three quarters of the money put aside to clean up toxic waste sites under the so-called Superfund law has been paid not for environmental safety but for lawyers and litigation costs. It is arguable that this is evidence against lawyers, much as absconding with a wallet left on the sidewalk is evidence adverse to the character of the man who does it; but I suggest that the problem here is one of finders/keepers, not one of moral turpitude. If Congress passes a law so dense and contradictory and ill-drawn that it invites lawyers to make fortunes pettifogging it, the real blame may lie not with the ethical standards of the legal profession or with the individual lawyers who walk away with what they found but with those who wrote and read and passed the law.

The late Reed Dickerson of Indiana University School of Law devoted most of his life to training legislative draftsmen and worked with the House Legislative Counsel in Washington as well as a number of state legislatures to demonstrate the difference between safe and dangerous language in terms of the disputes likely to result from the use of language. Unfortunately, we have permitted the legislative process in the United States to become so much one of compromise and consensus that people on both sides of a legislative issue are often willing to write deliberately vague language and leave the question of what it means to determination by the courts. As the director of the House Legislative Counsel's office once said when challenged to state the intention of Congress in a certain clause of a recent bill, "Oh, that was one of those times when it was possible to get agreement on language but not on substance."

If the motto of American government in the 1990s is "change," we must change such unworthy work at the heart of our governance. Our courts today are intolerably clogged. The backlog for civil cases in Chicago is now eight years, and a judge in New Orleans has declared that the entire court system of Louisiana is unconstitutional because delays prevent people from getting a fair trial.[27] The problem is not, as many people think, malpractice and product liability suits (900,000 in 1991); it is commercial litigation (1,400,000 cases in 1991).[28] The congestion has many causes, not least some lawyers' and judges' weak commitment to the task of getting the business done. But the taproot of much of this litigation is bad legislative drafting.

Nearly twenty years ago, Chief Justice Warren Burger called for legislation that would establish a "Judicial Impact Statement" similar to the "Environmental Impact Statement" that would be required before Congress passed a law or an administrative agency imposed a regulation. It is a viable idea. The American Law Institute, a self-perpetuating group of law professors and distinguished lawyers, meets annually to try to codify the judge-written common law and statutory interpretation that still govern our lives at least as much as any laws passed by elected legislatures. Nationally, in each state, and for each of the half-dozen most significant regulation-writing agencies, a tripartite body—judges, practitioners, law professors—could, for example, be formed under the aegis of the ALI to examine the language of the laws Congress and the state legislatures respectively are about to enact and to warn the legislators of ambiguities and invitations to sue contained in their bills.

Such a body would have to command the services of a sizable full-time staff, and its function would be to alert, not to decide. Nevertheless, the members of the committee would have to commit a number of hours a week during the seasons when legislatures give birth to laws—and they would have to be Vestal Virgins, pledged to renounce their own views and the interests of their clients and to look at proposed legislation from a strictly technocratic point of view. Service on such a body should be a great honor for any lawyer, a testimony to his colleagues' respect for his or her mind and probity.

The members of such a review committee could perhaps be appointed by the chief judge of the highest court in the juris-

diction with the presiding officers of the houses of the legislature. The legislatures would have to promise a delay of at least
a week between the conference agreement on the text of a bill
and the vote on it, to give the committee and its staff time to
read and parse the language. Over time, a significant part of
this job could probably be reduced to computer programs, but
much of it would require the judgment of experienced lawyers.
Reviewing legislation to judge its potential for creating court-
clogging litigation would take more time than anyone should be
asked to give pro bono and would overburden judges who were
not relieved of much of their normal caseload by the administrators of the courts. Arrangements would have to be made to
pay both the staff and the committee well for their time, and
the terms of the committee members should probably be quite
short, two years at the most.

This degree of elaboration might not be necessary, and certainly could not be part of the project from its beginning. Here
is an excellent place to use the possibility of the states as laboratories opened by the Constitution. In many states, legislative
drafting is primitive, dependent on volunteers from the private
sector who have their own agendas to serve. The creation of an
external, highly qualified office dedicated to reducing the litigation costs imposed by new legislation would be welcomed
in many states, and if the desired goals were achieved, the
demonstration effect might be considerable. At the least, a
functioning office for the avoidance of litigation costs would
permit lawyers to demonstrate why they were once considered
a democratic aristocracy.

CHAPTER 11

THE PROFESSION THAT CAN SAY NO

1

A few years ago, the chairman of Sony was listed as co-author of a book called *The Japan That Can Say No*, asking the Japanese to throw off what was considered to be the "domination" of the United States (where, incidentally, Sony made most of its money). The leaders of the law in America, historically, have been men who could say no, who preserved their autonomy, who served their clients with their hearts, their skills, their advice, their advocacy, and their friendship—but not with their souls or with their citizenship.

Not many years ago, the name of a businessman's lawyer, like the name of his banker, was a significant recommendation when the company sought to open accounts with suppliers or establish relations with large customers. Law firms were jealous of their reputation and would not risk having their name associated with shady operators. To some extent, acceptance as a client by a very prestigious law firm meant acceptance into a club, and the reason a firm took a client might sometimes be not his own reputation as a businessman or a citizen but his social status. But that was all the more reason for an entrepreneur to seek this seal of acceptance. And whatever the discrimination that lay behind the action of a leading firm in accepting or refusing a prospective client, the principle was clear—and practical, too: Over time, a law practice will be more stable as well as more personally rewarding if the clients come not just because there is a given piece of work they feel this firm will do especially well but because they feel that their association with this firm enhances their own status. Much of my hope for the future rests on the fact that every city still has its leading law firm and a few almost equally distinguished rivals, serving clients who have sought their representation rather than clients who have been recruited through a marketing department. The young lawyers who aspire to a practice built on reputation rather than salesmanship may yet have an opportunity to mend our tattered standard.

The values to the society of a legal profession that retains its independence are beyond measuring. In 1956, my collaborator on this book wrote a two-part article about the large Wall Street firms for *Harper's* magazine, which printed the second part under the title "Keepers of the Corporate Conscience." Who today would make such a claim? We are suffused with embarrassment in this country about the decline of morality and look for reasons in our government, our churches, our economists, our media. But among the most potent reasons must be the failure of many leaders of the legal profession to accept their role as law enforcers—to act as the keepers of their clients' conscience.

Speaking to a seminar on conflicts of interest at the 1972 American Bar Association convention, Richard H. Paul of Paul Weiss said that when he advised clients confronted with conflict situations: "My one and only touchstone is this: In assessing them, I ask myself, 'How would it look in *The New York Times*?'"[1] The psychologist Robert Lynd has pointed out that the drive to avoid shame is the force behind the construction and acceptance of ethical codes in all human societies, and the history of our century testifies horribly to what normal people will do when a Nazi or communist system seems to assure them against the exposure of their activities. Sunshine, said Justice Brandeis, is the best disinfectant. Paul's question is one lawyers should indeed ask themselves: How would I feel if the world at large knew that I was giving this client this advice? Some—I hope, most—would give clients the same guidance in public as they give in private; others might well feel that their reputation would be harmed if what they were telling a client were to become known.

The essence of the claim to professional status and professional privilege is that the members of the profession hold themselves to higher standards than other people. A businessman, after all, may properly make his prime goal the search for profits—indeed, his obligation to his stockholders is arguably that he do whatever the law permits that will be in their pecuniary interest. A lawyer must pass a stiffer test. He is supposed to be ethical, even when he could make more money by being unethical. Maintaining ethical standards, Justice Sandra Day O'Connor wrote in a dissenting opinion in an advertising case, "is a task that involves a constant struggle with the relentless natural forces of economic self-interest."[2] What makes the lawyer professional is his insistence that in the legal realm he sets the parameters of what he will and will not do—and he tells the client what he believes is in the client's interest.

NYU's legal ethics professor Stephen Gillers argues that with the spread of malpractice suits and the loosening of ties between client and lawyer, the fear of being exposed will repair some of the tears in the fabric of professional conduct. If the client follows his lawyer's advice and gets into trouble, he can claim in his defense that he was merely doing what his lawyer told him to do. Somewhere, however, there must be absolutes; the lawyer must say no.

Before the 1980s, it was universally understood that the lawyer should not become in any way a party to a client's action if that action violates the law. Until 1983, the Code of Professional Responsibility held that "[a] lawyer should bring to bear upon this decision-making process the fullness of his experience as well as his objective viewpoint. In assisting his client to reach a proper decision, it is often desirable for a lawyer to point out those factors which may lead to a decision that is morally just as well as legally permissible. . . . In the event that the client in a non-adjudicatory matter insists upon a course of conduct that is contrary to the judgment and advice of the lawyer but not prohibited by Disciplinary Rules, the lawyer may withdraw from the employment."[3]

Unfortunately, recent years have seen a serious decline from that standard. In 1992, the American Bar Association modified the Model Rules designed to govern such matters to provide that in representing corporations, lawyers may not withdraw, even when the client is pursuing a course "clearly" in violation of the law, unless the action is "likely to result in substantial injury to the organization." As Monroe Freedman angrily commented: "[I]f the company is likely to get away with its crime or if the penalty is not likely to be 'substantial,' the lawyer may not withdraw."[4] Roger Cramton of Cornell is equally outraged: "The organized profession's position on client fraud," he writes, "has been disingenuous and dishonest for many years, with ethics rules appearing to require prevention or rectification of client fraud while ethics opinions opt for virtually absolute confidentiality, ignoring authoritative pronouncements of law by federal agencies and federal and state courts."[5]

Even for those of us who believe that the older standards were the right standards, the context in which the lawyer is acting and his function in that context will be keys to judging his conduct. There is a great difference between prospective and retrospective attitudes. As Ray Patterson and Elliott Cheatham wrote in 1971: "[T]he lawyer in the courtroom shares no responsibility for the past conduct of his client; the lawyer in his office, by advising his clients as to future conduct, has responsibility in fact for the client's actions in accordance with that advice." And today the divisions probably must be much finer than that.

The NYNEX Yellow Pages for Manhattan in 1991–92 offered a *Guide of Lawyers Arranged by Practice*. There are forty three categories. Some are sizable specializations, some are not. To take every fourth listing, they range from adoption law to computer law to immigration law to landlord and tenant law to patent law to school law to taxation law to vehicle and traffic law. The ABA itself in 1990 expanded its traditional list of specialties for which standards had been promulgated (once only admiralty and patents) to no fewer than twenty-four categories. Clients for some of these specialties are very different from the clients for others—those who ask for help in civil rights law, estate planning, franchise law, international law, and military administration law do not have much in common.

It would be surprising if the duties of lawyers to clients and the bounds of acceptable behavior were to be the same regardless of the subject matter and the clientele, yet the focus is on trying to write codes of ethics for the entire profession. This means that the committee-bound writers of such codes, drawn from different disciplines, inevitably find common ground at the lowest common denominator. Professor Mary Moers Wenig of Bridgeport Law School argues that the problem is a kind of infection from the ethics of the trial bar (especially the criminal trial bar) to the ethics of the counseling world.

The highest standard of responsibility has been demanded from securities lawyers by the Securities and Exchange Commission. In early 1972, the SEC for the first time held an entire law firm—New York's very prestigious White & Case—liable for assisting a client, a high-flyer called National Student Marketing, which was defrauding the stockholders of a company the client was buying. The sellers were to receive NSM stock, not cash, as payment for their company. White & Case gave its client an opinion that the closing of the transaction had been conducted entirely according to law, even though it was aware that its client's auditors had urged a restatement of NSM's balance sheet before the papers were signed, for the information of the sellers, and the restatement had never been provided. The SEC sued, claiming that the entire firm, not just the partner who had handled the client, should accept responsibility and punishment. Private lawsuits then targeted White & Case—and other law firms as well—because there was no money to be got from National Student Marketing, which had descended rapidly from a market valuation of $144 a share to insolvency. The case came to an ambiguous resolution, but SEC Rule 2 (e) became recognized as a reasonable assertion that lawyers and law firms had obligations to third parties as well as to their clients when dealing with securities issues.

The Commission's argument, in essence, was that people relied on registration statements sworn to in a submission to the government and that *anyone* who submitted knowingly false information in a registration statement—whether it was the corporation selling the securities, the investment bank managing the sale, or the lawyer—could be punished for the fraud. Much of the profession was shocked by the National Student Marketing case. The argument made by many was that if a lawyer is compelled to look after his own interests, he will slight the client's interests. But surely when he knowingly abets a client who breaks the law, a lawyer violates the client's interests, too, as properly seen from the viewpoint of an independent professional. A bank robber's lawyer who drove the getaway car would not be easily excused on grounds of professional license, and it would be hard to persuade someone that a lawyer who knowingly collaborates with a dishonest operator from behind the door of his office should be more privileged.

Twenty years after the National Student Marketing suit, Harris Weinstein, chief counsel at what had become the Office of Thrift Supervision, took a similar position with regard to lawyers who had, to quote Cornell's Roger Cramton, "knowingly or recklessly assisted the managers of insolvent or nearly insolvent thrifts in cooking the books, lying to regulators, and defrauding investors and depositors."[6] And in 1992, the FDIC expanded lawyers' responsibilities to bank examiners still further, requiring that when a lawyer was consulted about a loan an insured bank wished to make, and believed that the loan was fraudulent and might subject the bank insurance funds to a loss, he was obliged to tell his client that he *must* not make it— and if the client made it anyway, to report the matter to the examining authority immediately. In adversary proceedings, in other words, it might be defensible to assist a client who is not telling the truth (though knowingly eliciting false testimony under oath remains punishable even under today's very permissive Model Rules), but securities registrations and bank examinations are not adversary proceedings. The Internal Revenue Service has insisted for years that lawyers who counsel their clients into tax evasion can be prosecuted when the clients are caught.

Clearly, there is a continuum from the criminal proceeding, where the lawyer is absolutely entitled not to "know" that his client is guilty (because only a jury reaching a verdict "beyond a reasonable doubt" can make that determination), to the securities registration, where the purpose of the law will be frustrated unless the unknown third parties who will buy the securities are given a claim on the due diligence and honesty of the lawyer who files the papers. In a criminal proceeding, the burden of accuracy is entirely on the government, and any hole the defendant's lawyer can find in the government's case can and should be used to help get the defendant off. In a registration statement and in documents provided to bank examiners, the burden to be accurate is on all those who submit the information. If a client cannot be dissuaded from making false statements to the government in such matters, the lawyer who knows the statements are false has no choice but to resign. (One should notice in this connection that National Student Marketing's original counsel, the Washington firm of Covington & Burling, *did* resign before White & Case was retained.)

Even in civil trials, there is a growing feeling among judges that a plaintiff's lawyer should carry a burden of investigating his client's complaint. As Chief Judge Judith Kaye of the New York State Court of Appeals pointed out in the discussion of Federal Procedure Rule 11 cited in chapter 8, lawyers bringing cases can now be held accountable if they fail to investigate their client's statements and proceed solely on the basis of what their client tells them. In short, there is not only a duty to reputation to say no when no should be said; there may also be a duty in law.

Peter Megargee Brown wrote an angry book (*Rascals: The Selling of the Legal Profession*) detailing shocking conduct in some of the nation's largest law firms and telling the story of his own summary dismissal from Cadwalader, Wickersham & Taft after twenty-seven years, the last of them as chairman of the firm's ethics committee.[7] His solution to the problem of declining ethical standards was that the legal profession should be bifurcated, that a smaller group

> directly involved in the administration of our judicial system, who can demonstrate to selected Bar commissions ability and willingness to abide by strict professional standards as "officers of the court," could be individually licensed by the state as "counsellors-at-law." This segment of the Bar—approximately 80,000—would in effect become the "law profession" on which the public could reasonably rely for service and honorable response. The balance of the existing Bar who forgo practice in our judicial system or who are unwilling or unable to meet the requisite high professional standards of conduct, would remain as "attorneys-at-law."[8]

But in fact the problem is not amenable to bifurcation, because the number of specialties to be separately governed runs into the dozens. The profession has profoundly resisted efforts to divide it into categories, but those divisions are now occurring without control and (except where agencies like the SEC have intervened) with the deterioration of rules of practice in the areas where once the standards were much higher. Geoffrey Hazard of Yale sees the problem as an overall decline of the profession's legitimacy:

> The effect has been no less demoralizing for not being acknowledged. The legal profession no longer enjoys an unchallenged sense of purpose and worth in its traditional practice of mediating through the courts between business enterprise and popular politics. The practice of the profession is no longer intelligible in the terms that prevailed in the century and three quarters between *Marbury* v. *Madison* in 1803 and *Roe* v. *Wade* [in 1973]. By the same token, the profession no longer presupposes its own identity as the aristocratic element in such a constitutional structure. Its governing norms no longer represent the shared understanding of a substantially cohesive group. They are simply rules of public law regulating a widely pursued technical vocation whose constitutional position is now in doubt.
>
> . . . Legalized regulation will undoubtedly continue to dominate the normative structure of the legal profession, through court-promulgated rules, increasingly intrusive common law, and public statutes and regulations. . . . The bar has become too large, diverse and balkanized in its practice specialties for the old informal system to be effective as an institution of governance. . . . Most lawyers now practice in multilawyer work groups, including independent law firms and the law departments of governments and private organizations. Specialized practice now predominates, including tribunal practice before courts and agencies with specific regulatory jurisdiction. For

better or worse, the law firm and specific tribunals, not "the bench and the bar," have become the centers of professional relationships among the lawyers. Whether "the bar" as such can remain a coherent entity seems increasingly doubtful.[9]

This seems to me unduly pessimistic. What Judge Stanley Sporkin has called "site-specific ethics" presents one plausible means to the maintenance of professional unity. The many different *kinds* of law are practiced today before many different kinds of tribunal, from traditional courts, probate judges, family courts, and bankruptcy referees to administrative hearing officers to arbitration panels, meetings with Internal Revenue agents, bank examiners, Food and Drug Administration doctors, environmental science reviewers, and others. Each of these institutions could—some already do, others will—have its own rules for acceptable or unacceptable behavior, especially the extent to which lawyers owe duties not only to their clients but also to others. Trusts and estates and divorce lawyers would carry obligations to specific third parties that other lawyers would not bear; securities and bank lawyers would carry obligations to the world of investors and to government insurance funds as well as to their clients; litigators would accept duties to the court and to opposing counsel as equal officers of the court. Prosecuting attorneys are already bound to a separate code to seek justice rather than a record of convictions, and Attorney General Janet Reno has warned U.S. attorneys around the country that she intends to enforce it.

The codes would be specific to their own areas, each determined with reference to practice before different courts and different administrative agencies. The work of constructing differing codes would be done by the judges and officers of the government agencies involved, together with the leading lawyers in the various specialties—lawyers whose pride is their profession itself, not the bottom line of law firms. And all the codes would be based on common principles of honesty, fair dealing, and equality before the law that define the professional obligations of the lawyer. Meanwhile, the bar as a whole would establish a core code of ethics stating the moral principles of the profession.

2

Agreement on a bedrock is needed because the nation relies on courts and lawyers to safeguard our most cherished rights. For ordinary people, the worst aspect of the diminished legitimacy of the profession is the danger that the abuse of impositional powers by corporate and personal injury and strike-suit lawyers will lead to government regulation of their use. Now so casually deployed to win advantage in lawsuits for money, these powers are the sword of democracy. There isn't much people can do alone to right wrongs done them by governments or great corporations, and writing a letter to a congressman only occasionally sparks any action that makes a difference. Lawyers can be the champions of the oppressed precisely because they can command corporations and governments to testify, to produce documents, to defend their actions. Subject that power to government regulation, and the first thing that will happen is that the government will exempt itself.

Indeed, one of the truly disturbing things that has happened in the United States in the last decade—in the prosecutions of Oliver North, John Poindexter, and Clair George, and in the aborted prosecution of Christopher Drogoul in the scandal of the Atlanta branch of Banca Nazionale del Lavoro—has been the willingness of courts to accept CIA statements that documents that might incriminate officers of the government are too sensitive to be shown to the lawyers who are trying to protect people from criminal prosecution—and even to the government's own prosecutors. The British, normally far less tender to personal liberties than we are, nevertheless allowed intelligence documents to be introduced in the trial of defendants cognate with those in the BNL scandal, resulting in the instant dismissal of the charges as an abuse of power by the prosecution.

Judge Learned Hand was certainly right when he evoked the commandment "Thou shalt not ration justice"; but it is not quite that easy. The relationship between law and justice is complex. Hand's contemporary Benjamin Cardozo noted: "[W]hen we use the word *justice* the quality we most frequently have in mind is charity." Hand himself, speculating on the lawyer's contribution, said, "I wonder whether the best mood or habit is not that, forgetting for the time our job as lawyers, we should think of human beings as a whole, we should look at life *sub specie aeternitatis* and yet believe that all specific choices may be momentous." Justice, moreover, is not immutable; it changes with time. "Laws and institutions," Thomas Jefferson wrote in a letter in 1816, "must go hand in hand with the progress of the human mind. As that becomes more developed, more enlightened, as new discoveries are made, new truths disclosed, and manners and opinions change with the change of circumstances, institutions must advance also and keep pace with the times. We might as well require a man to wear still the coat which fitted him when a boy, as civilized society to remain ever under the regimen of their barbarous ancestors."[10] Justice Oliver Wendell Holmes, Jr., in one of his devil's advocate moments, said that law was the governance of the living by the dead.

What we are normally (and correctly) concerned with when we speak of rationing justice is the availability of lawyers to people whose grievances exceed their resources. Once somebody has a lawyer, we believe (or want to believe) that he will receive his ration of justice. Lawyers can make their clients equal before the law because they have equal access to the information from which the judges distill the decisions that later—after other judges have ruled, after the legislature has considered, after other lawyers have tested for other clients— we will call the rule of law.

There cannot be a rule of law without lawyers—independent

lawyers, who, unlike house counsel, can choose their clients. And, as Supreme Court Justice Antonin Scalia has said, there cannot be a rule of law without a law of rules. Those rules, though Justice Scalia did not say it, must include rules of ethics, for in their absence the equality of information that defines equality of access will not occur.

3

The rule of law—"constitutional" democracy—is the essential American contribution to the world, and never has this contribution been so needed as it is today. Prior to the American Revolution, there were kings and princes, and no more than a distant recollection in books of the grandeur that was Rome, when elected tribunes ran what became an empire. After the American Revolution, there was a country based on an axiom that all men are created equal, and on the belief that the Constitution applied equally to everyone. At the depths of our self-interest in looking at the world, when we gave aid and comfort to tyrants because they proclaimed themselves the enemies of our enemy, these principles of American government still shone from our shores to people all over the world who wanted to believe. Today the necessity for the rule of law is more visible than ever before. So many nation-states have lost their legitimacy that tribalism rends the fabric of society. Everywhere we look outside this hemisphere, we see monstrous pogroms, wars, and atrocities caused in large part by the absence of law as a shield for the people. In the former Yugoslavia, in Sudan, in Sri Lanka, in Tajikistan, in Armenia and Azerbaijan, in eastern Turkey, in India, in Ethiopia, in Rwanda, in Somalia, people kill each other because they lack the security of law. And there may be worse to come.

Law is at its heart an organized, reasonable, accepted way for people to live together and settle their disputes without resort to force. To use battlefield imagery to describe the law is to betray the deepest meaning of the profession. All communities need law, and all the people who live in those communities need to feel they enjoy the equal protection of the law. Especially where ethnic rivalries seethe and people of different religions, colors, and loyalties must share the same pieces of land, it must be credible that all can come to the law and have their quarrels adjudicated without reference to their group. The great sin of Yugoslavia and the European attitudes toward Yugoslavia, the scholar-journalist Edward Mortimer pointed out even before the war acquired its full ferocity, was the attempt to separate out the pieces before the people who would be minorities in these new self-governing pieces had credible assurances that their rights and privileges would not change. In the Baltic republics on the Soviet borders, with less than a quarter of a century's independence in their history over the last two hundred years, the insistence that the Russians who immigrated a generation ago will not be citizens may come to threaten the peace of Europe.

For almost two years I was President Jimmy Carter's emissary to the negotiations dealing with the Palestinian problem after the Camp David Accords, and I came to know firsthand the corrosive residue from proceedings associated with one community's claim to lands another community regards as its own. In attempting to construct interim arrangements that would give the Palestinians self-government on a mutually acceptable basis, I found nothing so important as creating an atmosphere of belief that there would be agreed-upon rules enforced through mutually acceptable procedures—in short, due process of law. We were, I still feel, closer than those removed from the negotiations ever realized to developing a viable set of confidence-building institutions based on the desire on both sides to live under a rule of law. The Israeli-Palestinian agreement of September 1993 was built on those beginnings.

Elihu Root was secretary of state for President William

Howard Taft when the Second Hague Peace Conference met at The Hague in 1907 to improve on the so-called court of arbitration that had been formed after the first conference in 1899. He told the U.S. delegation to work toward a real international court, with judges "who are judicial officers and nothing else, who are paid adequate salaries, who have no other occupation, and who will devote their entire time to the trial and decision of international causes by judicial methods, and under a sense of judicial responsibility." A court embodying some of Root's hopes did come into existence after World War I, but the United States never adhered to the statute that established it. The International Court of Justice that now exists at The Hague, formed as part of the United Nations after World War II, is still a relatively creaky institution that often takes years to render a decision, but it is empowered to give advisory opinions. My feeling as both a lawyer and a former ambassador is that we should be leaders rather than (as we have been) reluctant followers and respondents in making use of it.

The International Court of Justice was not far from the center of the widest and most inclusive world vision of our time, that of Grenville Clark and Louis Sohn, who inspired an organization they called World Peace Through Law. A man of granitic integrity and stubborn brilliance, the law partner of Elihu Root's son, and a sternly just advocate, Clark spent the last dozen years of his long life traveling the globe trying to persuade political leaders that the time had come to bet the human future on process rather than force. The search for peace is lonely work, and it is the responsibility of lawyers to receive and disseminate the message of those who seek to undergird with legal machinery the moral case against war. When I think of the leadership of the bar, what it was and what it could be, I think of men like Elihu Root and Henry Stimson and Grenville Clark.

For American society, the challenge is to remain a beacon to those who wish desperately to see their lives governed by laws and not by men. When Americans come to distrust the law, the results are tragic for us and for the standard we seek to bear internationally. I was for several years chairman of the National Urban Coalition, which came into existence as a response to the race riots of the 1960s. Those riots were set off by black people's belief that they were abused by the police. The riots of the later 1980s and early 1990s were triggered by juries and judges whose verdicts and sentences were incomprehensible to many more than just the rioters. The conviction of large groups of our population that they do not stand equal before the law may be the greatest cause of civil unrest—and perhaps of crime—in our country.

I write about an unhappy profession. A study by Johns Hopkins University researchers in 1991 showed lawyers as the most depressed group among the 12,000 people surveyed.[11] The lead researcher on the project said he thought the high depressed state of lawyers "might be the result of operating in a moral ambiguity. They might be representing positions they may not like or believe in." *Working Woman* magazine reported in April 1993 on two surveys of women lawyers, one from 1967 and one from 1992. The questionnaire asked whether the respondent would have chosen law as a career if she had known ten years ago what she knew now. In 1967, 94 percent of the women questioned had said yes; in 1993, only 54 percent said yes. The article accompanying the survey blamed the dissatisfaction "largely on the competitive and acrimonious atmosphere at many law firms."[12]

Geoffrey Hazard, who was head of the American Bar Foundation before he became a professor of legal ethics at Yale, believes the situation is hopeless. Commenting on a law review article acclaiming the independence of lawyers, he wrote: "The conception of a legal profession that somehow operates free of an economic and political power base ignores what most lawyers do in their work most of the time, and depends upon implausible political-economic assumptions. Putting the point bluntly but respectfully, such a conception seems to me to fantasize about the legal profession no less, and perhaps more, than the profession may fantasize about itself."[13]

Yet every so often one finds reinforcement for happier beliefs. Elizabeth Perez, a thirty-year-old Cuban immigrant, went to New York University and Harvard Law School, worked for the Democratic party and in a presidential campaign, then for a corporate law firm and in Europe as a television reporter, and returned to Harlem to open a law office in a travel agency that caters to Spanish-speaking people. "I love talking to people," she told *The New York Times*. "I've never had real clients before." She helps people become citizens, find jobs, handle their marriages, negotiate with landlords. "I'll have to get an office downtown a couple of days a week," she said, "so I can support my little habit up here."[14]

Ellen Scully, who has run the Catholic University Legal Services clinic in Washington, D.C., for twenty years—lawyers and law students working together to help poor people with housing, consumer matters, public benefits, and domestic relations—speaks of herself as "especially *blessed*. I'm in the trenches because that's where I want to be. I would leave tomorrow if I could no longer work directly with the clients and the students."[15]

In August 1993, the American Bar Association gave a special award to Edward Kelaher of Myrtle Beach, South Carolina, who gives thirty hours a week to what he calls "free legal services" rather than pro bono. He thought his two partners should have prizes, too—they were "the enablers. . . . How could I do it, if they didn't back me up?" Lawyers, he told the ABA convention, "don't sell advice, don't sell paperwork. The thing that we sell is peace of mind."[16]

Dean Robert C. Clark of Harvard Law School reports that salmon have been seen in the Merrimack River for the first time in a century, and argues: "This environmental miracle was largely the work of lawyers." ("Lawyers," he explains in a footnote, "were involved in advocating and legislating environmental protection, making regulations, and counseling client companies about compliance.")[17] The claim is a little strong—there were likely more lawyers involved in fighting the legislation and looking for ways to avoid compliance than there were legal warriors for the salmon— but there can be no question that the effectiveness of our environmental legislation owes much to the band of lawyer-crusaders who planned strategies for the ecologists.

A study by Professor Donald Landon of the American Bar Foundation reports that young rural lawyers put a much higher value on ethical concerns than young Chicago lawyers, most of whom work in large firms. One explanation is that "the high levels of personal accountability typical of small communities make ethical sensitivity particularly salient. Lawyers in small settings live by their reputation."[18] To the extent that ethical behavior is a function of community, the separation of the profession into disparate specialties may create opportunities. It is not by accident that the Academy of Matrimonial Lawyers— more often attacked for their ethics than praised for them—has produced the strongest statement to date on the responsibility of lawyers to third parties. The divorce lawyers had seen child abuse by their clients, they had talked about it among themselves, and academic folderol that a lawyer owes a duty only to his client seemed to them a shameful abdication of humanity. The ABA's Model Rules did not demand that lawyers protect children, and therefore the Academy could not impose on lawyers an enforceable obligation to report child abuse by their clients. But they could and did say that a lawyer *should* do so.

Increasingly, the law schools are saying that the teaching of ethics should be every law professor's responsibility. Perhaps the bar association should say to its specialist groups that beyond a common core that is based on common sense and universal ethical principles, they are responsible for creating the rules that should govern their own community. These are the people who know each other, who know what constitutes fair dealing and what violates fair dealing in their own work.

In Geoffrey Hazard's terms, lawyers must find ways to "fantasize" about themselves and their profession—to see and thus to create the possibility of a legal profession that is once again independent, willing to sacrifice money for pride, eager to re-assert its role as the guarantor of rights. To make the contribution only lawyers can make to the future of our country and the world, we must accept rather than simply assert our responsibilities. When we look at our fellows and we decide whom we respect, civic leadership should count for more than hourly rate, the sense of justice for more than a record of victories at trial, service to those who need the law for more than representation of those who merely use the law. The fault is not in our stars but in ourselves.

NOTES

CHAPTER 1

1. Karl Llewellyn, "The Crafts of Law Re-Valued, *ABA Journal*, vol. 28 (1942), p. 801, cited in Geoffrey C. Hazard, Jr., "Four Portraits of Law Practice," *UMKC Law Review*, vol. 57, no. 1 (Fall 1988), pp. 2–3.
2. Simon H. Rifkind, *One Man's Word* (New York: Privately printed, 1986), pp. 502–3.
3. Everett C. Hughes, "Professions," *Daedalus*, Fall 1963, p. 655 @ p. 656.
4. Philip Shuchman, "Ethics and Legal Ethics: The Propriety of the Canons as a Group Moral Code," *George Washington Law Review*, vol. 244 (1968).
5. Warren E. Burger, *Delivery of Justice* (St. Paul, Minn.: West Publishing Co., 1990) p. 145.
6. Richard L. Abel, *American Lawyers* (New York: Oxford University Press, 1989), p. 247.
7. Lehman, "The Pursuit of a Client's Interest," *Michigan Law Review*, vol. 77 (1979), p. 1078 @ p. 1092.
8. Louis D. Brandeis, "The Opportunity in the Law," *American Law Review* vol. 39 (July–August 1905), pp. 559–61.
9. Robert T. Swaine, *The Cravath Firm* (New York: Ad Press, 1948), p. 97.
10. Laurie P. Cohen and Alex M. Freedman, "Tobacco Plaintiffs Face a Grilling," *The Wall Street Journal*, February 11, 1993, p. A-6.
11. Ellen Joan Pollock, "Divorce Lawyers Often Shortchange, Overcharge Women Clients, Study Finds," *The Wall Street Journal*, March 13, 1992, p. B-3.
12. Peter Megargee Brown, *Rascals: The Selling of the Legal Profession* (New York: Benchmark Press, 1989), p. 51.
13. Paul A. Freund, "The Legal Profession," in "The Professions," *Daedalus*, Fall 1963, p. 689 @ p. 693.

14. Charles P. Curtis, *Law Large as Life* (New York: Simon & Schuster, 1959), p. 156.
15. "Bounds of Advocacy, American Academy of Matrimonial Lawyers Standards of Conduct," AAML pamphlet, July 1991, p. 27.
16. *Fickett* v. *Superior Court*, 27 Arizona App. 793, 558 P.2nd 988 (1976).
17. Thomas M. Reavley, "A Perspective on the Moral Responsibility of Lawyers," *Texas Tech Law Review*, vol. 19, p. 1393 @ p. 1397.
18. Lis Wiehl, "Rural Lawyers: Representing 'Folks Not Entities,' *The New York Times*, September 1, 1989, p. B-8.
19. Curtis, *Law Large as Life*, pp. 181–82.
20. John R. R. Jennings, Q. C., "The Bottom Line," *New York State Bar Journal*, November 1990, p. 45.
21. *Shapero* v. *Kentucky Bar Association*, *U.S. Law Week*, June 14, 1988, 56 LW 4538.
22. Geoffrey Hazard, "The Future of Legal Ethics," *Yale Law Journal*, vol. 100 (March 1991), p. 1240.

CHAPTER 2

1. "The Legal Profession," *The Economist*, July 18, 1992, p. 13.
2. Ellen Joan Pollock, *Turks and Brahmins: Upheaval at Milbank, Tweed* (New York: Simon & Schuster, 1990), p. 266.
3. David Margolick, "At the Bar," *The New York Times*, April 8, 1993, p. B-16.
4. Ellen Joan Pollock, "Lawyers Go to Boot Camp for Sales Skills," *The Wall Street Journal*, April 1, 1993, p. B-5.
5. *Bar Report*, The Official Newspaper of the District of Columbia Bar, Washington, D.C., August–September 1991, p. 4.
6. Kim Isaac Eisler, *Shark Tank: Greed, Politics and the Collapse of Finley Kumble, One of America's Largest Law Firms* (New York: Penguin Books, 1991), p. 191.
7. "*. . . In the Spirit of Public Service*": A Blueprint for the Rekindling of Lawyer Professionalism, Report of the Commission on Professionalism to the Board of Governors and the House of Delegates of the American Bar Association, August 1986, in 112 Federal Rules Decisions, p. 243.
8. Randall Sanborn, "Anti-Lawyer Attitudes Up," *The National Law Journal*, August 9, 1993, p. 1 @ p. 20.
9. Richard L. Abel, *American Lawyers* (New York: Oxford University Press, 1989), p. 33.
10. Martin Mayer, *Emory Buckner* (New York: Harper & Row, 1968), p. 167.
11. Michael E. Parrish, *Felix Frankfurter and His Times: The Reform Years* (New York: Free Press, 1982), p. 58.
12. Mayer, *Emory Buckner*, p. 251.
13. Harold Obstler, general counsel for Colgate, told an *American Lawyer* symposium: "Just as the relationships of clients to law partners run the

whole gamut, so do relationships on the inside. . . . You are what you are. I consider myself highly professionalized. I don't think I changed when I came on the inside. It's caused friction sometimes within the company, but I stand by my principles just as the outside lawyer stands by his. . . ." (*American Lawyer* pull-out report "The Demand Side," June 1990, p. 50.)

14. George Bernard Shaw, "A Preface on Doctors," in *The Doctor's Dilemma* (New York: Brentano, 1911), p. xv.
15. Shaw, ibid.
16. Nancy Lisagor and Frank Lipsius, *A Law Unto Itself: The Untold Story of the Law Firm Sullivan & Cromwell* (New York: William Morrow, 1988), p. 234.
17. Abel, *American Lawyers*, p. 10.
18. Committee on the Profession, City Association of the Bar of the City of New York, "Is Professionalism Declining?," *The Record*, March 1992, p. 129 @ p. 174.
19. Annual Survey, *The National Law Journal*, September 27, 1993, pp. S1–S52.
20. Roy Grutman and Bill Thomas, *Lawyers and Thieves* (New York: Simon & Schuster, 1990), p. 28.
21. John Taylor, "Plus Ça Change," *New York*, January 18, 1993, p. 12 @ p. 13.
22. Paul Hoffman, *Lions in the Street* (New York: Saturday Review Press/Dutton, 1973), pp. 60, 61.
23. "Is Professionalism Declining?," pp. 163, 164.
24. Harris Weinstein, "Attorney Liability in the Savings and Loan Crisis," *University of Illinois Law Review*, vol. 1993, no. 1, pp. 53, 61.
25. Judge Stanley Sporkin, *The New World of Lawyering I*, Securities Regulation Institute, University of California at San Diego, January 22–24, 1992.
26. Geoffrey Hazard, "The Future of Legal Ethics," *Yale Law Journal*, vol. 100, no. 5, pp. 1239, 1255.
27. Pollock, "Lawyers Go to Boot Camp . . . ," pp. 263, 264.
28. Eric J. Cassell, "In Sickness and in Health," *Commentary*, vol. 49, no. 6 (June 1970), pp. 59–60.
29. From *American Lawyer* supplement "Short-Term Pressures, Long-Term Opportunity," September 1991, p. 33.
30. Emily Couric, "The Tangled Web: When Ethical Misconduct Becomes Legal Liability," *ABA Journal*, April 1993, p. 64 @ p. 65.

CHAPTER 3

1. Martin Mayer, *Emory Buckner* (New York: Harper & Row, 1968), p. 169.
2. Bernard Botein, *Trial Judge* (New York: Simon & Schuster, 1952), p. 149.
3. Jonathan M. Mozes, "Partners Losing Their Guarantee of Life Tenure," *The Wall Street Journal*, July 14, 1992, p. B-1.

4. David Margolick, "Pink Slips for Law Firm Partners as Tradition Bows to Tough Times," *The New York Times*, December 18, 1990, p. 1.
5. "The Association of the Bar of the City of New York," City Bar Association pamphlet, 1958, p. 30.
6. Stephen M. Bundy, "Commentary on 'Understanding *Pennzoil* v. *Texaco*': Rational Bargaining and Agency Problems," *Virginia Law Review*, March 1989, vol. 75, no. 2, p. 343.

CHAPTER 4

1. Ron Chernow, *The House of Morgan* (New York: Atlantic Monthly Press, 1990), p. 82.
2. Jean Witter, "Scandal in the Headlines: Theodore Roosevelt and the Panama Canal," *Columbia Library Columns*, February 1993, p. 23 @ p. 31.
3. See Nancy Lisagor and Frank Lipsius, *A Law Unto Itself: The Untold Story of the Law Firm Sullivan & Cromwell* (New York: William Morrow, 1988), p. 27.
4. Leo Gottlieb, *Cleary, Gottlieb, Steen & Hamilton: The First Thirty Years* (New York: Privately printed, 1983), p. 80.
5. Ibid., p. 218.
6. The information in the following pages is drawn in large part from Mark Pendergrast, *For God, Country and Coca-Cola: The Unauthorized History of the Great American Soft Drink and the Company That Makes It* (New York: Scribners, 1993).
7. Ibid., pp. 195–96.
8. Robert Swaine, *The Cravath Firm* (New York: Ad Press, 1948), vol. 2, p. 713.
9. Henry L. Stimson and McGeorge Bundy, *On Active Service in Peace and War* (New York: Harper and Brothers, 1948), p. 4.
10. Swaine, *The Cravath Firm*, p. 696.
11. *Panama Refining Co.* v. *Amazon Petroleum Corp.*, 293 U.S. 388, 55 S.Ct. 241 (1935).
12. Robert Banks, "Companies Struggle to Control Legal Ccsts," *Harvard Business Review*, March–April 1983.
13. Gary F. Torrell, "How to Work with In-House Counsel," *American Lawyer*, July–August 1992, p. 32.
14. Harrison Tweed, *The Changing Practice of Law* (New York: City Association of the Bar, 1955).
15. Internal memo on professionalism from Robert Banks, Xerox Corporation, May 4, 1981, p. 2.
16. Milton V. Freedman, "The Profession of Law Is *Not* on the Decline," *Dickinson Law Review*, Winter 1992, p. 96.
17. Ellen Joan Pollock, *Turks and Brahmins: Upheaval at Milbank, Tweed* (New York: Simon & Schuster, 1990), p. 117.

18. "Short-Term Pressures, Long-Term Opportunities," *American Lawyer* supplement, September 1991, p. 21.
19. "Succeeding in the Post Gold Rush Era," *American Lawyer* supplement, September 1992, pp. 38, 43.

CHAPTER 5

1. Lester Brickman, "Lawyers Fee Frenzy," *The Washington Post*, August 16, 1991, p. A-29.
2. Peter Megargee Brown, *Rascals: The Selling of the Legal Profession* (New York: Benchmark Press, 1989), p. 115.
3. Ellen Joan Pollock, *Turks and Brahmins: Upheaval at Milbank, Tweed* (New York: Simon & Schuster, 1990), p. 129.
4. The Committee on the Profession, City Association of the Bar of the City of New York, "Is Professionalism Declining?" *The Record*, March 1992, p. 129 @ p. 174.
5. Nancy Lisagor and Frank Lipsius, *A Law Unto Itself: The Untold Story of the Law Firm Sullivan & Cromwell* (New York: William Morrow, 1988), p. 193.
6. Robert Swaine, *The Cravath Firm* (New York: Ad Press, 1948), p. 329.
7. James R. Stewart, *The Partners* (New York: Simon & Schuster, 1983), p. 206.
8. Ellen Joan Pollock, "Big Law Firms Learn That They, Too, Are a Cyclical Business," *The Wall Street Journal*, August 15, 1991, p. 1.
9. Leo Gottlieb, *Cleary, Gottlieb, Steen & Hamilton: The First Thirty Years* (New York: R. R. Donnelley & Sons, 1983, p. 54.
10. Pollock, *Turks and Brahmins*, p. 80.
11. Steve Brill, "Dealing with Layoffs," *American Lawyer*, June 1990, pp. 5, 37.
12. Marc Galanter and Thomas Palay, *Tournament of Lawyers* (Chicago: University of Chicago Press, 1991).
13. "Pink Slips for Law Firm Partners," *The New York Times*, December 18, 1990, pp. 1, 46.
14. Galanter and Palay, *Tournament of Lawyers*.
15. Nancy D. Holt, "Are Longer Hours Here to Stay?" *ABA Journal*, February 1993, p. 62 @ p. 64.
16. Seth Rosner, "Professionalism and Money in the Law, *New York State Bar Journal*, September-October 1991, p. 26 @ p. 27.

CHAPTER 6

1. J. C. Furnas, *The Americans* (New York: Putnam, 1969, p. 256.
2. American Bar Association, *Legal Education and Professional Development: The Report of the Task Force on Law Schools and the Profession* (Chicago: American Bar Association, 1992), pp. 112–13.

3. "Talbot d'Alemberte on Legal Education," *ABA Journal*, September 1990, p. 52.

4. Quoted in Philip Lader, "The Need for Undergraduate Law Study," *ABA Journal*, March 1973, p. 266 @ p. 269.

5. Milo Geyelin, "More Law Schools Are Teaching Students Value of Assuming Clients' Point of View," *The Wall Street Journal*, September 17, 1991, p. B-1.

6. Richard D. Kahlenberg, *Broken Contract: A Memoir of the Harvard Law School* (New York: Hill and Wang, 1992), p. 5.

7. Stephen Gillers, "Making the Decision to Go to Law School," in *Looking at Law School*, edited by Stephen Gillers, 3rd rev. ed. (New York: Meridian Books, 1990), p. 5.

8. *Legal Education and Professional Development*, p. 236.

9. Anthony G. Amsterdam, "Clinical Legal Education—a 21st Century Perspective," *Journal of Legal Education*, vol, 34, p. 612 @ p. 614.

10. *Report of Commission on Professionalism*, 112 FRD 243 (1986), p. 268.

11. Martha Minow, *Making All the Difference: Inclusion, Exclusion and American Law* (Ithaca, N.Y.: Cornell University Press, 1990), p. 164.

12. Mark Tushnet, "An Essay on Rights," *Texas Law Review*, vol. 62 (1984), p. 1364.

13. *Proceedings*, 66th Annual Meeting, The American Law Institute, Philadelphia, Pa., 1989, pp. 333ff.

14. Lloyd Cutler, Robert Tyro Jones, Jr., Memorial Lecture on Legal Ethics, Cannon Chapel, November 24, 1981.

15. David Marston, *Malice Aforethought* (New York: Morrow, 1991), p. 69.

16. Junda Woo and Milo Geyelin, "Revised Ethics Classes Get Law Students More Involved," *The Wall Street Journal*, January 19, 1993, p. B-2.

17. Chris Goodrich, "Ethics Business," *California Lawyer*, July 1991, p. 40 @ p. 41.

18. Monroe Freedman, *Understanding Lawyers' Ethics* (New York: Matthew Bender, 1990), pp. 252–53.

19. Dr. Bernard L. Diamond, "Psychological Problems of Law Students," in Gillers, ed., *Looking at Law School*, p. 64.

20. Freedman, *Understanding Lawyers' Ethics*, p. 49.

21. Gary Bellow, "Clinical Studies in Law," in Gillers, ed., *Looking at Law School*, pp. 295, 296.

22. Elisabeth M. Fowler, "Law Schools Put Stress on Specialization," *The New York Times*, February 12, 1991, p. D-19.

23. "The Making of a Professional," *ABA Journal*, September 1990, p. 43 @ p. 46.

24. Stephanie B. Goldberg, ed., "Bridging the Gap," *ABA Journal*, September 1990, p. 44 @ p. 45.

25. Geyelin, "More Law Schools . . ."

26. John Sexton, "The Future of the Law School," *NYU: The Law School Magazine*, 1992, p. 40 @ p. 52.

27. Bellow, "Clinical Studies in Law," p. 300.

28. Goldberg, ed., "Bridging the Gap," p. 50.

29. Ibid., pp. 49–50.
30. Geoffrey C. Hazard, "Law Schools Must Teach Legal Ethics," *The National Law Journal*, October 7, 1991, p. 17.
31. Oliver Wendell Holmes, *Collected Legal Papers* (New York: Harcourt, Brace & Howe, 1920), p. 187.
32. Henry L. Stimson and McGeorge Bundy, *On Active Service in Peace and War* (New York: Harper and Brothers, 1948) p. xv.
33. Felix Frankfurter, "Advice to a Young Man Interested in Going into Law," in *Of Law and Men*, Philip Elmon, ed. (New York: Harcourt Brace, 1956), pp. 103-4.

Chapter 7

1. Richard L. Abel, *American Lawyers* (New York: Oxford University Press, 1989), p. 147.
2. Ibid., p. 143.
3. Judith S. Kaye, "Enhancing Competence and Professional Ethics," *Trial*, June 1988, pp. 41, 44.
4. *Report of Commission on Professionalism*, 112 FFD, p. 243 @ pp. 286, 287.
5. David Marston, *Malice Aforethought* (New York: Morrow, 1991), pp. 11–12.
6. Leonard E. Gross, "Legal Ethics for the Future: Time to Clean Up Our Act?," *Illinois Bar Journal*, December 1988, p. 196 @ p. 199.
7. *Report of Commission on Professionalism*, p. 276.
8. National Resource Center for Consumers of Legal Services, *Legal Plan Letter* (Special Census Issue, August 30, 1991, in *Legal Education and Professional Development* (Chicago: American Bar Association, 1992), p. 68.
9. *Legal Education and Professional Development*, pp. 57–58.
10. Stephanie Simon, "Mixed Verdict: Prepaid Legal Services Draw Plenty of Customers and Criticism," *The Wall Street Journal*, August 6, 1991, p. B-1.
11. *Legal Education and Professional Development*, p. 63.
12. Laura Mansnerus, "Bar Groups Are Happy to Find You a Lawyer," *The New York Times*, February 27, 1993, p. 24.
13. Barbara A. Curran, *1989 Survey of the Public's Use of Legal Services*, American Bar Association, Chicago, September 1989.
14. Stuart M. Speizer, *Lawyers and the American Dream* (New York: M. Evans, 1993), pp. 42ff.
15. Roger C. Cramton, "Mandatory Pro Bono: A Duty to Serve?" *Cornell Law Forum*, November 1991, pp. 7-12, as reprinted with changes from *Hofstra Law Review*, pp. 1113-39., pp. 7, 12.
16. Address by Edmund S. Muskie to a joint session of the Maine legislature, May 1, 1991, p. 3.
17. David Margolick, "Required Work for Poor Urged for Lawyers," *The New York Times*, July 11, 1989, pp. A-1, B-4.
18. *Legal Education and Professional Development*, p. 53.
19. Cramton, "Mandatory Pro Bono," p. 7.

20. Geoffrey C. Hazard, "After Professional Virtue," *The Supreme Court Review* (Chicago: University of Chicago Press, 1990), p. 6.
21. "Not All Pro Bono Work Helps the Poor," *The Wall Street Journal*, December 30, 1992, p. 7.
22. Stephen Gillers, "Words into Deeds," *ABA Journal*, November 1990, pp. 80, 81.
23. Statement of the Standing Committee on Ethics and Professional Responsibility on the Subject of Lawyers' Ancillary Business Activities, American Bar Association, January 1991, unpublished manuscript, p. 2.

CHAPTER 8

1. Interview with Kenneth P. Nolan, published in *Litigation Journal*, September 1984, and reprinted in Simon Rifkind, *One Man's Word* (New York: Privately printed, 1986), p. 467.
2. *In the Spirit of Public Service: A Blueprint for the Rekindling of Lawyer Professionalism*, Report of the Commission on Professionalism to the Board of Governors and the House of Delegates of the American Bar Association, 112 Federal Rules Decisions, pp. 243, 284.
3. Warren E. Burger, *Delivery of Justice* (St. Paul, Minn.: West Publishing Co., 1990), p. 143.
4. *DF Activities Corp.* v. *Brown*, 851 F2d 920, in Olson, *The Litigation Explosion* (New York: Dutton, 1991), p. 117.
5. *Zahn* v. *International Paper*, 414 US 291
6. Burger, *Delivery of Justice*, p. 145.
7. Ibid., p. 181.
8. *Report of the Commission on Professionalism*, 112 Federal Rules Decisions, p. 289–90.
9. Judith S. Kaye, "Enhancing Competence and Professional Ethics," *Trial*, June 1988, p. 43.
10. Herbert M. N. Kritzer, "The English Rule," *ABA Journal*, November 1992, p. 55.
11. *Report of the Committee on Professionalism*, pp. 284, 285.
12. Joryn Jenkins, "The Quiet Crusade," *Federal Bar News & Journal*, vol. 39, issue 5 (June 1992) p. 320.
13. Sherman L. Cohn, "First We Kill All the Lawyers," *Women Lawyers Journal*, Fall 1992, vol. 78, no. 4, pp. 6, 8.
14. Morris Janowitz, *The Last Half-Century: Societal Change and Politics in America* (Chicago: University of Chicago Press, 1978), p. 383.
15. ". . . Gerhard A. Gesell," *The Washington Post*, February 22, 1993, p. A-14.
16. Stephen Labaton, "Federal Judges Blame Money Woes for Slowdown," *The New York Times*, April 8, 1993, p. B-16.

Chapter 9

1. Don J. DeBenedictis, "Growing Pains," *ABA Journal*, March 1983, p. 52.
2. Ellen Joan Pollock, "Companies Cut Outside Legal Costs 24%," *The Wall Street Journal*, December 16, 1992, p. B-5.
3. "Succeeding in the Post Gold Rush Era," *American Lawyer* supplement, September 1992, p. 34.
4. Ibid., p. 32.
5. Richard B. Schmitt, "An Insurer's Sleuth Sniffs Out Lawyers Inflating Their Bills," *The Wall Street Journal*, July 21, 1992, p. 1.
6. Sam Benson, "Why I Quit Practicing Law," *Newsweek*, November 4, 1991, p. 10.
7. *Alternatives*, New York, May 1992, p. 71.
8. Richard L. Fricker, "Frankly Speaking," *ABA Journal*, December 1992, p. 76.
9. Linda Greenhouse, "Linowitz's Call for Lawyers to Be People Again," *The New York Times*, April 22, 1988.
10. Emily F. Mandelstam, "Malaise Is Growing at New York's Big Law Firms," *New York Observer*, March 12, 1990.
11. James M. Kramon, "Lawyers Look at the Practice of Law: Some Disquieting Observations," *The Maryland Bar Journal*, December 1986.
12. "Succeeding in the Post Gold Rush Era," p. 8.
13. Ibid., p. 17.
14. Ibid., p. 18.
15. *Alternatives*, July 1992, pp. 5ff.
16. "Succeeding in the Post Gold Rush Era," p. 11.
17. See Richard W. Moll, *The Lure of the Law* (New York: Viking Press, 1990), pp. 115ff.
18. Richard Lacakyo, "The Sad Fate of Legal Aid," *Time*, June 20, 1988, p. 59.
19. Barbara Buchholz, "The Melting Pots," *ABA Journal*, March 1993, p. 62.
20. Simon H. Rifkind, *One Man's Word* (New York: Privately printed, 1986), vol. 2, p. 540.
21. George H. Hettrick, "Doing Good," *ABA Journal*, December 1992, p. 77.
22. Ibid., p. 81.

Chapter 10

1. Alexis de Tocqueville, *Democracy in America*, translated by George Lawrence, edited by J. P. Mayer (New York: Anchor Books, 1969), pp. 268, 269.
2. Philip Nader, "The Need for Undergraduate Law Study," *ABA Journal*, March 1973, p. 266 @ p. 268.
3. Charles P. Curtis, *Law Large as Life* (New York: Simon & Schuster, 1959), p. 117.
4. Lester J. Cappon, ed., *The Adams-Jefferson Letters*, vol. 2 (Chapel Hill, N.C.: The University of North Carolina Press, 1959), p. 464.

5. Richard Hofstadter, *American at 1750: A Social Portrait*, (New York: Alfred A. Knopf, 1971), p. 159.
6. Bernard Bailyn, David Brion Davis, David Herbert Donald, John L. Thomas, Robert H. Wiebe, and Gordon S. Wood, *The Great Republic* (Boston: Little, Brown, 1977), p. 515.
7. Felix Frankfurter, *Law and Politics* (New York: Capricorn Books, 1962), p. 45.
8. Daniel Boorstin, *The Americans: The Democratic Experience* (New York: Random House, 1973), p. 417.
9. Carl Bridenbaugh, *Vexed and Troubled Englishmen* (New York: Oxford University Press, 1967), pp. 436–37.
10. Charles McIlwain, *Constitutionalism and the Changing World*, quoted in Bernard Bailyn, *The Ideological Origins of the American Revolution* (Cambridge, Mass.: Harvard University Press 1972), p. 190.
11. Edmund S. Morgan and Helen M. Morgan, *The Stamp Act Crisis*, rev. ed. (New York: Collier Books, 1963), p. 237.
12. Bailyn, *The Ideological Origins of the American Revolution*, p. 272.
13. Jacob E. Cooke, ed., *The Federalist* (Middletown, Conn.: Wesleyan University Press, 1961), pp. 420, 421.
14. Gordon S. Wood, *The Creation of the American Republic, 1776–1787* (Chapel Hill, N.C.: University of North Carolina Press), p. 407.
15. Jefferson to Philip Mazzei, Julian P. Boyd, ed., *The Papers of Thomas Jefferson* (Princeton, N.J.: Princeton University Press, 1954), vol. 9, pp. 68-71.
16. *United States Constitution*, Article I, Section 9; Article VI; Article III, Section 3.
17. Cooke, ed., *Federalist #84*, p. 579.
18. Wood, *The Creation of the American Republic*, p. 304.
19. Curtis, *Law Large as Life*, p. 112.
20. Cappon, ed., *The Adams-Jefferson Letters*, p. 423.
21. Ibid., p. 270.
22. Boorstin, *The Americans*, p. 623.
23. "A Just Man," *The Economist*, January 30–February 5, 1993, p. 27.
24. Alpheus Thomas Mason, *Harlan Fiske Stone, Pillar of the Law* (New York: Viking Press, 1956), p. 641.
25. Fred R. Shapiro, ed. *Oxford Dictionary of American Legal Quotations* (New York: Oxford University Press, 1993), p. 232.
26. Irving Dillard's collection of Learned Hand's papers and addresses entitled *The Spirit of Liberty* (New York: Alfred A. Knopf, 1952), p. 33.
27. "The Legal Profession," *The Economist*, July 18, 1992, p. 12.
28. "Reaching Common Ground," ABA Summit on Civil Justice System Improvements, December 13-14, 1993, Washington, D.C., Exhibit on Civil Litigation Caseload Volume.

CHAPTER 11

1. "Conflicts of Interest and the Regulation of Securities, a Symposium," *The Business Lawyer*, January 1973, p. 568.

2. *Shapero* v. *Kentucky Bar Association*, 486 US 466, 490.

3. "EC 7-8 ABA Model Code of Professional Responsibility as Amended," reprinted in *ABA/BNA Lawyers' Manual on Professional Conduct*. 1993, p. 1:333.

4. Monroe Freedman, "Corporate Bar Protects Its Own," *Legal Times*, June 15, 1992, p. 20 @ p. 22.

5. Roger C. Cramton, "Partners in Crime: Law Schools and the Legal Profession," *Cornell Law Forum*, March 1993, p. 2 @ p. 5.

6. Cramton, "Partners in Crime," p. 5.

7. Peter Mcgargee Brown, *Rascals: The Selling of the Legal Profession* (New York: Benchmark Press, 1989), p. 113.

8. Peter Megargee Brown, "Why Decline of America's Law Profession Is Dangerous to Society," mimeo, May 18, 1988, p. 10.

9. Geoffrey C. Hazard, "The Future of Legal Ethics," *The Yale Law Journal*, 1991, pp. 1239, 1278–79.

10. Charles P. Curtis, *Law Large as Life* (New York: Simon & Schuster, 1959), p. 54.

11. Andrew Herrmann, "Depressing News for Lawyers," *Chicago Sun-Times*, September 13, 1991.

12. *The Wall Street Journal*, March 27, 1993, p. B-12.

13. Hazard, "The Future of Legal Ethics," p. 1279n.

14. "At the Travel Agency, a Lawyer Finds Her Niche," *The New York Times*, July 30, 1993.

15. John Geenya, "In the Trenches," *The Washington Lawyer*, May-June 1993, pp. 17, 21.

16. Saundra Torry, "Inspiring the Legal Profession to Rebuild Its Image," *The Washington Post*, August 16, 1993, p. F-7.

17. Robert C. Clark, "Why So Many Lawyers? Are They Good or Bad?," *Fordham Law Review*, November 1992, p. 275 @ p. 292.

18. *Legal Education and Professional Development:The Report of the Task Force on Law Schools and the Profession* (Chicago: American Bar Association, 1992), p. 383.

INDEX

Library of Congress Cataloging-in-Publication Data
Linowitz, Sol M., 1913–
  The betrayed profession : lawyering at the end of the twentieth
century / Sol M. Linowitz with Martin Mayer.
      p.   cm.
  Originally published : New York : Scribner's, c1994.
  Includes bibliographical references (p.   ) and index.
  ISBN 0-8018-5329-X (pbk. : paper)
    1. Lawyers—United States.   2. Legal ethics—United States.
3. Practice of law—United States.   I. Mayer, Martin 1928–   .
II. Title.
KF300.L56   1996
174'.3'0973 — dc20   95–43782